G000067349

CYBERSPACE

CYBERSPACE

THE WORLD IN THE WIRES

Rob Kitchin

JOHN WILEY & SONS

Chichester · New York · Weinheim · Brisbane · Singapore · Toronto

OTHER WILEY EDITORIAL OFFICES

John Wiley & Sons, Inc., 605 Third Avenue, New York, NY 10158-0012, USA

WILEY-VCH Verlag GmbH, Pappelallee 3, D-69469 Weinheim, Germany

Jacaranda Wiley Ltd, 33 Park Road, Milton, Queensland 4064, Australia

John Wiley & Sons (Asia) Pte Ltd, 2 Clementi Loop #02-01, Jin Xing Distripark, Singapore 129809

John Wiley & Sons (Canada) Ltd, 22 Worcester Road, Rexdale, Ontario M9W 1L1, Canada

British Library Cataloguing in Publication Data

A catalogue record for this book is available from the British Library

ISBN 0-471-978612 (hardback)
ISBN 0-471-978620 (paperback)

Typeset in 9/12pt Caslon from the author's disks by Dorwyn Ltd, Rowlands Castle, Hants
Printed and bound in Great Britain by Bookcraft (Bath) Ltd

This book is printed on acid-free paper responsibly manufactured from sustainable forestry, for which at least two trees are planted for each one used for paper production.

A web of glass spans the globe. Through it, brief sparks of light incessantly fly, linking machines chip to chip and people face to face.

Cerf (1991, p. 41)

With politicians publicizing the democratic potentialities inherent in the construction of the information superhighway; popular business and computer magazines hailing the entrepreneurial opportunities available on the Net; the entertainment industry produc- ing and advertising video and music available on-line; and software companies introduc- ing virtual reality theme parks, it seems clear that there is a far reaching construction of the need to 'connect' and experience all the . . . wonders of cyberspace.

Bromberg (1996, p. 143)

We stand on the threshhold of turning life itself into computer code, of transforming the experience of living in the physical world – every sensation, every detail – into a product for our consumption. 'We now have the ability . . . to take the sum of human experience and give it a medium in which to flow'. . . . The implications of these new technologies are social; the questions these pose, broadly ethical; the risks they entail, unprecedented. They are the cultural equivalent of genetic engineering . . .

Slouka (1996, pp. 6, 12) quoting John Barlow

Cyberspace is opening up, and the rush to claim and settle it is on. We are entering an era of electronically extended bodies living at the intersection points of the physical and virtual worlds, of occupation and interaction through telepresence as well as through physical presence, of mutant architectural forms that emerge from the telecommunications-induced fragmentation and recombination of traditional architectural types, and of new soft cities that parallel, complement, and sometimes compete with our existing urban concentrations of brick, concrete, and steel.

Mitchell (1995, p. 167)

For Cora

and

my nieces and nephews, Adam, Alana, Becky, Daniel, Jenny, Joss and Lorcan, who will inherit the cyberspatial age

CONTENTS

PREFACE

The economics and politics of virtual culture; its material artefacts, processes, and human activities; its role in our systems of meaning and value – all must be interrogated if we are not to stumble blindly into the cyberspaces of our future, or be led in directions we might not wish to go by those with greater power to pursue their own interests.[1]

The need for criticism certainly is a matter of overwhelming urgency. While a number of critics have approached the new world of computerised communications with a healthy amount of scepticism, their message has been lost in the noise and spectacle of corporate hype – the unstoppable tidal wave of seduction has enveloped so many in its dynamic utopian beauty that little time for careful reflection is left.[2]

At present, most books concerning cyberspatial technologies can be divided into users guides (how to use/explore cyberspace), technical manuals (how cyberspace technologies work) and a range of academic, commentary and anecdotal accounts. This book examines the issues raised by the authors of the latter three and explores the social, cultural, political and economic implications of cyberspatial technologies and the 'world in the wires' they are creating; cyberspace. Cyberspace is an elusive word to define. In the context of this book, cyberspace refers to the emerging computer-mediated communications and virtual reality technologies. Both these cyberspatial technologies allow people to interact with other people or with computer simulated worlds through the creation of a virtual presence. As such, the discussion centres upon the development and appropriation of the Internet (the global network of connected computers), its close cousin, intranets (closed, private corporate telematic networks) and virtual reality (immersion) technologies. It is estimated that over 35 million people[3] are already connected to the Internet and, given that in advanced industrial societies nearly every home has a telephone connection and personal computers are becoming ubiquitous, the growth in cyberspace users is likely to continue at a rapid pace.[4] In addition to private users the Internet has also been opening up to business, with analysts predicting a rapid growth both in the amount of business being conducted in cyberspace and the profits to be made by cyberspatial companies providing both on-line and virtual reality services.[5]

It is probably fair to state that cyberspace is probably one of the most universally over-hyped terms of the latter part of the twentieth century. In general, this hype has been expressed through the popular and computing press; academic appraisal has, in the main, been more critical and reflective. Extensive commentaries, however, by both the popular media and the academic community mean that, in the developed world at least, the word has now been subsumed into everyday life. The reasons for this easy acceptance are numerous, not least of which is that cyberspace has captured the public's imagination as a place for exploration and interaction. For many social analysts and commentators, cyberspace captures a different imagination. For them, cyberspace embodies and helps to illustrate the changes in western society at the end of the twentieth century. Cyberspatial technologies are determined to be transformative technologies, changing the way we live our lives, just as the car, telephone and television did earlier in the century. Moreover, these technologies are going to affect the lives of individuals regardless of whether they actively use them or even want to use them (e.g. the effect of electronic banking on the world economy).[6] To many of these analysts, the advent of a cyberspatial age confirms the end of the modernist period and our entry into a postmodern world; cyberspace is altering our accepted notions of the body, identity, community and nature. Further, cyberspace is seen by some to raise fundamental questions concerning the democratic process, polity, regulation and ethics, and its form and use challenge our current thinking relating to ownership, privacy, confidentiality and deviancy. Within economic circles, commentators are observing that cyberspace is challenging capital with information as the dominant basis of local and global economies and is forcing a fundamental restructuring of organisational and employment structures by facilitating rapid globalisation. Moreover, some commentators envisage that cyberspace undermines and modifies both the urban fabric and our urban lifestyle by providing alternative bases of communication, work and leisure. At present, there are three main reasons given as to why cyberspace is instigating these changes: cyberspace is altering the space–time continuum; cyberspace is changing the basis of communication; and cyberspace is blurring the boundaries between the 'real' and the 'virtual'. In this book, each of these ideas is explored, intertwining the themes to try to gain a composite understanding of how cyberspace is impinging upon and changing our everyday lives.

Most academic, anecdotal and commentary texts tend to concentrate their analysis upon selective aspects of cyberspace and its current and potential implications, whether they be social, cultural, political or economic, and generally fail to draw differing themes together to address their wider significance. However, these different aspects of our lives are intricately entwined and interdependent. As a result, this book has been structured so that although a chapter is devoted to each of these themes, the discussion within each has been placed within the context of the other components, and within the wider context of the theoretical arguments developed. Thus, the target audience of the book is fairly wide ranging, encompassing many of the disciplines from the arts and social sciences, and it has been written for both academic use and to inform the lay person interested in assessing cyberspace's potential in the light of all the recent media hype. Inevitably, the text is a personal voyage through the landscapes of cyberspace, but care has been taken to try to provide a detailed comparison, synthesis and evaluation of theoretical positions and discussions, from a diverse range of sources that have sought to explain and understand the cyberspace phenomena (anthropology, cultural studies, economics, geography, linguistics, politics, sociology, urban studies, history of computing and popular science). It is not expected that everyone will agree with the assessments made or the arguments forwarded but it is hoped that people will find the diversity of issues raised and the structure of the book useful in developing an informed opinion of their own. It is inevitable, given the fast changing nature of cyberspace, that some of what is reported in this book will be obsolete by the time it reaches the shelves. However, despite these specific changes (in terms of technological developments or regulation) it is hoped that the main arguments outlined will retain a certain degree of shelf life.

Throughout the book a number of general theses are developed and critically evaluated. Central to my arguments is the tenet that cyberspace does, and will increasingly, matter in a number of fundamental ways. Cyberspatial technologies are transformative technologies that do affect everybody in one form or another. However, the book does not develop a strong utopian/dystopian vision of the future. Cyberspatial technologies, although in many aspects revolutionary, will be appropriated into everyday life as a natural evolution. It is suggested that to fully conceptualise how cyberspace does and will matter we need to base our analyses within a broader context, stepping back from the screen and taking off the 'glasses of hype' or 'goggles of despair'. At present, much of the writing concerning cyberspace, particularly in the popular press, is based upon sound-bite slogans and unsubstantiated opinion, and lacks empirical analysis. In addition, much writing is overly utopian, making false promises built upon the unrealistic pipe dreams of the intoxicated. We must realise that cyberspace is not going to be the panacea for all the world's problems. Further, in our inquiry we must not forget that the virtual does not and will not fully replace the material, but rather that the virtual is superimposed over the material in a symbiotic relationship. As such, we must be careful in our analysis not to be seduced by the powerful messages of hype emanating from both the computer corporate giants who have now colonised cyberspace and the popular media. Instead, we must seek to provide strong critical assessment of the cyberspace phenomenon based upon measured and reasoned analysis. As Lyon[7] points out, the over-optimistic hype concerning the social benefits of new technologies only serves as a distraction. In other words, meaningful social analytical questions are avoided, sidestepping crucial concerns relating to how these technologies are developed, introduced and appropriated. This does not mean that we have to adopt an overly critical approach – as you will read, I believe that cyberspace is introducing many benefits to society – but that we should not become blinkered in assessing cyberspatial developments. Such analysis has now been started in earnest by both academics and critical commentators, and I draw extensively from this work.

I argue throughout the book that to fully understand the implications of cyberspatial technologies we need to develop an overarching approach which acknowledges the inseparability of the social, cultural, political and economic. Current theories that have formed the bases of understanding the relationship between technology and society (determinism, utopianism, political economy and social constructivism) are too constricting and often too simplistic. A new integrated approach needs to be developed that recognises the value of postmodernist and feminist thought but which also acknowledges that much of cyberspace is rooted in the 'modern', post-industrial economic world. The approach developed seeks to integrate aspects of postmodernist thought with ideas from social constructivism and political economy. It is suggested that the appropriation and development of cyberspace is socially constructed at the local scale by the interplay between individuals and institutions, and mediated by a broader, more regional/global political economy through such structures as investment, policy, marginalisation, local economic conditions and status (levels of unemployment, poverty etc.), and the opportunity to exploit and break into both local and global markets. As such, there is a complex interplay between cultural and economic ideologies at both local and global scales. This approach recognises that cyberspace has important implications at the individual and local scale especially relating to identity and community and at regional and global scale especially in relation to economic development. These two spheres are not independent and there is a whole series of mediating factors that intricately entwine them in the form of politics and polity (democracy, ownership, regulation, access, ethics, laws). However, rather than develop a grand narrative, I suggest that we need to carefully deconstruct the various levels of interdependence, from the fluidity and multiplicity of on-line identities to the restructuring of the employment market. Further, we need to examine the linkages between the virtual and non-virtual worlds, the points of intersection, and the ways in which each impinges on and affects the other.

The book is divided into seven related chapters. Each chapter discusses a particular theme although the arguments for an overarching and integrated approach are developed throughout. In the first chapter, cyberspace is introduced, the basis of the hype surrounded cyberspatial technologies examined and the themes of the book outlined. In Chapter 2, the history and growth of cyberspace and cyberspatial technologies is explored. Both the Internet and virtual reality technologies have their origins in the US ARPA projects of the 1960s, although their subsequent development differed substantially. Individual timelines are developed and discussed. In Chapter 3, theoretical perspectives for understanding and studying cyberspace are critically appraised and a new approach linking aspects of postmodernism with political economy and social constructivism outlined. The potential social and cultural effects of cyberspace are explored in Chapter 4. Cyberspace, because of its disembodying and interactive nature, is thought to represent a catalyst for a broad and extensive change in society. At an individual level cyberspace is thought to have significant implications for identity and for how we come to understand identity. At a higher level cyberspace is seen as providing alternative communities to those experienced in non-virtual worlds. The political implications of cyberspace are critically appraised and explored in Chapter 5. In the first section of the chapter, the discussion focuses upon the effects of cyberspace upon democratic processes and structures, examining the two opposing views that cyberspace will either reinforce current systems or ultimately bring about the collapse of traditional government. In the following sections, the arguments concerning ownership and regulation, privacy and confidentiality, ethics and deviancy, and access, marginalisation and exclusion are examined. In Chapter 6, cyberspace's potential role within the emerging information economy and the implications of such an economy are assessed through the examination of organisational and employment restructuring, and the processes of urban–regional reconfiguration. Trends such as globalisation, office automation, back-offices and the slow rise in telework are examined. In the last chapter, the various social, cultural, political and economic themes are drawn back together and interwoven within the context of a combined postmodern, social constructivist and political economy approach, and possible futures discussed.

BACKGROUND TO THE BOOK

The germ for this book was planted in the spring of 1995, when the media hype surrounding cyberspace was probably at its highest, in a visit to the National Center for Geographic Information and Analysis (NCGIA) at the State University of New York, Buffalo. It was there that I met Mike Batty. I had just published a short piece in the *Geographical Magazine* concerning Internet resources for geographers and was just starting to become interested in wider debates concerning cyberspace. Mike had for a number of years been publishing work concerning the development of telematic networks and their effect upon urban–regional infrastructure. We spoke at length and agreed to keep in touch. A couple of months later, a chance remark by Tristan Palmer (then an editor at Routledge) provided the impetus for this book. At the time I was trying to generate interest in an idea that even now sits on the back boiler, and he asked if I knew anyone who might be able to write a book on cyberspace. I contacted Mike and we put together a proposal with Bob Barr from the University of Manchester. The book we planned *Digital Planet: Virtual Geographies of Cyberspace*, is clearly visible within this book although there are some quite significant differences. During the spring of 1996 I drafted out my three chapters. Mike withdrew from the project to concentrate on an urban modelling/virtual reality research contract he had just won and while I waited for Bob to reply to my e-mails I drafted out chapters that covered what he would be contributing. When Tristan Palmer moved to Wiley in the summer, I followed. The first draft of the manuscript was completed in September 1996. After review, and some quite extensive changes, the second draft was completed in May 1997.

During the two years from when I first met Mike Batty, a number of changes to my life have occurred. Probably the two most significant are that my intellectual reasoning is changing as I move out of the modernist framework to start embracing the ideas of postmodernism, and that I now live just outside Belfast, Northern Ireland, rather than in Swansea in South Wales. Moving to an area that is famed for 'the troubles' has placed cyberspace into context. Surfing the 'information highway', while providing a space of escapism, is not going to solve the deeply entrenched differences between the two communities that are in conflict here. Some might argue that the disembodied and anonymous nature of cyberspace might allow the creation of neutral spaces in which the two groups might engage in political dialogue without fear of reprisal – creating a platform that might be built upon in geographic space. I am not so sure. The people on the 'front line' are often from the poorest backgrounds, with little access to computer technology or the literacy to be able to use it. Cyberspace, despite utopian predictions, is not going to be the panacea for all the world's problems. Cyberspace, and the information economy, has reached Northern Ireland. British Telecom is building a large £30 million telematic centre in Belfast and some businesses are moving on-line and using e-mail.[8] The extent to which people are surfing the web or exploring on-line discussion groups is harder to fathom. In recent visits to the USA it is clear that people there seem enthusiastic about embracing cyberspace; the mood seems more upbeat and hopeful, and I am sure if I had written this book while living in California the tone would be different. I do not get the impression of an upbeat attitude to cyberspace in Northern Ireland – there are other, more pressing, issues on the agenda, so the corporate and media hype has not created a population desperate to get on-line. It is with these thoughts in mind that I have approached writing this book. While I think that cyberspace is going to have significant impacts upon our lives – the way we use our leisure time, the way the economy works – our analysis of how these effects will take place needs to be framed in the wider context in which we live our lives.

A number of people have made this book possible through their helpful discussions and readings of various chapters. I would like to take this opportunity to thank Bob Barr, Mike Bratt, Paul Cox, Neil Crump, Tom Delph-Januirek, Martin Dodge, Andy Gillespie, Stephen Graham, David Griffith, Keith Halfacree, Dan Jacobson, Nuala Johnson, Sheep, Richard Selby, Peter Shirlow, Ian Shuttleworth, Andy Smith and Spencer Wood. I would particularly like to thank Tristan Palmer, my editor at Wiley, who has kept this whole project on track, Gill Alexander for producing the illustrations and Mike Batty who started me on the process of writing and who was there still at the end.

Rob Kitchin
Belfast, May 1997

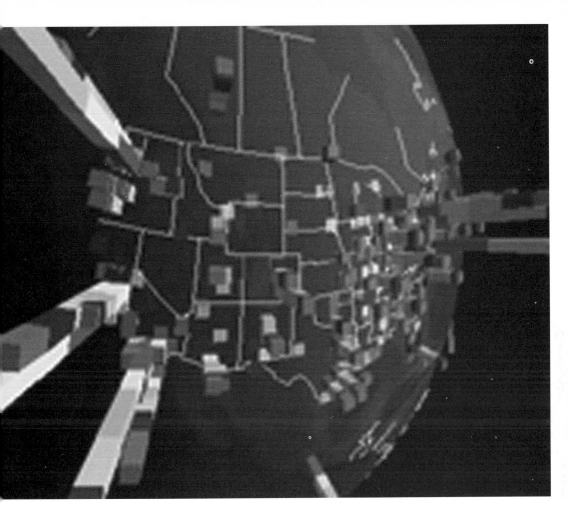

CHAPTER 1

INTRODUCING CYBERSPACE

CHAPTER 1
INTRODUCING CYBERSPACE

> A consensual hallucination experienced daily by billions of legitimate operators, in every nation, by children being taught mathematical concepts . . . A graphic representation of data abstracted from the banks of every computer in the human system. Unthinkable complexity. Lines of light ranged in the nonspace of the mind, clusters and constellations of data. Like city lights, receding . . .[1]

The above quotation is the often cited passage that William Gibson used to first describe cyberspace in his 1984 novel *Neuromancer*. Since Gibson published *Neuromancer* the word cyberspace has been subsumed into everyday life. It is a word that eludes concrete definition, with its elusiveness bound within the abstract nature of that which it seeks to describe and define. In *Neuromancer* cyberspace is a 'dataspace', a vast 'world in the wires'[2] known as 'the matrix', where transnational companies trade in information in a visual, Cartesian and electronic space. Here data reside in colourful architectural forms in a space the imagination enters and interacts with. Like films such as *Bladerunner, Terminator, Robocop* and *Johnny Mnemonic* (also written by Gibson), *Neuromancer* paints a dystopian picture of the near future where the urban fabric is in decay, technology and information is power and humans and machine merge to become one.

Since Gibson's seminal novel, the word cyberspace has been wrested free of its futuristic, dystopian moorings and generally been used to describe emerging computer-mediated communications and virtual reality technologies.[3] Both these cyberspatial technologies allow people to interact with other people or with computer simulated worlds. These technologies fit with Gibson's description of a consensual hallucination because, as Stone[4] explains through reference to Habitat, a real, on-line virtual environment, there are well-known consensual protocols or rules and because the medium of interaction loosely simulates real-world interaction. As we will see, however, the emerging technologies do more than just electronically simulate traditional forms of communication – they also provide new means of interaction. Cyberspace can generally be divided into three domains: the Internet, intranets and virtual reality. While the Internet and intranets are closely related, graphical virtual reality technologies have a different history and it is only in recent years that they have started to converge with communication media.

The Internet is a vast collection of computers linked to networks within larger networks spanning the globe – a huge anarchic, self-organising and relatively unpoliced system[5] which allows unlimited access to the other people connected, and the information stored on public databases and computer sites; 'a new network of virtual sites . . . superimposed on the world of places'.[6] As suggested, the Internet is not one networked space but consists of several separate but interconnected networked spaces (each consisting of thousands of individual networks), all linked through common communication protocols (ways of exchanging information). The diversity of these spaces can be illustrated in reference to John December's conceptual map of cyberspace (see Figure 1.1).

Anyone with a computer, a modem and a telephone can connect to one of the network spaces and through it to the rest of the Internet. To support those people without access to a machine there has been a growing number of cybercafes where users can log on at an hourly rate[7] (see Plate 1.1). At present, the Internet offers users a range of interactions allowing them to explore the world beyond their home. Users can browse information stored on other computers, exchange electronic mail, participate in discussion groups on a variety of topics, transfer files, search databases, take part in real-time conferences and games, and run software on distant computers.

The least sophisticated of these activities are accessing a remote machine using telnet and file transfer protocol (FTP). Telnet allows you to log on (attach) to a remote host computer. In effect, your computer becomes a terminal of the remote host allowing you to explore the files stored there. For example, you can use your computer at home (say, in London) to log on to a computer in a different location (say, Los Angeles). Even though you are physically sitting in your office, you can be searching directories, or deleting or copying files, thousands of miles away on the other side of the Atlantic. In general, you will need a log in name and a password to gain entry but there are some open access sites, including many bulletin boards. FTP allows you to 'download' or copy files from a remote computer to your own. Unlike telnet, which makes your computer a terminal of the host, when using FTP you can only look at the files and download them. Again, you need to have a username and a password. For open access sites the username is generally *anonymous*. Sometimes no password is required, but if it is, it is usual to enter your e-mail address.

Possibly the most used cyberspatial facility is the transfer of e-mail. E-mail allows people to send messages to each other via the computer. To send a message a person types into the computer the whole memo/letter and then sends the text, through the Internet, to the other person's specific, personalised address. In addition to plain text messages, most mailers also allow you to send files of various sorts (e.g. graphic or word-processed) across the Internet. Mail thus travels from point-to-point and to only the other person's address. Mailing lists are centralised, and in some cases monitored, forums for allowing a number of individuals to converse or swap information via e-mail on specific topics. Every e-mail message sent to the list is then redistributed to all the other subscribers, who then have the opportunity to respond.

An alternative to mailing lists is provided by bulletin boards. Bulletin boards, are centralised facilities that allow users to employ a number of functions. These can include access to newslists and chat facilities and the ability to connect to, and download information from, other boards. Newslists are centralised places to read mail, and

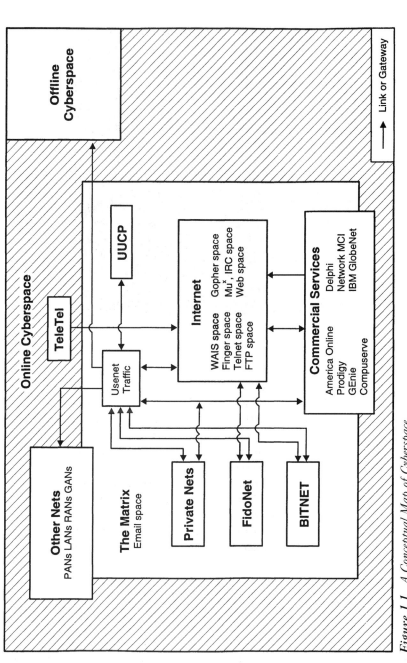

Figure 1.1   A Conceptual Map of Cyberspace

Plate 1.1   A Cybercafe

act like bulletin boards in real life. People can log on and check the board for messages, which are organised under subject headings. Within each subject there are normally several threads of conversations. Users can 'un-pin' a message, read it and choose whether to reply. As such, the system works in the opposite way to mailing lists. Whereas all mail on a mailing list is posted to all members of the list, on bulletin boards all users must go to the board to check for mail. Usenet is a particular example of a collection of newslists that is distributed across more than one bulletin board, so that people around the world can contribute. Within Usenet there are literally thousands of groups discussing the whole spectrum of human activity.

The World Wide Web (WWW) consists of multimedia data (mostly text and graphics) which is stored as hypertext documents (documents that contain links to other pages of information). Using a browsing program such as Netscape Navigator allows users to connect to a computer server and to explore and interact with the information stored there. For example, it is now possible to shop and bank on-line, find out about educational establishments or keep your children entertained, discover about places you might visit and even book your visit, and to keep abreast of local, national and global news via WWW pages (Plate 1.2). By clicking the cursor on a link (usually highlighted text or a graphical icon) the user is taken to that document. As such, the WWW allows people to 'jump' easily between documents, and search for other relevant documents. In addition to displaying documents, the introduction of JAVA script now means that programs can be run and downloaded across the web. Furthermore, companies are now

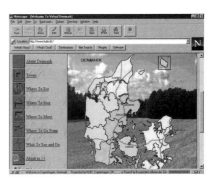

Plate 1.2   World-Wide-Web Pages

also using the web as a broadcast medium, channelling radio and television pictures direct to the host machine. Increasingly, businesses are noticing the advertising and marketing potential of web pages, and many conventional media (e.g. television and newspapers) now inform the viewer of the Internet address of the company's pages with enticements of special offers and more information.

Some Internet services allow real-time interaction with other people rather than stored information. Chat facilities, for example, allow a number of users to converse via the computer in much the same way as a face-to-face conversation might develop. As the user types in a message it simultaneously appears on the other user's screen, or else the text is typed and then sent. Because this does not have the benefits of normal face-to-face conversations such as voice inflection, eye contact and body mannerisms, chat users have developed a number of ways to impart such information through textual means (see Table 1.1). And some users, such as those described in Correll's[8] study of an on-line lesbian cafe, construct elaborate meeting places with the dialogue framed within the context of the setting. Similarly, textual virtual environments such as MUDs (multiple user domains; also known as MUSEs (multiple user social environments), MUSHes (multiple user social hosts)[9] and MOOs (multiple object-oriented)) provide a themed context for the interactions between people. The differences between these acronyms are mainly concerned with how each is programmed and the sort of interaction achievable in each. Whereas a MUD has been hard programmed to contain certain features, which would be textually described to a person entering a room, MOOs allow participants to alter and create environments, and to assign meanings and values to objects, which are then stored in a large database for future users. For the purpose of this book, I just use the MUD acronym to represent all the various textual worlds. The emergence and popularity of MUDs has led some commentators to argue that these virtual environments form new cultural spaces.[10]

The second main form of digital, networked space are called intranets. Intranets have the same general packet-switching, architectural form as the Internet, allowing the

Table 1.1 *Emoticons and the Feelings they are Used to Express*

Typical US/European emoticons		Typical Japanese emoticons	
:-)	regular smile	(∧—∧)	regular smile
:∧)	happy	(∧o∧)	happy
;-)	wink/mischievous	(∧ . ∧)	girl's smile
:-o	wow	(*∧o∧*)	exciting
:-|	grim	(∧o∧;)	excuse me!
:-||	anger	(—o—)	I'm sorry
:-(	sad	(;—;)	weeping
:∧(	unhappy	(∧ ∧;)	cold sweat
.oO	thinking	(∧—∧;;)	awkward

Source: Adapted from Aoki (1994)

transfer of multimedia data, but are private, corporate networks linking the offices, production sites and distribution sites of a company around the world. These are closed networks, using specific lines leased from telecommunications providers, with no, or very limited, public access to files[11] (company employees with knowledge of the correct password might gain entry from a public network). For example, most banks and financial institutions have national, closed intranets connecting up all their branches, offices and automatic teller machines (ATMs) to a central database facility which monitors transactions. Other systems might monitor orders and bookings, allow e-mail to be sent between different sites and allow teleconferencing. Such systems are protected by 'firewall' systems, which ensure that unauthorised users cannot gain access.

Virtual reality technologies partially or totally immerse users in an interactive, visual, artificial, computer-generated environment; instead of the users being spectators of a static screen, they are participants in an environment that responds.[12] By watching the screen or using head-mounted goggles users view a stereoscopic virtual world that phenomenologically engulfs them. When the user moves their mouse or head the 'surrounding' virtual world is continuously updated by the computer, providing the illusion that the user is partially or fully immersed in a three-dimensional, interactive space.[13] Virtual reality has three essential components: it is inclusive; it is interactive; and the interaction is in real time.[14] Because virtual reality integrates a whole series of computer-dependent media, Coyle refers to it as the new 'meta-media'.[15] Although at present it is mainly visual, developers soon hope to be able to fully include sound and touch. The aim is to create another world inside the computer where the experiences are the same as in the real world;[16] to make 'cyberspace into a place'.[17]

Heim[18] declares that 'virtual environments suck in their users with a power unlike any other medium' and argues that:

> tools that transform us, like fire and the wheel or the automobile, become integral parts of our destiny, part of ourselves. Such devices cause us to evolve and eventually mature. VR will very likely transform the culture that uses it.[19]

Virtual reality exponents argue that this transformation will be based upon the exhilaration of experiencing 'transcendence and liberation from the material and embodied world'.[20] At present, virtual reality machines are mainly limited to the military, academia and the arcade entertainment industry, but it is the potential to merge with the Internet that is really exciting commentators and analysts alike; from your own home you will be able to enter a virtual world, as envisaged by Gibson.[21] This convergence of technologies is rapidly taking place. In recent years, experimental virtual reality sites using VRML programming have been appearing on the web, allowing people to run virtual reality simulations via the Internet (see Plate 1.3) and also to take part in virtual reality MUDs (see Plate 1.4). Commercially, it is envisaged that virtual reality will have applications within architecture, planning, the military and surgery as places to explore possible eventualities.[22]

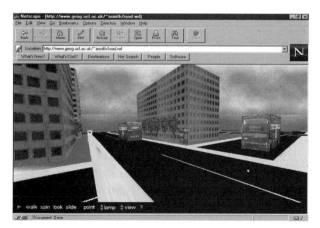

*Plate 1.3   Virtual Reality Simulations Across the Web
(http://www.geog.ucl.ac.uk/~asmith/road.wrl)*

Plate 1.4   Virtual Reality MUDs (http://ww3.blacksun.com/)

THE CYBERSPACE PHENOMENON

Cyberspatial technologies have caught the imagination of academics and the popular media alike. The reasons for this are numerous, and centre upon the fact that for many analysts cyberspatial technologies are determined to be transformative technologies, changing the way we live our lives, just as the car, telephone and television did earlier in the century. Moreover, these technologies are going to affect the lives of individuals regardless of whether they actively use them or even want to use them.[23] For example, whether we have a networked computer or not, cyberspatial technologies directly affect such things as the money markets and thus commodity prices. As such, cyberspatial technologies have been seized upon and used as a site for future projections to be cast upon. Whether these projections are utopian, dystopian or measured, cyberspace, for many social analysts and commentators, embodies and helps to illustrate the changes in western society at the end of the twentieth century. To many of these analysts, the advent of a cyberspatial age confirms the end of the modernist period and our entry into a postmodern world. For them, cyberspace is helping to transform society into a system fundamentally different from the one that gave rise to high technology.

In relation to culture and society cyberspace is providing a new laboratory in which to investigate and challenge the strictures of modernist thought, and is leading analysts to rethink accepted notions of the body, identity, community and nature. For example, researchers suggest that in cyberspace, identity – once described as rational, stable, centred and autonomous – becomes unstable, multiple, diffuse, fluid, and manipulable because the disembodied nature of communication and relative anonymity allows you to be accepted on the basis of your words, not your appearance or accent. Further, immersion within virtual worlds is leading some analysts to argue that cyberspatial technologies further the process of cyborging (the merging of technology and nature) and thus blur the boundaries of key dualisms that underlie modernist thought. For example, it is suggested that the dualisms of nature/machine and virtuality/reality both become unstable and untenable. Theorists such as Haraway[24] argue that the de-stabilisation of these dualisms creates a space in which some of the lynch pins of modernist thought can be recontested and renegotiated in an emancipatory and empowering way. In particular, she suggests that gender relations might be radically renegotiated in cyberspace. In addition, many analysts have been examining the potential effects of cyberspace upon notions of community. It is well documented that on-line communities are forming, centred on common interests and affinity rather than coincidence of location. Whereas social interaction, common ties and location are of importance in traditional notions of community, in cyberspace it is suggested that personal intimacy, moral commitment and social cohesion come to the fore. For some commentators such as Rheingold, cyberspace thus offers us the opportunity to reclaim public space and recreate the essence and nature of community on-line. Paradoxically, cyberspace is also helping to form off-line community groups in the form of cyberpunks and cyberians, who adopt a technology/new age based lifestyle.

In relation to politics and polity the development of cyberspace raises a whole series of questions concerning democracy, ownership, regulation and governance. Cyberspace, by providing a new medium of communication, is thought to provide a new space for political dialogue and democracy. Others suggest that cyberspace challenges space-based political order by rendering borders meaningless, and predict the breakdown of traditional polities and a new age of anarchic rule. Furthermore, cyberspace raises a number of issues concerning ownership, regulation and control. At present, there are few legal precedents concerning cyberspace, and whoever owns the 'wires' controls the network. As such, cyberspace is set to become a largely public space with private owners. Despite claims that cyberspace is an egalitarian space, access is clearly not universal and on-line discourse is predominantly Western. Cyberspace is also seen as a new space of deviancy, providing a new medium for pornography, perversion, antisocial behaviour and crime.

In relation to economics and regional development, cyberspace is seen as the technology *par excellence* as the 'information economy' starts to blossom and take shape, combining the communication of telecommunications with the storage and processing capabilities of computing. Cyberspatial technologies are set to revolutionise how we conduct business and alter our patterns of work. Poster[25] suggests that cyberspatial technologies are amongst those that are helping to replace the 'mode of capital and labour' with a new 'mode of information'. Such developments are leading analysts to examine how corporate and employment structures are being reorganised with the advent of office automation, telework and the adoption of back-offices operations. This corporate restructuring has important implications concerning urban–regional patterns of development and change, with analysts such as Graham and Marvin[26] suggesting that the new communication industries are leading to a radical restructuring of urban form and life as digital communication renders the friction of distance meaningless and reconfigures the functional structure of the city.

Mitchell[27] entwines some of these social, political and economic themes to argue that we are moving from a period when life is regulated by structures within space and time, to a period when the network will be the new agora with new, fragmented regulatory structures:

> The network is the urban site before us, an invitation to design and construct the City of Bits. . . . This will be a city un-rooted to any definite spot on the surface of the earth, shaped by connectivity and bandwidth constraints rather than by accessibility and land values, largely asynchronous in its operation, and inhabited by disembodied and fragmented subjects who exist as a collection of aliases and agents. Its places will be constructed virtually by software instead of physically from stones and timbers, and they will be connected by logical linkages rather than by doors, passageways and streets.

In combination, then cyberspace is set to revolutionise our social, political and economic lives. Cyberspace has a fundamentally different structure to the physical structures that currently organise everyday life, operating in new ways that will have serious repercussions concerning our lifestyles and the environments we live in.

NEW VOICES, NEW SPACES, NEW CATEGORIES

Commentators have focused upon one of three 'revolutions' to explain why cyberspatial developments are so significant. Firstly, cyberspace is challenging our traditional ideas concerning mass communication and the form of communication. Secondly, cyberspace is helping to radically transform space–time relations and create new social spaces. Thirdly, cyberspace is leading to a rethinking of concepts such as reality and nature. Although often discussed independently, these three 'revolutions' are highly interrelated.

For many, cyberspaces are changing the *nature of communication* in three main ways. Firstly, cyberspatial technologies are challenging the traditional mass medium model of one-to-many broadcasts and are thus transforming the way we produce and exchange knowledge.[28] Morris and Ogan,[29] for example, discuss the way in which the Internet plays with the traditional source–message–receiver features, sometimes retaining the same configuration, sometimes using different configurations. They detail that producers and audiences can be grouped into four categories:

- One-to-one asynchronous communication, such as e-mail.
- Many-to-many asynchronous communication, such as Usenet, bulletin boards or mailing lists.

- Synchronous communication on a one-to-one, one-to-few and one-to-many basis, as found on Internet Relay Chat, chat rooms and MUDs.
- Synchronous communication where the receiver seeks out information from a provider, such as web sites, gopher and FTP.

Unlike traditional mass media such as television and newspapers, which are based on a one-to-many model where an editor, publisher or producer decides upon what should be seen and when, the 'consumers' of cyberspace are also the 'producers', so that we have a merging of the traditional boundaries. In addition, in cyberspace it is easy, fast and relatively inexpensive to produce many copies and to redistribute information.[30] Until recently, all cyberspatial connections involved interactivity. As a result, they required more effort than sitting watching a television or listening to a radio. However, television and radio are now receivable over the Web, and it is predicted that we will now see the emergence of two distinct cyberspatial populations: 'the interacter and the interacting'.[31] While some might argue that the Internet is yet to become a mass medium (i.e. 10–20% of the population has adopted the innovation) it is clear that in North America this figure, if not already surpassed, is within sight.

Secondly, the various forms of cyberspace are providing new forms of communication. Castells, for example, suggests that cyberspace is leading to the formation of a new meta-language as, for the first time, the written, oral and auditory modes of communication are integrated in the same system. He argues that cyberspace is fundamentally changing the character of communication:

> Because culture is mediated and enacted through communication, cultures themselves, that is our historically produced systems of beliefs and codes, become fundamentally transformed, and will be more so over time, by the new technological system.

At present, cyberspace is limited to mainly textual interaction. As such, whereas social presence and emotion are often communicated through visual means in face-to-face discussion, in cyberspace other means have to be found to express personality and feelings. Analysts contend that cyberspace provides a unique space of communication, blending together written and oral styles to produce a new linguistic register and to create new rules of language. Written interaction within settings such as a MUD display a novel form of communication as users convert normally verbal communications into a written style. To communicate, users usually only have access to the 'lower end ASCII' character set (upper and lower case letters, numbers and some commonly used mathematical and punctuation symbols such as (,), $, % and +). Given this restricted character set and the fact that writing takes longer than speech, a relatively sophisticated shorthand has been developed to speed up communication while creating and sharing meaning. For example, '=' is used to mean the same as; s/tume/time indicates a correction to misspelt type; rkitchin <− Belfast means that rkitchin lives in Belfast.[32] The extent of these unusual words can be confusing for the newcomer but they are generally learnt quickly with experience. To add emotional content and substitute for physical expression a series of emoticons have also been developed. These can be used to express a whole range of feelings. As Table 1.1 demonstrates, these emoticons do have a cultural basis varying for different countries. For example, unlike the US-inspired versions where the emoticons are read side-on, the Japanese emoticons are designed to be viewed traditionally. In addition, these emoticons are interpreted slightly differently by US/European and Japanese users. Whereas US/European emoticons are often used in a joking or ironic way, Japanese emoticons are often interpreted literally. CAPITAL letters are used to indicate shouting and groups of periods pauses (e.g. 'yeah . . . right').

In addition to the writing style, the nature of interaction is also changing. In face-to-face conversations it is usually only possible to follow one or possibly two discussions at any one time. This is mainly limited spatially (the number of people within earshot) but also through our need to be able to distinguish the signal we want to listen to from other noises. However, within chat rooms and MUDs it is not uncommon for several threads of conversation to be running simultaneously. Skilled users can follow these multiple threads and contribute to many of them simultaneously. This is equivalent to being able to listen and contribute to everyone's conversations within a cocktail party, not just those of the people immediately around you. However, when several people are 'speaking' at the same time within the same MUD room the text can quickly scroll up the screen and following the conversations becomes more difficult. In addition, whereas with face-to-face conversation people can make long speeches and the other person must wait for them to stop speaking,[33] the nature of MUDs forces people to type short messages otherwise the other person is left thinking 'when will they start speaking?'. Messages are composed and then sent rather than appearing as composed. Users refer to the time delay between messages as the 'lag'. This gives an on/off form of communication. Some experienced users use this lag to good effect, talking about two topics simultaneously: while one person is replying to one conversation, the other is composing a reply to the other conversation.[34] In this way, neither person is left idle.

Thirdly, cyberspace allows people to construct their self-presentation much more carefully and to play with their on-line identity, adopting roles that they would not usually undertake.[35] For example, people can experiment with gender roles, pretending to be male or female, or even adopting gender-neutral positions, and play with personality, choosing to be shy or loud and boisterous. Although some researchers predicted that computer-mediated communication would be cold and anonymous and lack social presence because of the absence of non-visual cues, analysts now suggest that this could not be further from the truth. Play on-line is expressed in a number of different ways through the masking and unmasking of identity, engaging with word-play and the use of innuendo and irony.[36] It is suggested that this playfulness is due to the relative anonymity and disembodied nature of the medium coupled with a clear sense of interactivity and more equal power relations between discussants (traditional social hierarchies disappear in the ether). The screen acts as a mask, much like masks within a carnival. The flip-side of this level of anonymity is that people are more open and frank with their views and this often leads to open hostility and what has become known as flaming. Flames are abusive messages where people dispose of diplomacy. For some analysts the nature of cyberspace thus allows people to explore their identity further but also highlights to those experimenting with identity the world of those they are pretending to be (e.g. gender-swapping highlights the ways in which gender structures human interaction).

Other commentators suggest that rather than changing the nature of the communication, it is the *transformation of space and time* that lies at the heart of potential impacts of cyberspatial technologies: social transformation is occurring through spatial transformation. Indeed, Soja[37] argues that space (and place) is central to today's postmodern society, contending that 'the contemporary period of restructuring has been accompanied by an accentuated visibility and consciousness of spatiality and spatialisation, regionalisation and regionalism'. Harvey[38] argues that there has been a collapse of spatial and temporal boundaries, with cyberspace and telecommunication technologies leading to a radical space–time compression. Whereas innovations such as the railway reduced communication times substantially, telecommunications makes them near instantaneous. Not only have the effects of spatial separation been negated, but expenditure on delivery has been substantially reduced in real terms. The increasing efficiency of communication is translating into greater and more efficient productivity. The 'wiring of the world' is leading to a corporate, decentralised globalisation. This has led some commentators, such as Benedikt,[39] to question the 'significance of geographical location at all scales'. For Benedikt,[40] 'we are turned into nomads . . . who are always in touch' with the 'spatial dynamics of the whole world collaps[ing] to those of a pinhead'.[41] Castells[42] refers to a change from the 'space of places' to a 'space of flows'. Gillespie and Williams,[43] however, warn that it is misleading to think of near-instantaneous telecommunication technologies as mere 'distance shrinkers'. For them, telecommunication technologies, including cyberspatial technologies, challenge fundamentally classic economic geographies based upon the ideas of 'friction of distance':

> The idea of telecommunications as 'distance shrinking' makes it analogous to other transport and communications improvements. However, in so doing the idea fails to capture the essential essence of advanced telecommunications, which is not to reduce the 'friction of distance' but to render it entirely meaningless. When the time taken to communicate over 10,000 miles is indistinguishable from the time to communicate over 1 mile, then 'time–space' convergence has taken place at a profound scale. Because all geographical relationships are based, implicitly or explicitly on the existence of the friction imposed by distance, then it follows that the denial of any such friction brings into question the very basis of geography that we take for granted.

As such, 'geography and time are no longer boundaries'.[44]

In contrast to this radical position, where the Internet is seen as a space–time destroyer, shrinking distance and time to zero, others suggest that while cyberspace does have a significant influence concerning space–time relations, geography and time will not be eliminated. Space and time remain significant for three main reasons. Firstly, cyberspatial connections and bandwidth are unequally distributed both within and between Western countries and in comparison to developing countries. Globalisation is not an egalitarian process aimed at creating an equitable distribution; it is designed to reproduce capital most effectively. Secondly, while information on-line might seem geographically dislocated, information is only as useful at the locale within which the body resides. For example, a gay man who physically lives in an area of homophobia or where homosexual practice is illegal will still be unable to openly act on his desires regardless of the information gathered on the Internet.[45] Thirdly, cyberspace depends on real world spatial fixity – the points of access, the physicality and materiality of wires. There is a world outside of the wires in the form of other infrastructures, and local and global markets. Location is not going to become irrelevant because cyberspace does not annihilate all of the other determinates of commercial location such as face-to-face social networks, skilled workforce and access to materials and markets. Paradoxically, globalisation is thus exerting the simultaneous pressures of unity and fragmentation.[46] Far from eliminating variances between places, cyberspatial technologies actually permit the exploitation of differences between places by capitalising on cheap wages, reduced standards of work conditions, cheap sites etc. Castells,[47] for example, while acknowledging some of the decentralising tendencies of informational technologies, argues that geography currently remains paramount. In many cases, information technologies reinforce centralising tendencies because they are tied to the telecommunication infrastructure and social milieu of large metropolitan areas. Similarly, those services that can be decentralised have to locate in areas of suitable skilled-labour and conventional transport links. As such, the local is not insignificant. As Morley and Robins[48] state:

> If we have emphasised processes of delocalisation, associated especially with the development of new information and communications networks, this should not be seen as an absolute tendency. The particularity of place and culture can never be done away with, can never be transcended. Globalisation is, in fact, also associated with new dynamics of re-localisation. It is about the achievement of a new global–local nexus, about new and intricate relations between global space and local space. Globalisation is like a jigsaw puzzle: it is a matter of inserting a multiplicity of localities into the overall picture of a new global system.

Castells[49] thus suggests that we are witnessing a division of spatial logic into two distinct forms. The 'space of flows', he suggests, is emerging to dominate the old 'space of places'. The space of flows is the space of managerial elites and the dominant interests in our society. This space of flows overlies the space of places. At present, then, real space is merely being overlain by a virtual space in a symbiotic fashion,[50] allowing organisations to be more flexible in relation to real-space geographies.

Cyberspace, as well as affecting traditional space–time relations, is also seen to be providing a new social space,[51] a place where people can meet and interact; a place with a new uncharted virtual geography which bears little resemblance to geography outside the wires.[52] In recent years, planners and geographers[53] have been arguing that real-world spaces are not just Cartesian spaces, absolutely defined and understood with Euclidean geometry, but are also socially constructed. Here, it is argued that our access to certain spaces is strongly regulated through social and cultural practices and beliefs. In effect, certain spaces are socialised by certain homogeneous groups who regulate and exclude 'unwelcome' visitors. Social spaces, as found in any city, are thus contested through processes of domination and marginalisation. We can thus identify social spaces that are constructed through identity politics relating to gender, race, ethnicity, disability and sexuality.

MUDs, discussion lists and IRC are spaces that are socially constructed; they do form social spaces. Cyberspace is a social space free of the constraints of the body, you are accepted on the basis of your written words, not what you look or sound like. Cyberspaces are 'social spaces in which people still meet face-to-face, but under new definitions of both 'meet' and 'face'.[54] Gibson[55] remarks that 'everyone I know who works with computers seems to develop a belief that there's some kind of *actual space* behind the screen, someplace you can't see but you know it is there'. In many respects, the actual space Gibson identifies is a consensual social space devoid of any of the qualities of formal, real-world space. Indeed, Mitchell[56] describes cyberspace as:

> profoundly *antispatial* . . . You cannot say where it is or describe its memorable shape and proportions or tell a stranger how to get there. But you can find things in it without knowing where they are. The Net is ambient – nowhere in particular but everywhere at once. You do not go *to* it; you log *in* from wherever you physically happen to be. . . . the Net's despatialization of interaction destroys the geocode's key. [original emphasis]

For others cyberspace is a significant technological advance because it continues the *blurring of modernistic dualisms* such as virtuality with reality and technology with nature. For example, Benedikt[57] argues that cyberspace causes 'a warpage, tunnelling and lesioning of the fabric of reality'. Cyberspace rapidly increases the blurring of reality and virtuality first started with the printed word, and further developed by radio, television and film. Each of these media provides us with a representation of the real; a copy of the original;[58] simulations which Baudrillard terms hyperreality (more 'real' than reality).[59] Baudrillard has closely examined the ways in which capitalism has subtly moved from an ethic of production to one of consumption. Tied into this change has been a growing consumption of cultural representations. Baudrillard seeks to expose how, despite the desire by modern institutions to portray these representations with true value, they are produced in deliberate ways to seduce consumption. As such, he suggests that much of our postmodern culture is an illusion, full of objects and buildings masquerading as the real. America is seen as the capital of the postmodern hyperreal, where styles and objects from all countries are merged and where the fake substitutes itself for the real and in the process becomes more real than the real. Disneyland is often seen as the 'apotheosis of the hyperreal . . . a fantasy more real than reality'[60] with Las Vegas and Los Angeles the archetypal cities. Virilio[61] argues that rather than simulating reality, 'virtuality will destroy reality'. He argues that rather than being a simulation, virtuality is a substitution. He explains:

this is a real glass, this is no simulation. When I hold a virtual glass with a data glove, this is no simulation, but substitution ... As I see it, new technologies are substituting a virtual reality for an actual reality. . . . there will be two realities: the actual and the virtual. . . . This is no simulation but the coexistence of two separate worlds.

Castells,[62] however, argues that 'virtual reality' is a misleading term. He suggests that there has always been a separation of reality and symbolic representation because we always interpret everything we encounter through some system of meaning. He contends that we are constructing a real virtuality where reality is entirely captured by the medium of communication so that our everyday lives are increasingly structured around what we have read, seen or heard: 'make-believe is belief in the making'.[63]

For Slouka[64] the danger is that many of us are now willing to accept the copy as original, and put our trust in those that re-represent the world to us – to accept simulation as substitution. We are too willing to accept the virtual for real. Virtual reality technologies, in particular, are specifically designed to immerse users into a parallel, artificial world that mimics the real. Their appeal is that actions in virtual space do not have material consequences; 'it gives the user the sense that they may do anything, but in terms of consequences, they do nothing'.[65] To many, this replacement of reality with virtuality means that cyberspaces are spaces where we can explore and recontest our identities without material consequence. Slouka,[66] however, fears that these are self-indulgent technologies that will make it increasingly difficult to separate real life from virtual existence. For many of the people Slouka met, cyberspatial interactions on chat and MOO facilities were a reality. The new identities they had formed had blended with their former persona; the virtual was blurring with the real. Slouka's fear is that we are increasingly 'seeing' and understanding the world in isolation, staring through glass windows, whether that be a house window, a car windscreen, a television or a computer screen.[67]

Theorists such as Haraway[68] and Plant[69] argue that, at present, the boundaries between people, their bodies and the outside world are being significantly reconfigured.[70] Balsamo[71] suggests that the boundary between nature and culture serves several ideological purposes. Most importantly, it affirms a proper order and installs a hierarchical relationship between nature and culture. Balsamo argues that this hierarchy serves to reinforce the belief that through technology, humans will prevail over their encounters with nature. However, to many, the boundaries between technology, nature and culture are currently blurring, with the strict hierarchies crumbling and merging through a deep restructuring process. As a result, the divisions between these concepts become unrecognisable. For example, biotechnological advances are leading towards a biochip, which Escobar[72] explains will determine how nature is known and remade. Here, nature will be built the same way as culture, but the 'making of nature will take place through the re-configuration of social life by micropractices originating in medicine, biology, and biotechnology'.[73] For Stone,[74] cyberspatial technologies further help to blur the relationships between the social and technological, biological and mechanical, natural and artificial, with the resultant mergers forming the keystones for the new social space. As we will discover in Chapter 4, the blurring of the relationships between technology, nature and culture, through biological, medical and computing advances, is leading some theorists to hypothesise that we are becoming nations of cyborgs. Here, human and machine merge, with the machine replacing or supplementing the flesh. We are being reconfigured in new ways that challenge traditional identities.

LOOKING THROUGH ROSE-TINTED SCREENS?

From the discussion so far it is clear that the development of cyberspace raises a number of interesting questions relating to the nature of the 'world in the wires' but also in relation to real-world space. Cyberspace is providing a new medium of communication, altering space–time relations and leading some to challenge traditional notions of reality and nature. Within their analyses a large proportion of the literature is optimistic and utopian in its predictions concerning the development and adoption of cyberspatial technologies. While critical responses are now becoming more common, particularly from within academia, the popular press continues to hype cyberspace and its possible implications, particularly those relating to disembodiment, community, democracy and business. Indeed, Slouka[75] suggests that the amount of hype surrounding cyberspace is unprecedented:

> Rarely in . . . history . . . has a new technology been sold so effectively; not since the advent of television have such outrageous claims been made for one; never, to my knowledge, has one steamrolled so completely the voices of caution and dissent. We seem . . . to have bought into the New Age lock, stock and modem. . . . nearly every [newspaper article is] filled with the kind of positive-thinking, forward-looking, onward-marching rhetoric usually reserved for re-election campaigns and times of national crisis.

However, to what extent is this hype warranted? To some critics, utopian commentators are looking through rose-tinted screens. For example, Stallabrass[76] argues that utopists are drawing upon a number of old bourgeois dreams, which include the ability to survey all the world from within one's home, to grasp the totality of all data from within a single frame, to recapture a unified knowledge and experience, and to create a total and eternal archive. He suggests that, ironically, the brave new world that they envisage is based upon the Enlightenment paradigm but defended by postmodern theory. To Stallabrass and others, the utopists are painting a poor picture of how cyberspace will affect society. Castells[77] laments that it seems the historical fate of new technologies to be surrounded by prophecies rather than serious social and spatial analysis. Many technologies, despite grand claims, have only partially fulfilled their promise. For example, the development of home video equipment led to claims that everyone would be able to manufacture their own programmes and public access television would challenge the mainstream channels. While there are critical analyses, prophecies still pervade much of the cyberspace literature. Critical Art Ensemble suggest that utopian claims are based around five key virtual promises: the new body; new consciousness, community;

democracy; and convenience. As such, the promises of the utopians take on a variety of forms but normally manage to include words such as liberation, empowerment and revolution, heaven and dreams. As Slouka[78] notes, we are being sold the promise that cyberspace will allow us to solve all our problems, to shed the constraints of materiality, space, time, our bodies and mortality. These are grand claims, effectively suggesting that cyberspace will allow us to become gods, to transcend, and even make, nature.[79] For example, Brenda Laurel[80] writes:

> With virtual reality systems the future is quite literally within our grasp. . . . [It will] blow a hole in all our old imaginings and expectations. Through that hole we can glimpse a world of which both cause and effect are a quantum leap in human evolution.

As Stallabrass[81] notes, cyberspace seems to attract breathless, hyperbolic writing of a quasi-religious nature. For example, Michael Heim,[82] has suggested that cyberspace is 'more than a breakthrough in electronic media . . . cyberspace is a metaphysical laboratory, a tool for examining our very sense of reality'. Elsewhere, Heim,[83] discussing virtual reality, gushes that 'cyberspace transcends the physical by replacing it with the electronic heaven of ideally organized shapes and forms'. Tomas[84] preaches that cyberspace is a 'powerful, collective, mnemonic technology that promises to have an important, if not revolutionary, impact on the future compositions of human identities and cultures'. Novak[85] is also intoxicated with cyberspace's promises, proclaiming 'cyberspace is the place where conscious dreaming meets subconscious dreaming, a landscape of rational magic, of mystical reason, the locus of triumph of poetry over poverty'. Sherman and Judkins[86] argue of virtual reality that 'it is the most dramatic, and potentially most far-reaching, computer development since the silicon chip. It is science fiction come true – it is science fact'. They continue to rejoice that virtual reality is 'truly the technology of miracle and dreams'[87] and go on to exult in the abilities 'to play god' and proclaim that virtual reality 'is the hope for the next century. It may indeed afford glimpses of heaven'.[88] Nicole Stenger[89] enthuses that 'in this cubic fortress of pixels that is cyberspace, we will be, as in dreams, everything', with cyberspace providing 'a wavelength of well-being' opening up 'a space for collective restoration, and for peace . . . our future can only take on a luminous dimension! Welcome to the new world'.

The notion that cyberspace represents a 'new world', or a least a 'new frontier', waiting to be colonised is one oft-repeated. Cyberspace is popularised as a place of exploration and discovery; an unmapped territory to be inhabited and economically exploited:[90]

> The early days of cyberspace were like those of the western frontier. . . . a vast, hitherto-unimagined territory began to open up for exploration. Early computers had been like isolated mountain valleys ruled by programmer-kings; the archaic digital world was a far-flung range in which narrow, unreliable trails provided only tenuous connections among the multitudinous tiny realms. But networking fundamentally changed things. . . . Cyberspace is still a tough territory to travel, though, and we are

just beginning to glimpse what we behold. . . . This vast grid is the new land beyond the horizon, the place that beckons the colonists, cowboys, con-artists, and would-be conquerors of the twenty-first century.

Benedikt[91] argues that 'we are contemplating the arising shape of a new world'. Just as the space age was going to allow us to escape our earthly mistakes, travel to new galaxies to start afresh and create a new world, it seems that the cyberspatial age is going to perform the same role.[92] Penny[93] writes:

> With geography filled up and the dreams of space colonization less viable every day, the drive to the frontier has collapsed on itself. The space remaining for colonization is the space of technology itself.

Instead of looking outside and towards expansion the fatalists have turned to the inside and disembodiment as a means of deliverance. Tomas[94] actually goes so far as to state:

> cyberspace . . . does indeed hold the promise of . . . postorganic lifeforms. . . . For there is reason to believe that these technologies might constitute the central phase in a postindustrial 'rite of passage' between organically human and cyberphysically digital life-forms as reconfigured through computer software systems.

It seems that we will be able to shed our 'meat' (body) and slip behind the screen into the datascape – immortality will be ours.

The utopian claims concerning community, democracy and business follow similar lines of arguments. Cyberspace will provide a new space to reform our ailing communities; a new, egalitarian medium that will provide a truly democratic system of government; and will increase business and profit while increasing leisure time and the standard of living. These claims have not been left unchallenged; a number of commentators have criticised these utopian visions as the pipe dreams of the intoxicated. For Mnookin,[95] cyberspace is the new stage of dreams for utopists who believe that humanity will be saved and transformed by moving to a new space:

> Cyberspace has clearly become the latest site within this lineage of utopian dream-spaces, and in this new world as surely as in the ones that preceded it, utopian dreamers are destined to be disappointed.

Robins,[96] and others such as Sardar, Stallabrass and Slouka,[97] endeavour to grab the heels of the intoxicated, and pull their heads back out of the clouds. They try to burst the bubble that cyberspace, and in particular virtual reality, is the panacea for all the world's problems. Robins[98] develops an argument that contemporary social and cultural theorists have, like Gibson, created a 'consensual hallucination':

> There is a common vision of a future that will be different from the present, of a space or a reality that is more desirable than the mundane one that presently surrounds and contains us. It is a tunnel vision. It has turned a blind eye on the world we live in.

While not denying that cyberspace does raise a whole series of questions relating to identity and community, Robins persuasively contends that these theorists have neglected to realise that we do live in a real world, and despite the problems each of us struggles with everyday, 'there is not some perfect world of cyberspace'[99] that we will be able to migrate to. He suggests that it is time to 'relocate virtual culture in the real world' and 'de-mythologise virtual culture if we are to assess the serious implications it has for our personal and collective lives'.[100] Novak[101] states that 'cyberspace is a habitat for the imagination'; we must remember that real space is the habitat we *do* live in. It is easy to get carried away on the wave of hype, but at present most home computers are just used for word processing, record keeping and game playing.[102] Those who connect to the Internet are generally swapping mail or seeking specific information. The Web currently has little long-term entertainment value (surfing soon becomes tedious) and although those taking part in mailing list discussions number millions, MUD users only numbered about 20 000 in 1991.[103] As Dery[104] proclaims:

> Visions of cyber-Rapture are a fatal seduction, distracting us from the devastation of nature, the unravelling of social fabric, and the widening chasm between technocratic elite and the minimum-wage masses. The weight of social, political and ecological issues brings the posthuman liftoff from biology, gravity, and the twentieth century crashing down to Earth.

Roszak[105] develops a stronger argument, suggesting that while computing does have some benefits these will only be recognisable in the short term and will soon be followed by long-term liabilities. For him, cyberspace is a false promise, and a promise with hidden consequences:

> The computer is the latest entry in . . . history, still bright with promise for its enthusiasts but surely destined to join the lengthening file of modern technological treachery that Aldous Huxley began compiling in his prophetic *Brave New World*. . . . there will never be a machine that leaves us wiser or better or freer than our own naked mind can make us – nor any that helps us work out our salvation with diligence.

Robins[106] contends that we must remember that cyberspace is not a fundamentally different world. Rather, cyberspace overlies real space in a symbiotic relationship. He argues that the changes that cyberspace is predicted to bring about must be placed within the broader context of the social and political upheaval that is taking place in the world today. For him, many commentators have made the error of dealing with technological innovation as self-contained and autonomous, rather than situating their thoughts within the context of wider debates and changes. It should also not be forgotten that cyberspatial technologies are the children of military-funded inventions, and it will be business and industry that will nurture future developments and seek to pocket the rewards. Cyberspace is not divorced from the economic realities of the real world, and wherever there is the potential to make money commercialisation will inevitably follow. As such, some commentators suggest that cyberspace merely represents the creation of new markets – the next frontier for exploitation – and to replicate the dominant pan-capitalist ideology.[107] As Rheingold[108] points out:

> Research and development in the late twentieth century is a hybrid of *capitalism*, science and technology. Discoveries and technologies lead to products; the demand for products, and the money they bring in, drive research to uncover principles that lead to new technologies and improved products. [My emphasis.]

These critics are reminding us that cyberspace technologies did not just appear from nowhere – plenty of hard cash has been spent on developing them, and those doing the developing are at some point going to want to recapture their initial outlay and then to reap large profits. The monthly phone bill (to those outside the USA who have to pay for local calls) and subscription charges to service providers must surely shatter the illusions of many cyberspace users hyped-up on the utopian visions of a 'heaven beyond the screen':

> It is easy to forget that bullshit like 'the fastest route from imagination to reality' is not really for greasing the skids upon which we ride into the future, it is for greasing up potential customers.[109]

This discussion has sought to highlight some of the hype that surrounds cyberspace and the counter-claims of others. In recent years we have witnessed the slow growth of studies which rather than taking a classical utopian or dystopian approach have started to relate cyberspace and virtual lives to our societies within real space. It is this vein of work that we must seek to build upon, critically analysing the implications of cyberspatial developments. As Lajoie[110] states:

> Perhaps it is time to look at the mess outside the windows, rather than pass through the looking-glass of narcissism the computer screen represents into a spectacular hall of mirrors.

THE NEED FOR AN OVERARCHING AND INTEGRATED APPROACH

This book builds upon the arguments of Robins and others and seeks to evaluate the role of cyberspace in everyday life and contemporary society. It is important to realise that just because I do not take a utopian perspective I do not necessarily conceive of cyberspace as a 'bad thing'. To the contrary, I contend that cyberspace does and will matter in a number of fundamental ways. However, we must be careful to chart and analyse its development within the context of the world we do, and will continue to, inhabit, carefully deconstructing the points of intersection between virtual and real space and the ways in which actions within one have consequences in the other.

Not only do we need to base our analysis within the 'real' but we also have to recognise that the social, cultural, political and economic implications of cyberspace are inseparable. Cyberspace does have and will continue to have many implications for our everyday lives. These implications, however, cannot be easily decontextualised because they are intricately entwined. For example, social implications relating to say, identity or community, are not entirely divorced from cultural or political or even economic implications. Both identity and community are bound within larger structures than the purely social and depend on a whole host of intertwined components. My call is for an integrated and overarching approach, which seeks to appreciate the complexity of cyberspace's current and future implications and developments.

Throughout the book such an integrative approach is developed by adopting a perspective that seeks to link postmodernist thinking with ideas from political economy and social constructivism. This approach is outlined in more detail in Chapter 3, but basically it acknowledges that technology and society are bound and intimately woven. As such, cyberspace is best understood by appreciating that technology is both a sociocultural *and* political–economic construct. Essentially, at the local scale technology is socially produced and mediated through culture. Here, different individuals and institutions interplay to determine how technology is socially produced and used. This local scale feeds into and feeds off a much larger set of wider economic relations and dynamics that underlie the global economy. For example, regional and national policies implicitly influence local economic development through specific initiatives that interact with local attitudes, culture and desire to determine how a specific technology is adopted, appropriated and used. The social and economic contexts are thus part of the same structure and are dynamically related to each other, so that cyberspaces are socially constructed within the broader framework of the capitalist political economy. However, it must be noted that I am not seeking to produce some new grand narrative, seeking universal truths. Instead, I am forwarding a position that seeks to deconstruct the complex ways in which the local and global, sociocultural and politico-economic intersect and are played out; a framework in which the fragmentation, decentring and restructuring of society can be read and interpreted.

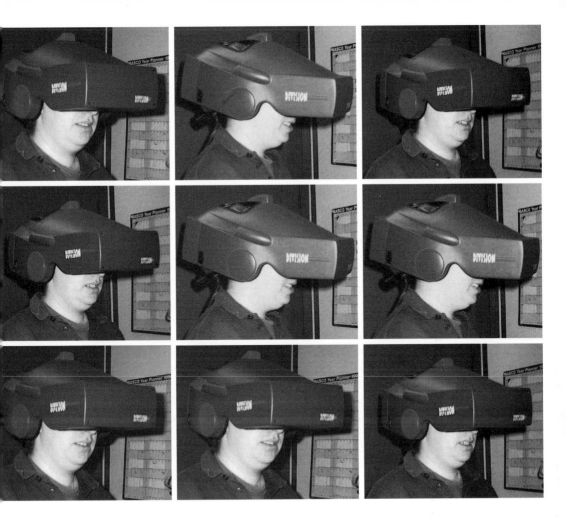

CHAPTER 2
THE HISTORY AND GROWTH
OF CYBERSPACE

CHAPTER 2

THE HISTORY AND GROWTH
OF CYBERSPACE

To fully understand the growth of cyberspace, its history within the 'information revolution' must be appreciated. The advent of cyberspace has not been achieved independently and is bound within the histories of computing and, to a lesser extent,
telecommunication technologies. Today, the world is increasingly becoming wrapped
in 'gigantic invisible cobwebs'[1] of electronic spaces, clothed in 'optic fibres, copper
cables, wireless, microwave and satellite communications networks'.[2] Predictions about
the future are rife and we are already witnessing the Internet and virtual reality technologies merging and coalescing to form a powerful set of cyberspatial technologies. As
a result, in this chapter, the development and growth of both Internet and virtual reality
technologies are detailed (Figure 2.1). It must be appreciated that most of the key
developments, either by large corporate and state-sponsored initiatives or home-brew
tinkering, were made by US computer scientists and enthusiasts and much of this
history has a strong US bias.

Both the Internet and virtual reality technologies can be traced back to the first
computers. These massive machines, using a system of valves and controlled using
punch cards, were originally developed to crack Nazi war codes and to try to compute
the trajectory of missiles.[3] Beyond a few visionaries, such as Bush, Engelbart and
Licklider, their usefulness beyond military and industrial applications was generally
unforeseen, with many believing that we would not need much more powerful machines to fulfil our future needs.[4] By the 1960s, however, people were starting to
become more convinced that computers had the potential to fulfil a number of wider
applications. At this time, machines although reduced in size, were still large and almost
strictly used as scientific machines for research or payroll devices/databases for
businesses.

The course of computers changed when the Soviets launched the Sputnik 1 satellite
in 1957, quickly followed by Sputnik 2 and the moon landing of Luna 2 in 1958. To
keep pace, and once again overtake the Soviet developments, the US Department of
Defense created the Advanced Research Projects Agency (ARPA). ARPA's mandate
was to rapidly advance technological development. In order to leapfrog the Soviets,
ARPA actively sought visionaries who could see clear ways to advance technological
development, and where necessary they bypassed conventional proposal refereeing. As

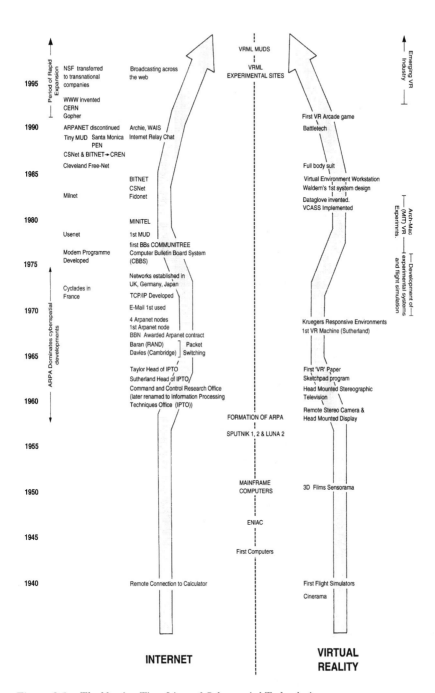

Figure 2.1   The Merging Time-Lines of Cyberspatial Technologies

such, ARPA sought to fund people who wanted to re-invent computing as it was then practised.[5]

In 1961 J.C.R. Licklider was appointed head of ARPA's Command and Control Research Office, which quickly widened its brief and became renamed the Information Processing Techniques Office (IPTO), with a mandate to seek new ways to use computing in relation to the military and scientific community.[6] Engelbart, after a decade of championing innovative computing, headed Stanford Research Institute's (SRI) Augmentation Research Center (ARC) and sought ways to make computing more interactive, and to liberate computing power for non-computer-literates to use. By 1963, Licklider had written to a number of leading researchers describing his desire for communication and cooperation among them and signed two contracts to conduct research into networking computers. At the same time, ARPA sponsored a number of other computing projects at 17 different sites.[7] At MIT, researchers such as Fano and Minsky sought to make a central computer time-shareable,[8] that is, allowing many people to simultaneously interact with the computer via terminals rather than having to wait in line for computer operators to submit their programs. At Lincoln Lab, at the University of Utah, Sutherland, Kay and other researchers sought interactive graphics and a suitable human–computer interface, exploring the first virtual reality displays. The aim of these groups was multiple-access computing where time-sharing, group communication and interactive graphics converged.[9] By the mid-1960s, the IPTO projects had advanced to the stage where multiple users could interact with a central machine. However, because IPTO projects had led to the development of several different systems located at various points across the US, to share resources it had to find a way to connect several, incompatible systems that were geographically separated.[10]

THE INTERNET

The idea of remote connection to a machine can be indirectly traced to George Stibitz, of Bell Laboratories, who in 1940 demonstrated to attendees of the American Mathematical Society a remote connection to the Complex Number Calculator (Bell Laboratories Model 1) over a distance of 230 miles.[11] During the war calculators advanced to become computers and the origins of the Internet can be directly traced back to ARPA's IPTO initiatives and the development of the world's first computer network. The network created by the Department of Defense to fulfil the aim of connecting computers was called ARPANET. The ARPANET project grew directly out of Licklider's work, with first Sutherland and then Taylor carrying on the work when he left IPTO in 1964. In 1966, Taylor decided to start a network project and approached Larry Roberts to head the venture. Roberts came to IPTO from (Massachusetts Institute of Technology, where he and Thomas Marill had been experimenting with linking two computers via a 1200 bps dedicated phone link. Roberts organized a number of meetings with principal investigators concerning the development of a network. At the ACM conference later that year, Roberts was introduced to the packet-switching work of Davies and colleagues at the National Physical Laborary (NPL), and on return contacted Paul Baran.[12]

In 1964, Baran, a member of a RAND Corporation think-tank, proposed a framework for packet-switching. Baran was concerned with finding a way to secure communications, command and control for the US military in the event of a thermonuclear attack. This, however, was not an intention of the ARPANET group, who wanted to enhance the environment for conducting computer research by fostering collaboration and the swapping of ideas and code.[13] Baran outlined the basis of a computer network with no central control. His idea was to design a system that could continue to operate, allowing the transfer of information and data, even if any part of the network was lost. Baran proposed that the information, data or messages to be sent should be broken into units of equal size. These units would then be sent along functioning paths (i.e. those not destroyed), with the identity of their intended recipient, to their destination, where they would be reassembled. So, for example, if one section of the network were removed, the units would find an alternative route to their destination. This also means that individual units do not have to take the same route. Donald Davies, at NPL in the UK, in 1965, independently came to the same conclusions as Baran, and described dividing messages into 'packets' for storage and forwarding using a process of 'packet-switching'. The idea is to allocate all of a system's capacity to one user for a short period of time. In this time, a packet is transmitted. Each packet is passed from one packet-switch (node on a network) to another until it arrives at the intended destination. Packets arriving at a switch may be held temporarily until the transmission line is free. At the destination, all of the separate packets are reassembled into the proper sequence using individual identifiers.

In late 1967, SRI was awarded a four-month contract to study the design and specification of a computer network, and in early June 1968 a program plan was submitted to the director of ARPA. The plan was approved in late June, with a fiscal budget of $500 000, and the request for proposals/quotations for the network design for ARPANET was published by Roberts.[14] The request was sent to 140 potential bidders. The specifications for this system had to be such that all computers in the network did not have to be connected to all the others, that interactive response times were good, and that there was added functionality.[15] Bidders were requested to submit a plan for a network involving thirteen nodes, but to price for a four-node network. The successful bidder was to be given a thirteen-month performance period to build and have operational four nodes.

A think-tank at Bolt Beranek and Newman (BBN), under the guidance of Robert Kahn, a professor of mathematics at MIT, Frank Heart, a computer engineer, and Severo Ornstein, wrote the successful application to develop ARPANET. BBN built a purpose-designed system for the ARPA contract called an Interface Message Processor (IMP) as initially conceived by Clark in 1967. The IMP was essentially a minicomputer that acted as a translator. The host system would talk to the IMP, which would then convey the message to the destination IMP that translated for the destination system.[16]

IMPs thus performed the functions of dial-up, error checking, re-transmission, routing and verification on behalf of the participant's computer.[17] In this way, destination systems did not have to be fully compatible and any changes that needed to be carried out could be done to the IMPs and not to the host machines. An essential feature of the IMP was the implementation of packet-switching architecture, which could transfer packets to other IMPs via 56 kbps leased telephone wires.[18]

The first ARPANET node was installed at UCLA in September 1969 connecting the IMP to a Sigma 7.[19] The second IMP was installed at SRI in October, and on 21 November the computers at UCLA and SRI first communicated. By December 1969 there were 4 nodes (UCLA, SRI, University of California, Santa Barbara, and University of Utah), expanding rapidly to 13 in January 1971, 23 in April 1972, 62 in June 1974 and 111 by March 1977[20] (Figure 2.2). Within 16 months ARPANET was a genuine packet-switching network, with at least two available routes between all the nodes.[21] In 1972, a new device called a Terminal IMP (TIP) was implemented, which allowed users to connect to the network via remote terminals using the public switched telephone network (PSTN).[22] IPTO strictly limited who had access to ARPANET but was more open concerning network information, with details of how the network was designed and run reaching the broader computing community through publications and conferences.[23]

The initial network used dedicated switching protocols called Network Control Protocol (NCP).[24] The Department of Defense, however, wanted a system that could link up machines of different makes, that ran at different clock speeds and used different sized packets, and that could link to satellites and packet radio systems, which did not have the same format as ARPA packets. The resulting Transmission Control Protocol/ Internet Protocol (TCP/IP) network protocol was developed by Cerf and Kahn in 1973 and has, because of its flexibility, become the standard switching protocols for interconnecting networks. Cerf and Kahn also wanted to connect to the networks developing elsewhere in Europe. TCP/IP was, after a brief tussle with OSI, adopted as standard for ARPANET in 1983 and the current Internet still uses the protocols, despite advances in networking design.[25] These protocols have allowed the Internet to flourish by allowing the transfer of data between platforms that could not be mediated by IMPs. In fact, the Internet literally refers to all networks connected by TCP/IP protocols.[26]

E-mail was a key development on ARPANET. E-mail services had first been used on the multi-access projects of the mid-1960s. Here, users of a common machine could leave messages for each other and thus exchange information.[27] In 1970, Ray Tomlinson at BBN wrote the first program that allowed mail to be sent across a distributed network. The program was quickly circulated between all of the ARPANET sites,[28] and by 1971 the two most widely used applications were e-mail and remote login services.[29] Thus, long-distance personal computer-mediated communication was born.

In 1973, Robert Metcalfe developed the idea for a multi-access channel where many packets could be transferred at high speeds along coaxial cable. Along with David Boggs, Metcalfe developed Ethernet, a shared communication channel. In 1978 the system was standardized by Xerox, Intel and DEC and upgraded from 3 Mbps to 10

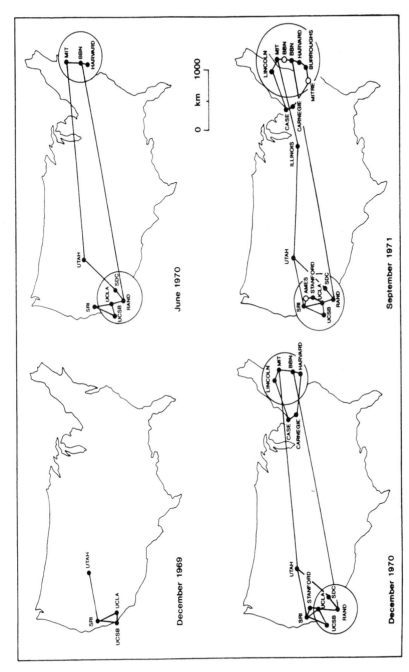

December 1969

June 1970

December 1970

September 1971

Figure 2.2 The Development of ARPANET (1969–1971) Source: Based upon Salus (1995)

Mpbs. Ethernet consisted of a coaxial cable, up to 500 metres long, where all stations share one channel and receive every transmission which is filtered by the host interface. Ethernet provided the basis for the first local area networks (LANs) with several users able to connect with and transfer data to a host machine.

At the same time, ARPA researchers were developing a way to transmit packets via satellite to link up military establishments around the globe (SATNET). In May 1973, a satellite link had been established between Hawaii and an IMP in California. By September of the same year a link was established to the Royal Radar Establishment in Norway, and from there by a dedicated line to University College London. From 1975 to 1989 SATNET was used to connect research institutions in the US, the UK, Norway, Italy and Germany.[30] The ARPANET was starting to become international. In 1974, network services also became commercial with BBN operating Telenet, the first public, packet data service, and in 1975 the operation of ARPANET was transferred to the Defense Communication Agency (DCA).[31]

As noted, however, network developments were not solely sought by the US. Davies and colleagues at NPL in the UK were working on packet switching in the 1960s, and by the early 1970s a host of countries were developing national networks. The earliest to develop was CYCLADES, engineered by the French. CYCLADES was first demonstrated in November 1973 and quickly developed to form a basic national network (Figure 2.3). Networks were then established in the UK, Germany and Japan in 1974 forming the bases for larger more successful future networks such as the UK's Joint Academic Network (JANET) and France's Minitel. Minitel was born in 1981 as a videotext system to supply users with public information and quickly grew to be, by 1987, the world's largest e-mail system.[32]

The wider computing and hobbyist community took note of the leading research developments and by the late 1970s were themselves interconnecting personal computers (then an emerging market) via modems and telephone lines to make early bulletin board systems (BBSs).[33] These systems were essentially places where people could post messages for others to read and comment upon and, importantly, a means by which PC owners could communicate and form interactions. The roots of BBSs can be traced back to Ward Christensen and Randy Suess, who in 1977 devised a program MODEM for transferring files via the telephone system between microcomputers. In 1978 they created Computer Bulletin Board System (CBBS). In November of that year, *Byte* ran a feature on the system and how to create a similar version. In 1979, they updated the MODEM program to XMODEM and went on-line to the public in Chicago. The conversation was limited to personal computing. Communitree, based in Santa Cruz, California, whose efforts paralleled those of Christensen and Suess, went on-line in 1978 but had a more structured base for discussion.[34] Communitree divided messages into open discussions each with a central theme.[35] The themes, however, were not computer based but centred on spirituality and religion – a distinct move away from computer talk. The efforts of Christensen and Suess and Communitree formed the basis for the emerging BBSs.

In 1993, *Boardwatch* magazine estimated that there were 60 000 BBSs operating in the BUS alone, with BBS culture spreading rapidly throughout Japan, Europe, and Central

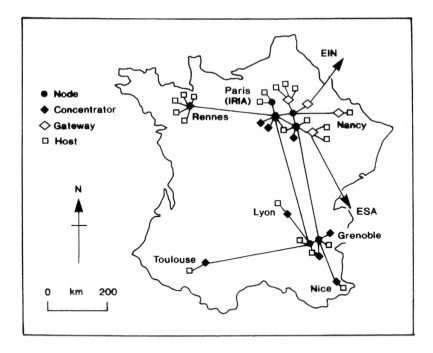

Figure 2.3   CYCLADES (1982). Source: Based upon Salus (1995)

and South America.[36] BBSs started out as localised, community-based projects, but with changes in network architecture and a convergence of cyberspatial technologies some are expanding to incorporate a wider audience. Bulletin boards were particularly important for two reasons. First, they were the forerunners to general file sharing and public access services.[37] Second, they were the start of non-academic/computer scientists becoming involved with computer-mediated communication.

Of these bulletin boards, or discussion groups, Usenet and Fidonet have grown to be the most successful, quickly developing national and then international audiences in the 1980s. Usenet's success was dependent on the fact that the information within a discussion group was not limited to one site but forwarded to many subscribing sites. Rheingold describes it as a 'network-scale conferencing system'. Usenet was initially conceived by Steve Bellovin from the University of North Carolina (UNC) in 1979 in response to an administrative need, a rudimentary news system for disseminating information about UNIX within UNC.[38] A number of newsgroups were set up and each subscriber could subscribe to as many or as few as desired. At the same time, Tom Truscott from Duke University and Bellovin were trying to set up a UUCP (UNIX-to-UNIX Copy) link via modem between UNC and Duke (neither was connected to the Internet).[39]

Truscott and Jim Ellis (also at Duke) felt that other people might appreciate Bellovin's UNIX news reports. They proposed a network, with Duke as the hub, which would distribute news concerning UNIX's latest news and bug reports. Using an auto-dialer they would contact other sites to pick up any inbound mail and redistribute news items. The system works so that when the next computer in the network gets the message, it checks to see which newsgroups it holds, copies all the relevant messages and disregards the rest. Because each message has a unique code no message is copied twice. Unlike mailing lists, which copy to every subscriber, Usenet postings are placed into a single newsgroup file that anybody can read. The system does, however, also support personal e-mail. Initially, Usenet began with two hosts, one at UNC and one at Duke, with a third added at Duke in 1980.

In January 1980, Ellis distributed a pamphlet describing the Usenet system at the Boulder USENIX conference. At the summer Newark USENIX conference, News software was made available on computer tape. At this time there were 15 sites; within a year there were over 100 participatory sites and 25 articles per day.[40] In this form, UUCP was unable to cope with demand and the Usenet software underwent the first of four transformations. Bellovin first revised the code, rewriting it in C. Next, Steve Daniel and then Truscott rewrote the code into 'A News'. In 1981, Mark Horton (UC Berkeley graduate) and Matt Glickman (high school student) rewrote 'A News' into 'B News'. Horton continued to update and release versions of 'B News' until 1984, when Rick Adams at the Center for Seismic Studies took over maintenance and control. At this point, Usenet was distributed widely.

Lastly, in 1987 Henry Spencer and Geoff Collyer of the University of Toronto produced 'C News'. Usenet has continued to grow exponentially. By 1986 there were 221 groups and 1414 sites. By 1988, there were 11 000 sites with 4 million bytes being posted every day. By 1991 there were 1732 groups and 14 565 sites. By 1992, it was estimated that Usenet postings were distributed via 4129 groups at 23 253 sites, with an estimated readership of 2.5 million people and over 35 million bytes posted each day. In 1994, there were 58 402 sites and 10 696 groups.[41] For Rheingold[42] it was Usenet that was the first system to fulfil Licklider's dream of a computer community and, along with ARPANET's full conversion to TCP/IP, marked the start of the Internet's rapid growth.

FidoNet started life in 1983 as a single BBS, Fido, run by Tom Jennings in San Francisco. Unlike Usenet, FidoNet links personal computers running Dos rather than University Unix hosts. After Jennings converted the Fido BBS to run on another brand of computer, Fido BBSs started to grow in number, as the software for running a Fido system was available for download from any other Fido BBS. In 1985, Jennings released the FidoNet software, and Fido BBSs started to communicate with each other using cheap calls in the early hours of the morning. Mail messages were sent between other nodes using a coding system. As the number of nodes began to cluster, instead of dialling and sending to each individual node, one node became a gatekeeper and then redistributed to other local nodes, thus cutting telephone costs. In 1986 there were about 1000 nodes supporting at least 10 000 users. By 1991, the network had grown to over 10 000 nodes with at least 100 000 users, with 40 gateways via the Internet around the globe,[43] and Hardy[44] reports that as of June 1993 there were 24 800 nodes serving an estimated 1.56 million users.

In 1980, computer communities of a different type first came on-line, in Essex, UK. Multi-User Dungeons (MUDs), later to become Multi-User Domains and mutate into several different acronyms (e.g. MUSE), are gaming systems allowing hundreds of people to take part in an interactive, textual, adventure game. The original system, developed by Roy Trubshaw and Richard Bartle, was an on-line version of Dungeons and Dragons, allowing individuals to create an identity, explore a textual world and take part in an adventure, encountering computer-made people and creatures, and also converse with other adventurers connected to the game from all over the world.[45] In 1989, James Aspenes, a student at Carnegie Mellon University, started TinyMUD, a virtual world with the fantasy role-playing element removed. These early systems were hard-programmed, with users encountering set scenarios. However, LamdbaMOO (multi-object oriented), developed by Pavel Curtis at Palo Alto, was the first system to allow users to alter their surrounds and build new parts of the world. MUDs, MOOs and their hybrids quickly grew in popularity, providing places where on-line users could interact in more informal settings. By April 1993 there were 276 publicly announced MUDs based on twenty different kinds of software on the Internet.[46]

In the early 1980s, two new special purpose networks, modelled on ARPANET, were built. CSNet was designed to give access to electronic mail to non-defence-contracting computer science departments and was funded by the NSF. BITNET was aimed at the wider academic community and was partially funded by IBM.[47] The brainchild of Ira Fuchs, then Director of CUNY Computer Center in Manhattan, BITNET (Because It's Time Network) was a store-and-forward network. This meant that the system was ideal for mailing lists but could not support remote login or general file transfer.[48] BITNET was also limited by hardware, originally only running on IBM hosts. IBM did, however, fund an expansion programme across the US and also into Europe.

In 1989, CSNet and BITNET were merged to form CREN (Corporation for Research and Educational Networking).[49] The principal constituents of CREN are BITNET/CSNet, NetNorth in Canada, EARN in Europe and some sites in Japan, totalling over 3400 host sites[50]. With its limited functionality, however, it is unlikely that CREN will be able to continue to compete with other major networks.

The growth of ARPANET, BITNET and CSNet led in the late 1970s and early 1980s to strong public support for the federal government to build a public network accessible to all private and public research facilities. In the late 1970s, the Computing for Education and Research (CER) programme was established at the National Science Foundation (NSF). In 1980 the NSF obtained Congressional approval to build five supercomputer centres.[51] The selection of sites took place in 1983–84, and they were built in 1985–86 at Cornell, Princeton, Pittsburgh, Illinois at Urbana/Champaign and San Diego. In 1986–87, four more sites (Delaware, Purdue, Washington at Seattle and Minnesota) were added to the NSFNET plans.

To allow scientists from other sites to use the supercomputer sites, it was decided to link them together to form a nationwide network. The NSF first approached ARPA with a view to connecting the sites using ARPANET. The Department of Defense was in the process of trying to expand ARPANET, which in 1983 was divided into two networks, MILNET and the residual ARPANET, which was finally decommissioned in 1990. MILNET would be a strictly military network. MILNET was granted approval to be expanded dramatically from 40 to 3600 nodes (later merged with Defense Data Network (DDN)). However, because of staff shortages it was proposed to expand MILNET and NSFNET/ARPANET simultaneously.[52] This expansion, however, did not occur because of long delays in acquisition orders and the delivery of circuits. As a result, the NSF decided to push ahead on its own, using a temporary 'do-it-yourself' network running at 56 Kbps, whilst its request for proposals was completed. The award of the network building contract was awarded to a three-company, non-profit team, ANS.[53] Merit was responsible for management and administration, MCI was responsible for maintaining the system and IBM provided the software and the switches, based on its machines. By July 1988 NSFNET was fully in place, capable of transferring data at 1.5 Mbps using TCP/IP protocols (Figure 2.4).

By 1992 NSFNET, through ANS, was upgraded to 45 Mbps on trunk routes (T3) (Figure 2.4). At this time, 10% ($60–100 million per year) of the operational and maintenance costs were met by the Federal government. The rest was picked up by the local and state governments. In 1991 Merit, IBM and MCI formed another joint venture, ANS CO+RE, as a for-profit subsidiary. ANS CO+RE was the first company to offer network services over the Internet on a commercial basis after NSF lifted commercial restrictions on the Internet (although MCI and CompuServe had both been offering e-mail services since 1989, and The World had been providing a commercial Internet dial-up service since the previous year[54]). This caused some controversy, as the publicly owned Internet was being used for purely commercial concerns. In 1993, the NSF created InterNIC, which contracted out the most important Internet administrative functions for $12 million. Assigning Internet addresses and gaining access were awarded to Network Solutions, maintaining directory and database services were assigned to AT&T, and maintaining Internet services and modernisation of tools to General Atomics.[55]

While the NSF was trying to create a large, super-network, universities were starting to form campus networks or LANs using Ethernet connections. The NSFNET, in effect, became a Wide Area Network (WAN), linking these local networks into a larger structure. The Internet was thus expanding rapidly at both a global and a local scale. So, for example, the nodes detailed in Figure 2.4 really represent mid-level networks connecting the local to the national.

At the same time, Usenet, BITNET, CSNet and FidoNet were all expanding, and there was the development of the first free-nets and Public Electronic Networks (PENs). Also called community networks, public-access networks, civic networks and telecommunities,[56] these systems developed as on-line community-based democracies aimed at improving the lives of local residents. The first on-line free-net was Cleveland's, linking together information from the city's community organizations. The free-net was essentially a community BBS. Established in 1986, the free-net now has 40 000 registered users and 16 000 logins a day.[57] Santa Monica's PEN was launched in 1989 with the donation of $350 000 of hardware from Hewlett Packard.[58] The city distributed

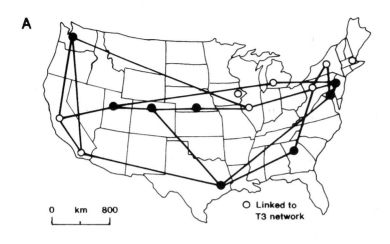

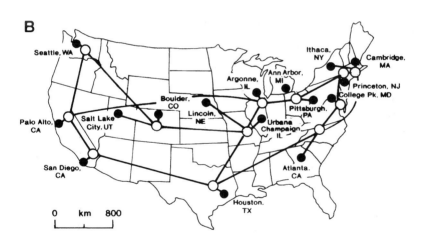

Figure 2.4 *The T1 (1988) and T3 (1992) NSF Backbones. Source: Based on Hart* et al.
(1992)

free accounts and placed machines in libraries, schools and city buildings for ease of
access. The system allows participants to take part in the democratic process, as they
can e-mail city officials and take part in public conferences. They can also access
information about services and policy, and on-line library services. National Public
Telecommuting Network (NPTN), established in 1989, is an organisation formed to

help set up and link free-net systems worldwide. NPTN currently links 50 free-nets and 120 organising committees in the process of developing their networks. Also in this period, Internet Relay Chat (IRC) was developed by Jarkko Oikarinen, allowing real-time 'conversations' between users at different machines.

Since 1990, a number of developments have occurred to make the Internet more popular. Firstly, and probably most importantly, personal computing has expanded rapidly, with real advances in both capability and functionality. Accordingly, with the increase in the number of personal computers, the potential number of users of the Internet has increased. Secondly, the Internet has become more user-friendly and accessible to the layperson, with a succession of helpful applications. For example, Archie, a device for searching ftp sites was released in 1990. Prior to this, the contents of anonymous ftp sites could only be determined by searching them personally. Also in 1990, Wide Area Information Servers (WAIS) was released and similarly browsed for information. In 1991, Gopher, an application for searching and retrieving information, was circulated. However, the main breakthrough came in 1992 when Tim Berners-Lee at CERN, Geneva, developed the World Wide Web. Here, text, images and sound could combine to provide a range of information. The documents created were also hypertext documents, allowing users to link directly to other relevant sites. Mosaic, an interface for WWW pages quickly followed, as did search engines. The most popular browser at present, Netscape Navigator, also allows users to employ other functions such as gopher and telnet. In March 1995, the WWW became the service with the greatest traffic on the Internet, overtaking ftp.

As a result of these developments, since 1990 the number of Internet users has rocketed. From ARPANET's four nodes in 1969 the Internet had grown dramatically to a global network with nearly four million nodes by the end of 1994.[59] Some estimates now place host numbers at over 9.5 million (Figure 2.5). With each node supporting between 1 and 10 users, the Internet connects between 4 and 95 million people world-wide. This growth can be demonstrated by the rapid increase in the number of packets transmitted, the growth of host computers and the explosion of smaller NSFNET networks (Figure 2.5). The Internet has also been growing in popularity around the world, although in 1994 the US still had by far the most hosts (65%). Germany, the UK and Australia had 5% each, while the majority of the remaining 20% were located in Western Europe. Figures 2.6 and 2.7 demonstrate the geographical diffusion and growth of the Internet illustrated through the number of hosts in each country.

The explosion of users has led to a number of recent changes. In 1991, Senator Al Gore proposed and Congress approved the High Performance Computing Act, providing funding for a National Research and Education Network (NREN). NREN was envisaged as a way for the US to re-establish some of its international competitive-ness and to provide an educational facility for both schools and the public. This bill authorised the NSF to spend $650 million, DARPA $388 million and the Department of Commerce's National Institute of Standards and Technology (NIST) $31 million on developing and testing faster network technology.[60] In 1992, Bill Clinton, then a presi-dential candidate, announced a vision of a new national technology initiative. In 1993,

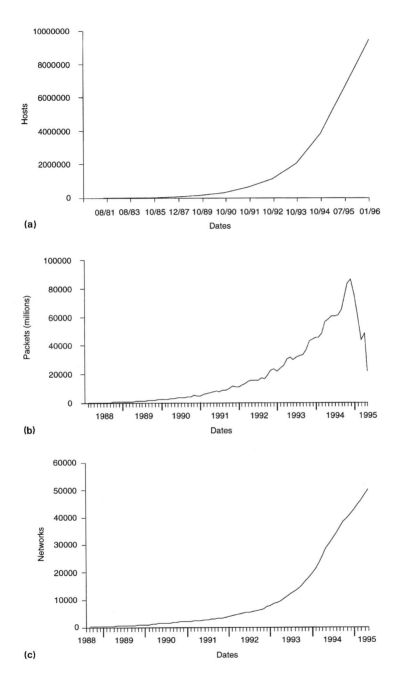

Figure 2.5 *Growth of Packet Transfers, Host Computers and NSFNET Networks.*
Source: http://nic.merit.edu/nsfnet/statistics/history.hosts

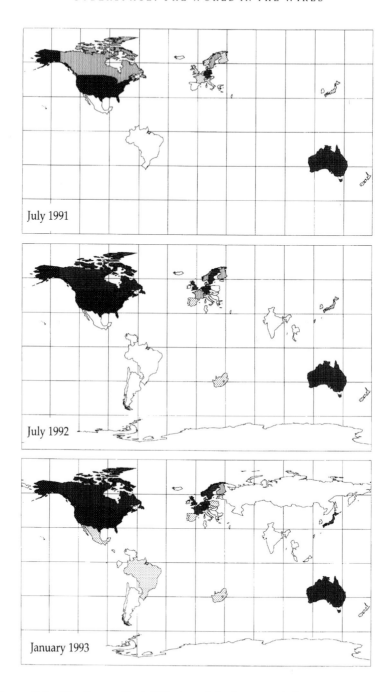

Figure 2.6 *The Geographical Diffusion of the Internet. (July 1993 and January 1994 opposite) Source: Batty and Barr (1994)*

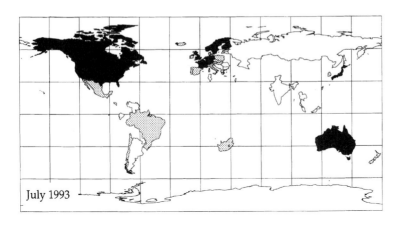

July 1993

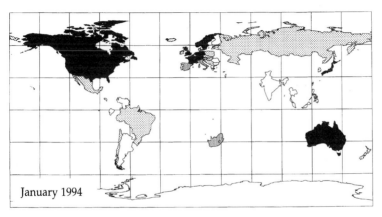

January 1994

Number of Hosts 1991-1994

■ —	1000000 to 5000000	(1)
■ —	100000 to 1000000	(1)
■	50000 to 100000	(3)
■	20000 to 50000	(6)
▨ —	10000 to 20000	(4)
▢ —	1000 to 10000	(19)
▢	1 to 1000	(18)

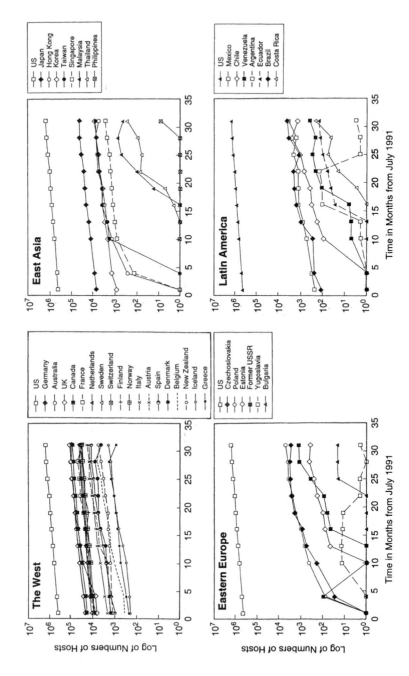

Figure 2.7 The Growth Rates for Different Countries. Source: Batty and Barr (1994)

Gore outlined plans for a National Information Infrastructure (NII) and in 1994, addressed the International Telecommunication Union (ITU) in Buenos Aires, Argentina, calling for the development of a Global Information Infrastructure (GII). Later in 1994 the White House issued plans for the NII, with several key objectives to be achieved by the year 2000 (Table 2.1).

Table 2.1   NII Objectives

---

1. Invite private investment.
2. Assist and protect competition.
3. Allow open access to the network.
4. Avoid creating a polarised (haves/have-nots) information society.
5. Advocate flexible government action.
6. Safeguard Protect privacy and copyright.
7. Ensure that USA remains a leader.
8. Provide for inter-operability.
9. Create new employment, new businesses, new commodities.
10. Enrich delivery of health care.
11. Reduce prices.
12. Create diversity of choice.
13. Encourage economic growth.
14. Democratise information.
15. Provide long-distance learning opportunities.
16. Connect citizens to their governments.

Source: Salus (1995)

Gore's vision of a GII was to provide a global community with stronger democracies, improved education and health and a greater sense of planet stewardship.[61] Based on the NII model, Gore's proposal suggested that such a GII should adopt the guiding principals of private investment, competitive service provision, open access to network providers, flexible regulation and universal service. Gore's vision is of a hierarchical system of networks linking the individual to the local to the regional to the national to the global. Everyone should be able to access an 'information superhighway'. For Hollifield and McCain[62] both the NII and GII are going to be the major shapers of the emerging network, affecting design, regulation, applications and availability of resources during development. Both aim to be commercially operated but universally accessible networks. The majority of the systems discussed so far have had restrictions on who used them, with access generally limited to academics, researchers, Net owners and commerce.

In Europe, there have been similar developments to the US with the European Multi-Protocol Backbone being built, linking the networks of different countries such as the UK's JANET (see Figure 2.8). These country networks are themselves mini-NSFNETS and have a series of mid-level nodes beneath them. This backbone is being built to enable the Internet to handle networks using several different languages or protocols and to promote unity between European neighbours.

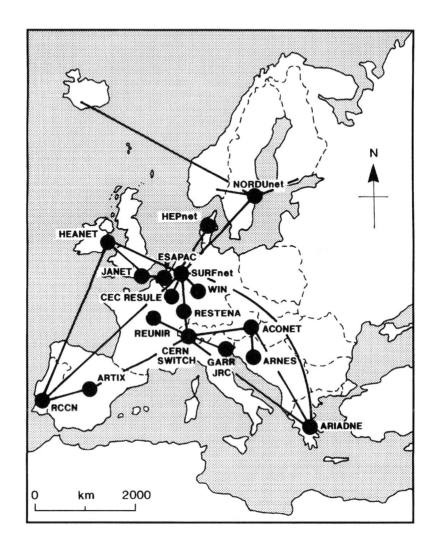

Figure 2.8 *Europe's Multi-Protocol Backbone with Country Nodes. Source: Based on Batty and Barr (1994)*

In 1995, the NSF relinquished control of the NSFNET. Main US backbone traffic is now routed through interconnected network providers.[63] With the growing commercialisation of the Net, there has also been an explosion of service providers such as CompuServe, AOL, Pipex and Prodigy and a host of spin-off industries such as those that design and maintain Web pages and cybercafes where you can connect to the Internet while having a coffee. The proliferation of these industries is likely to continue for some time, especially as digitally based industries collide and merge. In addition, the telecommunication companies are positioning themselves for a slice of the pie by laying thousands of miles of fibre optic cable capable of transmitting the images, text and sound of cyberspace and cable TV at high speeds, and by forming alliances. For example, Stix[64] reports that Corning, makers of fibre optic, estimated that 55 000 miles of cable consisting of 12–200 fibres were laid in the USA in 1993. In April 1993, Tele-communications Inc. (TCI) announced a $2 billion, four-year plan to lay fibre throughout its network. The telephone companies are not sitting back to let the cable companies 'steal' the potential market. They have been developing an integrated ser-vices digital network (ISDN), which will supplant analogue modems. ISDN supplies 64 000 bps and an additional channel of 16 000 bps. ISDN is costly but is becoming more competitive, supplying most of the capabilities of a broadband network. Since 1994, the Euro-ISDN has been implemented, with 26 network operators in 20 countries adopting the standard to improve information exchange.[65] Both the cable and telephone companies are aiming to be the 'on and off ramps' and toll booths to the 'information superhighway'.[66]

Many companies are forming alliances and strategic partnerships to take the best advantage of the developing market, aiming to give themselves future market domi-nance and also ensuring corporation survival when certain media win through. In par-ticular, telecommunication and entertainment companies are seeking to realign their interests.[67] Stix[68] reports that US West has teamed up with TCI, the largest cable supplier in the US, and has also formed a partnership with Time Warner; AT&T has formed an alliance with Viacom; Southern Western Bell has bought two cable com-panies. Other large transnational companies such as Murdoch's News Corporation, Sony and Disney have all been diversifying across digital terrains.[69] For example, Disney has purchased Capital Cities, owner of the ABC network, 10 TV stations, 21 radio stations, and newspaper and magazine properties in order to become a supplier as well as a producer of entertainment services.[70] This jostling for position for the emerging global market is likely to continue for some time, given the instability and uncertainty over which particular transmission technologies are going to win (e.g. cable, ISDN, cellular, satellite) and regulation stopping a complete, market free-for-all.[71] The outcome, however, is likely to be six to ten colossal transnational companies dominating the global communications market within the near future.[72]

VIRTUAL REALITY

Like the Internet, virtual reality's history can be traced back to the 1960s and an ARPA researcher. Sherman and Judkins[73] trace virtual reality's inception to Ivan Sutherland's 1965 paper, 'The ultimate display', in which he outlined his ideas for an immersive, three-dimensional display for computer graphics. Sutherland replaced Licklider as head of IPTO in 1964 before joining Harvard/MIT in 1966 and later the University of Utah.[74] Three years previously, while a graduate at MIT, Sutherland had invented Sketchpad, the first interactive computer graphic system, and from 1966 and into the early 1970s he created the first three-dimensional head-mounted display. The Philco corporation had developed a remote stereo camera and head-mounted display in 1958, and Heilig patented a head-mounted stereophonic television display in 1960, but Sutherland's system was the first to involve computer generated graphics, albeit crude three-dimensional displays of outline-style cubes.[75] Sutherland's approach was to try to place humans 'inside' the computer graphics displayed. The head-mounted display he developed used binocular computer screens each displaying the same image and a gaze-tracking device, which helped mimic three dimensions. Sutherland's head-mounted display was so heavy that it had to be suspended from the ceiling.

Rheingold[76] traces virtual reality's roots back further to the visual, immersive qualities of Cinerama, 3D films and Sensorama. Cinerama was invented by Fred Waller in the late 1930s. Waller, who wanted to create a way of presenting films that took up the whole field of view, experimented with multiple projectors and screens. He secured a contract with the US Air Force to build the visual displays for the first flight simulators. Using a system of five cameras and projectors, Waller aimed to fill as much peripheral vision with imagery as possible. After the war, he tried to interest Hollywood in a Cinerama, three-camera/projector system with limited success. When television started to compete with Hollywood during the 1950s Hollywood also experimented with three-dimensional movies on wider screens. Sensorama aimed to go one step further and allow the viewer not only to be visually immersed but to feel, hear (in stereo) and even smell the sights portrayed.[77] These technologies were the first in which you not only saw the images but also experienced them – they projected the illusion of reality. As broadcast media, however, they did not allow interactivity.

During the 1970s, unlike computer networking, virtual reality research progressed slowly. The components and computing power were expensive. Many components were one-offs unable to be made commercially with the technology of the time. Virtual reality was an idea waiting for suitable enabling technologies to mature: electronic miniaturisation, computer simulation and computer graphics. Research focused upon the technologies that converged to produce virtual reality: interface design, flight and visual simulation and telepresence technologies.[78] Most of this work was based around Sutherland's ideas for creating 'machines that help you think'. Sutherland's vision was based around the notion of creating ideal human–computer interfaces, of helping minds and machines to work together more effectively. Here, VR is seen as the ultimate human–computer interface, as interaction is based within natural gestures and using your hands to manipulate objects. In this way, the computer is opened up to more effective use by people who are limited in programming skills. In other words, rather than shaping human behaviour and skills to the computer, the computer is designed to accommodate human needs and abilities.

For example, Brooks at UNC started to work on the three-dimensional, interactive visual modelling of biochemical structures in 1969, later developing ways to use haptic VR to conduct molecular docking. Brook's work led to a VR-centric research programme tackling a wider set of problems such as architectural walk-throughs and medical imaging using head-mounted displays. At MIT, the Architectural Machine Group

(Arch-Mac) led by Nicholas Negroponte and Richard Bolt was experimenting with merging other audio-visual media with computer technology to produce 'exploratory computer environments', and seeking ways to couple human minds and computers. At the University of Utah, Sutherland's team continued to work, with John Warnock developing a method to superimpose objects onto, or in front of, other objects and hide the relevant parts of the background object. In 1969, Myron Krueger started to experiment with 'responsive environments', creating artificial realities where an environment responds to the occupant. First with Glowflow and a year later with Metaplay, he constructed environments controlled by a computer which reacted to video cameras and 800 pressure sensitive switches. Krueger's future projects, Psychic Space and Videoplace, both used a mix of video, computer graphics and gesture/positioning technologies. In Videoplace people in rooms separated by a geographical distance could interact with each other. At Xerox, Palo Alto, researchers were developing the work of Engelbert's ARC, by starting to implement for a mass personal computer market the first iconic interfaces, removing the programming element needed to operate a computer. The ideas developed at Xerox fed directly into Apple's 'windows' interface.

Several key ideas emerged from Arch-Mac (later Media Laboratory). In the late 1970s and early 1980s, Christopher Schmandt and Eric Hulteen, working under Bolt, performed several key experiments in VR development. They combined a wall-sized display, a voice recognition system and a gestural (pointing) input device. The operator, sitting facing the screen and using a combination of pointing and voice commands, could move, resize and shape objects displayed on the screen. Other work determined ways to transmit facial expressions and gaze direction via telecommunications, where facial movements would be altered in synchrony with physical movements. Arch-Mac researchers also further developed the work of Kenneth Knowlton, who in the 1970s, while working for Bell Laboratories, developed a virtual desktop workspace for telephone operators. The system worked by projecting virtual images onto physical objects such as a keyboard. The Media Laboratory created a small virtual space that the operator could reach into and manipulate the keys using his hands. In addition, they created a 'Dataland' using wall-sized screens, eye-tracking, voice input and gestural tracking devices and controlled using a Spatial Data Management System (SDMS) for visually navigating through databases. The aim was to create navigable information spaces. In 1978, Scott Fisher and Andrew Lippman (again within Arch-Mac) created an information tool, 'Movie Map', another important precursor to VR. Movie Map (Aspen Map) simulated a three-dimensional environment in which the user was immersed. This environment, though, was also interactive, allowing users to explore it. Rather than using head-mounted displays, users sat in a room surrounded on all sides by a photographic representation. Pointing in a direction started to move the view that way. Houses could be zoomed in on and even entered. Unlike today, the information was stored on a videodisk.[79]

In the early 1980s Fisher made another breakthrough. He created an interactive three-dimensional virtual world (Movie Map was two-dimensional) by combining stereographic three-dimensional technology with videodisk image storage and retrieval technology. Using two videodisks, each containing matched but different images, one for the right eye the other for the left, and linked to a computer that charted the user's position, the user could view a three-dimensional image of the surrounding environment on a monitor, using special glasses that rapidly alternated the images seen by each eye. The system was limited in that the view in every direction had to be known at every point the user could be situated. However, the system did demonstrate that the system could give an authentic feeling of travelling.[80] These developments in the late 1970s and early 1980s were laying the foundation stones for affordable VR systems.

For Rheingold,[81] VR really started to take shape in the mid-1980s when a group of researchers all ended up working at the NASA Ames Research Center in Mountain View. It was there that the first affordable, head-mounted displays, three-dimensional audio devices and glove input devices were used to interact with complex, three-dimensional computer-generated graphics. By altering the position of the head or hands, users of the Virtual Interactive Environment Workstation (VIEW) developed by NASA altered their field of vision and could control virtual objects. The work at Ames built directly upon the work of the Atari Research Laboratory, where many of the Arch-Mac veterans such as Fisher, Naimark, Hooper and Hulteen had moved. Joined by Brenda Laurel and Susan Brennan, their remit was to dream up the entertainment and education future; they dreamt of immersive, interactive environments. It was here that Thomas Zimmerman invented the DataGlove used by Jaron Lanier's visual programming language. Atari Research fell apart but many of its staff worked together again at Ames and Apple. Ames's head-mounted display was invented by Michael McGreevy and James Humphries in 1984 and was modelled on the highly expensive Air Force simulator helmets. Rather than costing millions, their headset cost hundreds. In 1985, NASA commissioned the Virtual Environment Display System and hired Fisher, who incorporated VPL's (Lanier's) glove-based input device and experimented with three-dimensional audio devices. Again the team fell apart, but they had provided an affordable system that was starting to capture people's imagination, and their research, along with Atari's, kick-started the commercial VR business.

The front-runner in the early 1990s was VPL Research, whose poor performance and reliability ultimately led to its fall and reorganisation,[82] and the ousting of its charismatic head, Jaron Lanier. Since the early 1990s, several start-up companies, such as Fakespace and SENSE8, have formed and are being joined by several more every month in an effort to capitalise on a growing market. VPL worked with NASA at Ames and in 1987 they developed a full bodysuit. In conjunction with SEGA and Mattel, they developed the PowerGlove for use with Nintendo games and between 1988 and 1990 VPL was the vendor for both gloves and headsets for the research community. By this stage, early force-feedback gloves were being introduced, capable of allowing pressures to be exerted on the gloved hand via tiny electronic motors.[83] Systems, however, were expensive: over $100 000 for the bottom of the range and over $500 000 for a system that two could share. Most of the cost was for the computing power to make it work: the basic system cost $25 000, plus another $50 000 if you wanted a bodysuit.[84] By the early 1990s VPL was quickly trying to diversify into entertainment arcade machines, surgical simulation and aircraft design. However, a poor-performance market product led to its demise. By 1989, Autodesk was also demonstrating its first prototype system costing $25 000, but this system could be powered by a personal computer costing a couple of thousand dollars. The problem with these early commercial systems was that they failed to pass from conceptual demonstration to useful work.[85]

In 1989, the Human Interface Technology Laboratory (HIT Lab) in Seattle joined the academic and commercial scene, signalling the arrival of relatively unknown military research. The laboratory's director, Thomas A. Furness III, was formerly the head of the US Air Force's VR research programme, with over 25 years of VR research. Over that 25-year period, the Air Force had spent hundreds of millions of dollars developing sophisticated flight simulators and on-board virtual systems. Since 1966, Furness had been involved in visual displays for the simulators. In the late 1960s/early 1970s the Air Force started to employ computer graphic displays and in 1982 they produced the first working model of the Visually Coupled Airborne Systems Simulator (VCASS). The system used head-mounted displays and allowed pilots to fly through three-dimensional digital terrain models in real time while also providing attendant data. By 1986, VCASS had developed gaze-tracking and voice command, and the Super Cockpit was initiated. New helmets were developed that could add a virtual overlay over cockpit controls, plus a three-dimensional acoustic sound system and special gloves.[86] With a vastly superior budget, the Air Force had created more sophisticated virtual systems. These included simulators with moving-bases, using a series of hydraulic jacks mounted under the simulator's base to add to the sense of movement.[87] With Furness's departure, some of that knowledge could be imparted to the wider academic community. HIT Lab is currently developing a laser scan system that scans images directly onto the retina, avoiding large head-mounted displays containing LCD screens.[88]

Another parallel to the Internet is, that until the mid-to-late 1980s, virtual reality development was almost exclusively American. At this time, both Japanese and European researchers began to take an interest. Although VPL developed the first commercial systems, the first cheap, mass-orientated, helmeted VR product was not developed in the US but by Jon Waldern in Leicester, UK in his garage in 1988.[89] Waldern, an electronics buff, had discovered some of the work of Jim Clarke, whose PhD was supervised by Sutherland, in 1981. By 1984 he had designed his first system and he published details in 1985. Waldern's company, W Industries (now Virtuality Entertainment Systems), continued to develop the project and released the world's first arcade game VR system – the 1000 SD – on 22 March 1991. On 31 July they released the world's first shared, virtual reality game, Dactyl Nightmare, where two players stalked and shot at each other. One week later they released Total Destruction, where four drivers race each other round a virtual track. Virtual reality had made it to the games arcade. In 1990, another group VR gaming system but without helmets was unveiled in Chicago. Battletech Center utilises simulation software. Each participant is enclosed in a small motion-platform, sound-and-vision simulation and fights group battles. There are now over thirty centres worldwide but individual systems are not available in general arcades.

Elsewhere in the UK, several different enterprises had been working on telerobotic applications and telepresence control. From Law and Fluck's 'Spitting Image' puppets to Government-funded European Space Agency work, robotic applications were being controlled remotely, mimicking human movement. Telepresent VR controlled robots could have important applications in industry (e.g. repairs in highly radioactive places), health (e.g. surgery undertaken remotely) and public service (e.g. remote fire rescue/ fighting machines). The space industry in particular is interested in controlling robots from a distance. Other groups such as Division, a branch of INMOS, were developing transputers linking together many specific, cheap chips to generate the supercomputer powers necessary to run VR systems. Whereas a supercomputer processes everything in parallel, transputers divide tasks into components, which are tackled simultaneously by several chips. Division markets a multi-user VR system, dVS, with specialised hardware additions such as accelerator cards (ProVision and SuperVision) and a mouse.[90] All of these developments were being taken by Robert Stone of ARRL (Advanced Robotics Research Limited) to develop a Virtual Human–System Interface Demonstrator, a remote navigation vehicle which could be remotely controlled through a virtual interface, giving the user the impression of actually being seated in the vehicle.[91] ARRL received £5 million in start-up funds spread over 5 years to be matched by funds from 12 shareholder companies and has recently diversified outside of telepresence into simulation.[92]

Other European countries, such as Germany, the Netherlands, Sweden, France and Switzerland, were at the same time starting to develop VR research programmes, although in the main they are seldom funded by national governments.[93] The IGD (Fraunhofer Institute for Computer Graphics) and GMD (German National Research Centre for Mathematics and Computer Science) in Germany have both been developing VR systems. IGD, funded through industrial contributions, currently employs 10 researchers and 20 students to develop a virtual toolkit called Virtual Design to create walk through virtual environments. GMD are examining more technical issues such as rendering techniques, collision detection and motion guidance to improve interaction. Other developments in Germany include Fraunhofer Gesellschaft, an applied research organisation which launched a five-year VR initiative in 1993 to demonstrate VR applications using commercial systems through four demonstration centres; ZGDV's gesture recognition software; and industrial and manufacturing VR-controlled telerobotics by Fraunhofer IPA. In the Netherlands, the FEL (Physics and Electronics Laboratory) of the Netherlands Organisation for Applied Scientific Research (TNO) have been developing a VR training and simulation VR centre. In Sweden, the Swedish Institute for Computer Science (SCSI) have developed the MultiG Distributed Interactive Virtual Environment (DIVE), a development platform for multi-user VR applications. France has several of Europe's leading research centres for machine vision, robotics and other technologies that affect VR and is just beginning to explore VR development.[94]

By 1989, the Japanese had also entered the fray. Advanced Telecommunications Research Institute International (ATR), a consortium of 140 telecommunication and computer companies, had an annual budget of $50 million in 1991. Two of their four laboratories focus on televirtual communications, with $5.3 million guaranteed over ten years for a project 'Communications with realistic sensations'. Their Systems Research Laboratory opened in Kansai in 1989. Most of ATR's backers are Japanese transnationals such as Hitachi, NEC, Mitsubishi and Toshiba, and they are investing heavily, banking on VR's potential to revolutionise telecommunications and provide mass-market products.[95] Whereas American VR companies tend to be small, entrepreneurial enterprises such as VPL Research, SENSE8 and Fakespace, Japanese companies are predominantly transnationals looking to increase their computing applications' market share. Similarly, in contrast to the *ad hoc* nature of much of the US's research programme, ATR is a systematic research programme aimed at long-term competitive advantage fully backed by MITI (Ministry of International Trade and Industry), which helps to direct the long-term future goals of the Japanese economy. Unlike the US move to head-mounted displays and gloves/bodysuits, ATR is exploring the concept of a 'VR room' along the lines of the experiments of Krueger and the Media Laboratory in the 1970s. The aim is to produce a 'virtual meeting place' with three-dimensional graphics that does not require head-mounted displays or gloves/bodysuit, but instead uses eye-tracking devices and gesture sensing. The CAVE system at the Electronic Visualization Laboratory at the University of Illinois is a US equivalent. Other developments include NTT's three-dimensional realityphones, MITI telepresence experiments controlling a remote robot through virtual reality projections and force feedback experiments at the University of Tsukuba, Tokyo Institute of Technology and Product Science Research Institute.[96]

Japanese giants such as Nintendo, Fujitsu and SEGA are also targeting the entertainment and education markets. For them VR orientated software is the next evolution of games and educational packages and they are investing billions of yen so that they might reap the future benefits. Compared to the US and the UK (which operates on a shoestring budget), Japan is aiming to buy and then sell the shop, not just the sweets. A government-led industrial policy is leading to cooperation between companies and a rapid convergence of technology. In Japan, there is a coordinated strategy linking telecommunications and robotics with computing hardware and software. Fujitsu has interests in all of these markets plus the entertainment market. Fujitsu's ultimate aim is to entwine these themes into a personalised system which uses neural networks to be individually responsive: the machines will learn our behaviours and react accordingly.[97] Nintendo also clearly envisages that VR is the next stage from dedicated games platforms and has already invested in co-developing a PowerGlove (a cheaper version of the DataGlove).

Virtual reality does not have to be visual either. Scientists at the University of California, Santa Barbara are working on auditory environments to help people with severe visual impairments and blindness to navigate around the real world. Developed by a geographer, Reg Golledge (himself blind), and a psychologist, Jack Loomis, the system works by combining global positioning system (GPS) software with geographic information held within a geographic information system (GIS).[98] The GPS uses satellite positions to work out exactly (within 1 metre) where on the earth's surface the user is located. This information is fed into the GIS map database, which tracks the route the person is taking. The system then uses this information to update the user about his or her location and the buildings and features in the immediate locale. However, rather than just stating 'building A is on your right', the system uses stereo sound that allows the buildings to sound as if they are calling you: they sound as if they are where they are – they exist simultaneously within an virtual auditory space and real space (although direction is all right, ranging distance is proving more tricky – a problem common to all VR systems). Other teams around the world, such as the European joint venture MOBIC, are developing similar prototype systems.

In the past five years, virtual reality has developed rapidly, with an increasing amount of research and commercial projects. Applications tend to be as simulators, allowing users to experience a particular environment and learn how to react to a series of situations. These applications are diverse, ranging from medicine, to learning to drive, to emergency situations, to overcoming vertigo plus many others.[99] Recent developments include Advanced Distributed Simulation (ADS), which builds upon the technologies underlying BattleTech (SIMNET) to link together several simulators within one cooperative environment using a combination of synthetic environments, synthetic forces and computer networking.[100] However, virtual reality technologies are not as advanced in development, or in the numbers of users, as the Internet. At present, they have not crossed the threshold of usability, with display resolutions rendering the user legally blind, head- and hand-tracking devices inaccurate and limited in range, and lag times that can ruin the sensation of immersion.[101] Ellis warns that we should be cautious about singing the praises of VR too soon.[102] He suggests that the reason why VR has had little 'real' success outside of flight simulators and basic research is because to produce systems sophisticated enough costs millions of dollars, with cheaper systems usually being flawed, with poor performance and usability. As such, development costs are likely to remain high and confined to specialized fields.

However, virtual reality technologies have shown real promise and are rapidly advancing in sophistication, with an estimated 60% growth rate and $250 million worth of VR products shipped in 1994, rising to an estimated $1 billion by 1997.[103] Boman reports that head-mounted displays can now be obtained for less than $1000 with $200 video game versions not far off.[104] It is anticipated that once it has merged with the Internet and other technologies such as high definition television (HDTV), it will really capture the public's imagination.[105] There are a number of test VRML sites allowing virtual reality to be broadcast over the Internet but these are often crude and slow. Prior to 1990, virtual reality was practically unheard of but since then it has rapidly been wrapped in a ball of hype. Much of this hype, however, relates to potential and non-tactual current capabilities. In 1991, VPL was planning Reality Net and a national virtual telecommunication network exploring the possibility of plugging a headset into the Net and visually exploring and interacting in 'Dataland'. ATR, and many of its Japanese backers such as NTT, are exploring similar scenarios. It will probably be another 10–20 years before immersive VR technologies become as advanced as the

Internet, and another 10–20 years after that before they become ubiquitous and move out of the laboratories and arcades and onto desks. However, there is little doubt in the minds of many commentators that VR will reach the same status as the Internet, and that the two will merge to become one to revolutionise the way we live. Indeed, we can see the start of such a merger with the increasing prevalence of virtual reality web sites that allow web users to interact with a 'game space'.

THEORETICAL PERSPECTIVES

APPROACHING CYBERSPACE

CHAPTER 3

THEORETICAL PERSPECTIVES
APPROACHING CYBERSPACE

Graham and Marvin,[1] in their discussion of the growth of telecommunications and their impacts upon the city, identify four main theoretical perspectives that seek to under-stand and explain the relationships between technology and society. These are utopianism-futurism, technological determinism, social and political constructivism and political economy. These four approaches represent traditional modernist approaches to the relationships between technology and society. In recent years, we have seen the emergence of the more critical postmodernist, poststructuralist and feminist ap-proaches. In this chapter, these approaches and their relationship to cyberspace are explored and a new integrated approach, combining aspects of postmodernism with social constructivism and political economy, is developed. This integrated approach is used to provide the context for the remainder of the book.

APPROACHING CYBERSPACE

UTOPIANISM AND FUTURISM

Utopists and futurists seek to forecast how technological innovation will affect future societies. As Graham and Marvin[2] suggest, forecasts tend to be bound up within some form of the 'grand metaphor' approach whereby 'western society is seen to be moving *en masse* to some new and novel stage in its development as some form of 'information society'. Writers within this vein generally enthuse about new ways of life and construct some kind of utopian future filled with hope and benefits for all. The general ideology is that virtually all of our problems – ethical, economic, political – are subject to technical solutions.[3] Roszak[4] explains that utopian visionists tend to be either reversionist, seek-ing a pre-industrial lifestyle with an economy based on handicrafts and farming and a communal governing system, or technophiles, seeking a mature urban-industrial society, a new order of science and technology. Within the context of cyberspace, many utopian visionists have tried to imagine a future that combines reversionary tastes with technology. Here, technology would be framed within an organic and communitarian political context, be decentralised and humanly scaled, and be used to link community groupings.[5] Other visions either centre on the shredding of constraints such as materiality and the body, or on the potential economic and lifestyle improvements championed by what Kroker and Weinstein[6] term the 'virtual class' (those industries with a vested interest in cyberspace's future). The basic tenet is that we will use technology to progress and that potentialities will be realised simply because they are possible.

Gray and Driscoll[7] suggest that these future visions are, in the main, wishful thinking and, at worst, misguided efforts at engineering social reality. Yet there can be little doubt that much of what is written about cyberspace is utopian. As noted in Chapter 1, the hype surrounding cyberspace's development is unprecedented. However, much of this writing is unsubstantiated and based upon dreams and hopes rather than any empirical evidence. Such utopian writing centring on the automatic production of a better world has been termed 'mythinformation' by Langdon Winner.[8] As Robins[9] argues much of it is a 'consensual hallucination', a common vision un-tethered from the realities of the world; the dreams of imagination. While I personally remain optimistic that cyberspace will do more good than harm, I find it difficult to become as enthusiastic and intoxicated as some analysts, who seem to write with a religious fervour in technological tongues. As we will discuss in Chapter 5, there will not be benefits to all; there is little to suggest that access to cyberspace in the future will become more democratic or that a radical alteration and coming together of social divisions will occur. Cyberspace is not going to be the clear and simple answer, the panacea, for all the world's troubles.

TECHNOLOGICAL DETERMINISM

Technological determinists argue that the social, cultural, political and economic aspects of our lives are determined by technology; 'technology is culture'. Technical innovations, themselves uncaused by social factors and essentially inevitable,[10] are for the determinists, the dominant shapers of society and the way we think and act. Technology is independent, active and determining, and culture and identity dependent, passive and reactive[11] so that technical change is seen as autonomous, that is, 'outside society'.[12] Here, as Woods[13] posits, '[technological] design is a means of controlling human behaviour, and of maintaining this control in the future' where:

> Technological change seems to have its own logic, which we may perhaps protest about or even try to block, but which we appear to be unable to alter fundamentally.[14]

In this vein, cyberspace is seen to directly *cause* changes in our everyday lives in fairly linear, simple cause and effect relationships. For example, for the determinists, cyberspace *will* lead to the formation of new communities, *will* lead to changes in business practice, *will* change how we live our everyday lives. For them, the questions concerning cyberspace centre on how society can adapt to and learn to live with the effects of cyberspace rather than focusing upon how we can use, alter and reshape cyberspace to our benefit.[15] While not denying the influence of technology upon our lives – one only has to think of our over-reliance on the automobile as an example – it is easy to argue against the prophetic assumptions and our 'enslavement to the technology'.[16] As Penley and Ross[17] state:

> technologies are not repressively foisted onto passive populations, any more than the power to realize their repressive potential is in the hands of a conspiring few. They are developed at any one time and placed in accord with a complex set of existing rules or rational procedures, institutional histories, technical possibilities, and last, but not least, popular desires. All kinds of cultural negotiations are necessary to prepare the way for new technologies, many of which are not particularly useful or successful.

Here, Penley and Ross effectively reverse the argument and alternatively suggest that technology is mediated by culture, not culture by technology. Given that technologies do not give rise to themselves but are the product of our imagination and endeavours, bound in historical systems and dependent on structured relations between people,[18] this argument seems wholly reasonable. As Bijker and Law[19] argue, 'technology does not spring, *ab initio* from some disinterested font of innovation. Rather it is born of the social, the economic, and technical relations that are already in place'. As such, it is easy to counter-argue that technology does not simply *cause* an event or societal development. As White[20] describes, 'a new device merely opens a door; it does not compel one to enter'. Evidence for this position is derived from the fact that the same technologies have not led to the same societies when used in different situations, and that technology is not always used as intended by the developers. For instance, the Internet was developed to link computer centres funded by a government agency, ARPA, to advance research and overtake Soviet technical advances. It is a technology that has been re-appropriated – the original ARPANET was never intended to be used for personal communications and interactions. Technology, it seems, is always being reread and reinterpreted within the context of local cultures and local politics.[21] Returning to one of our examples, it is clear that cyberspace will not create new communities in a cause and effect manner. On-line communities are the product of like-minded people finding a common 'place' to interact. Cyberspace will not force the formation of community, in the same way that we do not have to drive a car. Rather, a community may form and develop through a complex set of interactional processes.

SOCIAL CONSTRUCTIVISM

The arguments against technological determinism essentially form the basis of social constructivism. Constructivists argue that technology is a social construct and that technology and society cannot be separated but are intimately entwined with each other and with nature.[22] For example, Lemos[23] contends that 'contemporary technology is embraced, diverted and reappropriated by everyday life'. Escobar[24] explains that the general belief is that:

> technology systems are regulated according to flexible technosocial arrangements which, within certain structural constraints, constitute social closure around concrete developments.

As a social construction, cyberspace is mediated and understood through culture as a social process.[25] Here, it is recognised that human beings are reflexive in nature, with the capacity to choose between alternatives.[26] As such, different individuals can interpret cyberspace in alternative ways. Cyberspace, therefore, is a social artefact, as it mediates a series of social interactions and is itself a product of social mediation. Human beings conceptualise the interaction, others encode this into a formal language, others use the resulting program and the results lead to situations that impinge upon other people's lives.[27] As a consequence, social constructivism rejects the social determinist ideas that structures of capitalism and the power of political-economic forces dominate how cyberspace has and will develop.[28] Social constructivists are interested in the micro-level social processes of human agency used in shaping and reappropriating cyberspace with the aim of identifying, analysing and explaining:

> causal relationships between social, institutional and political factors and the development and applications of technologies . . . The purpose of research in the [social constructivist] tradition is, therefore, to understand how technology and its uses are socially and politically 'constructed' through complex processes of institutional and personal interaction, whereby many different actors and agencies interplay over periods of time.[29]

Social constructivism itself, however, is not free of criticism. Escobar[30] explains that social constructivism underplays the roles of science and industry in technological developments and takes for granted the deeper cultural background that shapes interpretation. In addition, by focusing upon how technologies arise, and are appropriated and maintained by certain social constituencies, it is suggested that social constructivists fail to explore the specific effects of cyberspace on people, communities, economies and power relations.[31] Social constructivists counter that it is impossible to define all-encompassing impacts of cyberspace because the effects are the aggregate results of countless individual examples of the social construction of the technology.[32]

POLITICAL ECONOMY

Like social constructivists, political economists suggest that technologies are not separated from society. In contrast, however, they suggest that the relationship between technology and society is bound within capitalist modes of production and the associated political, economic and social relations that underlie capitalism. To the political economist, cyberspace's relation to everyday life cannot be understood without considering these broader relations and dynamics of capitalism of advanced industrial society.[33] This approach focuses upon the relations that underpin capitalist power and how they are changing. In general, arguments are neo-Marxist in emphasis with the suggestion that capitalism is still a dominant shaper of today's society, that cyberspace will help to reproduce the political and social relations of capitalism and that although we might be moving into a postindustrial phase, the balance of power remains and will continue to remain the same. Technologies are rarely neutral, but are developed in the interests of industrial and corporate profits.[34] Bound within this is a belief that technological development could provide a new social deal and 'deliver the goods' to society 'in return for which the culture surrender[s] its autonomy to the technological imperative'.[35] This prospect of general and individual increases in the level of material welfare renders the modern unavoidable and capitalism compelling.[36] As such, technological development helps reinforce hegemonic structures while allowing standards of living to improve, thus propagating modernism. As such, the information society or economy is seen as a myth developed to serve the interests of those who initiate, manage and benefit from the information revolution (e.g. governments, military establishment and transnational corporations).[37] It is no more than the latest ideology of the capitalist state, so that capitalism has merely been extended, deepened and perfected rather than transcended.[38]

While much of the global Internet was publicly (nationally) owned, it has been increasingly privatised and commodified, with transnational companies seeking to provide customers with value-added services. In this light, as suggested, it is possible to argue that even with a shift to a mode of information, this mode will still be underlain fundamentally by capitalist desires and old power; power on-line will equate with traditional capitalist power. As such, information allows 'capitalists to tighten their grip on the mode of production'.[39] In a sense, information technologies provide fresh sources of power, so the system of production and consumption,[40] wage-labour relations and social divisions, at both local and global scales, are perpetuated. Here, the 'information' revolution has 'wrenched us out of the age of factory capitalism and hurled us into the postindustrial era of transnational corporate capitalism'.[41] In many ways, a cyberspatial era widens social divisions, particularly at a global scale, where not only does a capital rich/capital poor dichotomy exist but an information rich/information poor dichotomy is also growing, reinforcing current divisions.

Kroker and Weinstein[42] suggest that the rise of virtual reality technologies is another opportunity for hegemonic structures to commodify 'reality' and further the trend of global capitalism. As such, the fundamental restructuring and merging of the telecommunication, cable, entertainment and computer industries to form massive, global, multimedia conglomerations who own both the means of production and communication can be seen as a move to realign to new opportunities and sources of capital. Here, traditional capital values can be seen to be driving restructuring and the associated cultural and social reforms. Indeed, Interrogate the Internet,[43] an interdisciplinary working group, suggest that we are on the threshold of a new age of supra-cybernetic capitalism where the Internet will become the ultimate site of both production and consumption. However, instead of the traditional model of owners and subservients, this group suggests the advent of a third class of people who are both. They further warn that as the power on-line increases there may be a fundamental decline in economic determinism and a rise in technological determinism. Indeed, Tomas[44] envisages a future where data, rather than capital, will structure social activity; the haves and the have-nots will be divided by direct access to information, hardware technologies and software expertise. Such views lead Slouka[45] to fear that far from empowering us, the advent of a cyberspace age further empowers traditional capitalist concerns; far from leading to more freedom, enlightenment or rationality, cyberspace in the capitalist's hands will result in oppression, passivity and irrationality.[46]

The approach of political economists, like the other approaches, is not without criticism. Graham and Marvin[47] suggest that political economy often neglects the social processes, as detailed by the social constructivists, overplaying the role of capital in shaping technology and the way it is adopted and used. As such, it 'ascribes simple and all-encompassing powers to abstract and macro-level capitalist structures while neglecting the ways in which structures are themselves created by innumerable individual and institutional actions over time'.[48] Given this criticism, Graham and Marvin construct a theory that combines social constructivism with political economy as a way to explore the recursive relationship between urban places and telecommunications.

POSTMODERNISM AND POSTSTRUCTURALISM

The conceptualisations of the futurists, determinists, constructivists and political-economists remain part of the landscape of modernity. Postmodernism challenges modernist thinking, which is deemed outdated and dead. To Dear,[49] modernism concerns the search for a unified, grand theory of society and social knowledge and seeks to reveal universal truths and meaning through meta-narrative and meta-discourse. He argues that this has led to a variety of internally consistent but mutually exclusive approaches whose meta-narratives fail to adequately account for differences between peoples and places.[50] Druckery[51] furthers this argument by stating that:

> the concept of a singular – one might even say modernist – ideological structure no longer serves to rationalize cultural change, nor to sustain the unity of conditions of difference.

At one level, postmodernity refers to a new way of understanding the world. Here postmodernity is concerned with developing an attitude towards knowledge, methods, theories and communication, and posits that we move away from questions relating to the 'things actually going on . . . to questions about how we can find out about, interpret and then report upon these things'.[52] Here, 'knowledge as traditionally conceived evaporates, to be reconstituted as constructed surfaces'.[53] As such, 'the very possibility of acquiring knowledge or giving an account of the world is called into question'.[54] To the postmodernists, modernist methods are fundamentally flawed in six main ways. These are characterised by Rosenau[55] as:

1 the failure of modern science to produce the dramatic results promised, with slow, marked efforts to improve model predictability and studies plagued with short-term errors, some with devastating consequences (e.g. Thalidomide);

2 the growing misuse and abuse of science by those in power to reinforce certain positions and policies;

3 the growing gap between how science is meant to be practised and how it actually is;

4 an ill-founded belief that science can actually solve all the world's problems;

5 a dismissal of mystical and metaphysical dimensions of human existence as trivial and unworthy; and

6 that science has little to say about normative and ethical issues about the uses of science.

These six flaws have led to the exploration of new, postmodern approaches. McHale describes these new approaches as embodying a shift from ways of knowing and issues of truth, to ways of being and issues of reality.[56] Here, postmodern science rather than seeking 'truth' takes on a functionalist approach aimed at creating human solidarity by adopting a pragmatic theme.[57] As such, organised, objective science is being replaced by a postscience, which acknowledges the position of scientist as agent and participant. Essentially, there is a broad-gauged re-conceptualisation of how we experience and explain the world around us, which includes focusing attention upon alternative discourses and meanings rather than goals, choices, behaviour, attitudes and personality; the dissolution of disciplinary boundaries; and a re-emphasis on that which has largely been ignored by Modern scholars – namely the excluded, marginal and repressed.[58] As such postmodernists offer 'readings' not 'observations', 'interpretations' not 'findings', seeking inter-textual relations rather than causality.[59] For Rosenau, this raises many endless challenges as postmodernism:

> rejects epistemological assumptions, refutes methodological conventions, resists knowledge claims, obscures all versions of the truth, and dismisses policy recommendations.[60]

At another level, postmodernity refers to an object of study – postmodernity is the study of the temporal and spatial organisation, and the complex interaction, of economic, social, political and cultural processes in the late twentieth century. In this framework, postmodern culture is often presented as an alternative to modernist visions of society, which are presented as fundamentally flawed and structurally weak.[61] Postmodern theorists argue that in a number of fundamental ways modernist societies and the relations that underlie them are changing and breaking down. We are moving into a more unstable age; an age where individuals are not rational, autonomous, centred and stable but unstable, multiple and diffuse;[62] an age of fragmentation, pluralism and individualism.[63] As such, the ideas of Enlightenment, of progress through scientific and technological improvement leading to economic development, are beginning to be questioned.[64] Instead, it is argued that attitudes are changing away from the modernist ideals as people begin to realise that the promises of jobs, income and improved social conditions are actually materialising as unemployment, urban decay, rural poverty, illiteracy, drugs and dysfunctional communities. Here, modernity is no longer seen as a force for liberation but rather as a source of oppression and repression. Postmodernists therefore criticise all that modernity has engendered including industrialisation, urbanisation and the nation-state.[65] As a result, analysts argue that we are moving to a culture that denies depth and history, to a culture where alternatives are mixed and blended, a culture of pastiche, superficiality and 'depthlessness'.[66]

This postmodern culture has its roots in the sixties counter-culture (although its intellectual heritage can be traced back to Nietzchse and Heidegger[67]), where its proponents saw themselves as fighting against everything modernism stood for (e.g. authoritarianism and elitism) and typified by mass demonstrations, the merging of pop art with pop music, the emergence of 'new wave' in cinema and the 'new novel' in literature.[68] It is these early movements, challenges to modernism's sensibilities, that led to theorists such as Foucault to re-constitute 'man-as-subject' in the form of discourses, symbols and images, and to develop the bases of postmodern theories. Perfectly timed as its natural ally, the emerging concept of a postindustrial society was accompanied by the concept of an emerging postmodernist culture. As such, postmodernism has become 'the culture of postindustrial society'[69] and represents a shift in both world-view and civilisation as we move to a new era of culture and social organisation.[70]

For many, then, the emerging postmodern culture is closely tied to technology,[71] with theorists envisaging technology as an agent of change; technology is helping to break down the modern and is producing new forms of relations, expressions and society.[72] Druckery[73] suggests that just as modernity matured in the economies of capitalism and science and formed the basis of culture over the past two centuries, postmodernism is being ushered in on a shift to the economies of information and technology. He sees technology as the 'essential media of postmodern culture, a pastiche of instrumentality and speculation' and the 'amorphous foundation of a new social order'.[74] These changes have led social critics, such as Poster,[75] to argue that we are on the verge of massive cultural reorganisation as we enter what he terms the 'second media age'. To Thu Nguyen and Alexander,[76] network-generated operations, such as cyberspace, fundamentally undermine political discourse based within modernity and upon notions such as agency, action, territory, progress and development. These, they argue, are being replaced by usership, operation, non-linearity, recursivity and chaos. Quoting Emberley,[77] they claim:

> The old economy of production, of industrial policy, of state initiative, of discrete and singular actors and audiences, of centers and margins, form and contents, in brief, the great order of reverential finalities where the world was compartmentalized, taxonomically ordered, and prescriptive – all this is over.

For them the turn to postmodernity is a necessity not just a choice. Given these links between postmodernism and technical change, its closeness to the emergence of a postindustrial, information society, it is no surprise that many of the ideas surrounding cyberspace and the changes they are implementing are postmodern in nature.

To the postmodernists, change seems to be occurring at two levels. At the first level, economic and political systems have been evolving, with a global movement away from the local, accompanied with a vast restructuring. We are living in times of fragmentation, decentring, disorientation and disenchantment as we enter a postindustrial phase. Here, the postmodernists' emphasis 'is on the nature and experience of the new spatiality' caused by increased globalisation.[78] The second level tends to focus on the local and the individual, and how traditional modernist notions are being challenged and reconceptualised. Here, postmodern theorists focus upon the conceptualisations and meanings of identity, the body, community and place, and how these concepts are bound and affected by the social production of space and the blurring of boundaries between reality and virtuality, nature and culture. As we will discover in Chapter 4, cyberspace and virtual reality in particular are highly relevant to the arguments being forwarded. Cyberspace is providing new, less formalising and formal, disembodied spaces where identities can be constructed and contested; cyberspace is providing a new locale for communities, uprooted from the traditional boundaries of place; cyberspace is providing explicit spaces of artificial realities.

Poststructuralists argue that the relationship between technology and culture is mediated through language. In contrast to postmodernism, much of the focus is upon the individual, and methodological and epistemological issues, rather than society and cultural critique.[79] For Poster,[80] a human being is configured and given cultural significance through language. As such, the way we live our lives within society, and the constraints and empowerment that operate take effect in language. Therefore, if we are to understand the relationship between technology and society we need to explore the positioning of an individual in relation to language and how the individual is configured by language.[81] Such an approach examines society by interpreting and deconstructing cultural dissemination to gain understanding. Peet and Thrift[82] explain that poststructural work assumes:

> that meaning is produced in language, and not reflected by it; that meaning is not fixed but is constantly on the move . . . and that subjectivity does not imply a unified, and rational human subject but instead a kaleidoscope of different discursive practices. . . . the kind of method needed to get at these conceptions will need to be very supple, able to capture the multiplicity of different meanings without reducing them to the simplicity of a simple structure.

Researchers, then, should focus on textuality, narrative, discourse and language as these do not just reflect reality but actively construct and constitute it. As language precedes us and exceeds us so that it is something into which we are initiated and which governs our actions and thoughts, when each of us reads a text, or views a landscape or a building, we see and interpret them in different ways.[83] Poststructuralists thus propose that the way to gain an understanding of the social, cultural, political and economic factors that shape our lives is to deconstruct the multiple messages being conveyed to us by the objects we encounter – in our case, cyberspace and its different forms. Deconstruction is a technique for 'teasing out the incoherencies, limits and un-intentional effects of a text'.[84] A poststructuralist approach seems well suited to analysing cyberspace as web pages and MUD interactions are literally constructed through the language of the programmers and the actions of the players.

Morley and Robins[85] express concern that we must be careful and cautious when trying to apply the abstract notions of postmodernity to avoid the pitfalls of generalisation. One of postmodernity's claims is the focus on difference rather than sameness, and through over-generalisation, say concerning globalisation, postmodernists risk ignoring these differences. As Morley and Robins[86] state:

> There is . . . the tendency of theories of postmodernity to fall into a kind of formalist, poststructuralist rhetoric, which overgeneralizes its account of 'the' experience of postmodernity, so as to de-contextualize and flatten out all the significant differences between the experiences of people in different situations, who are members of different social and cultural groups, with access to different forms and quantities of economic and cultural capital. The point is 'we' are not all nomadic or fragmented subjectivities, living in the same 'postmodern' universe.

While accepting that there is something significantly new about contemporary society, they further caution against the claim that 'our contemporary experience is so significantly new and different from all that has gone on before'.[87] Bromberg[88] is willing to admit that cyberspace technologies are characteristically postmodern by virtue of their fluidity and malleability but then goes on to claim that it is this nature that makes them ideally suited to combat the postmodern condition, to bring society back within a modernist framework. Interrogate the Internet,[89] of which Bromberg is a member, furthers the argument, stating:

> We see the Internet as an expression of, and even the salvation of high modernism. Its development is consistent with the logic of late capitalism. It above all else, promises the possibility of achieving the ends of the Enlightenment: a sense of mastery and escape from the limits of the frailties of incarnation. As the product of a prolonged period of incubation, mediation and scientific development, it represents . . . the scientific solution to the death of God.

To them, far from challenging modernity, cyberspace both reproduces and reinforces existing hegemonic structures. We are in times of restructuring the modern rather than moving to some fundamentally different postmodern condition. In this scenario, cyberspatial technological development and promotion are bound within capitalist modes of production. Here, cyberspace is a commercial product to be economically exploited, and to be used to provide the basis for opening new markets of opportunity. While cyberspace is ushering in a new 'age of information', information is being used as the basis for reinforcing the mode of capital; information is capital. The dominant bases of the modernist agenda, enquiry, discovery, innovation, progress, internationalisation, self and economic development, are, however, still the principles underlying Western society.[90] Indeed, as Kumar explains, the concept of an information society fits well with the liberal, progressive tradition of Western thought:

> It maintains the enlightenment faith in rationality and progress. Its current exponents belong generally to the centre of the ideological spectrum. To the extent that knowledge and its growth are equated with greater efficacy and greater freedom, this view, despite its pronouncement of a radical shift in societal arrangements, continues in the line of thought inaugurated by Saint-Simon, Comte and the positivists.[91]

As such, these commentators suggest we are living in a time of economic and commercial restructuring, not some fundamental shift to a new age, underlain by new values. Society has taken no fundamental new principle or direction and 'new technology is being applied within a political and economic framework that accentuates existing patterns, rather than giving rise to new ones'.[92] For Berman,[93] postmodernism is just an aesthetic word game, a clean-hands, non-desk-leaving approach to studying life. To him, postmodernism is a farce, a re-enactment of much modernist thought but unanchored from its moral and political context; a set of ideas unhinged from life in the 'real' world:

> They [postmodernists] announce the end of all things in tones of serene aplomb, proclaim incoherence in elegant neoclassical antitheses, and assert with dogmatic self-certainty the impossibility of truth and the death of the self. Where is this voice coming from? It sounds as if, after the failure of their one great leap into actuality, back in May 1968, they resolved never to go out again, and dug themselves into a grand metaphysical tomb, thick and tight enough to furnish lasting comfort against the cruel hopes of spring. . . . We should not be surprised to find, even in this dead air, modernism born again.[94]

To him, postmodernists are denying the central theme of progress that motivates many people's lives as they try to make the modern world their own – modernism is still the overridingly dominant basis of everyday life, visible from every Western window. These queries have led Rosenau[95] to ask whether postmodernism is merely a product of affluence, the child of those more interested in liberty rather than necessity (postmodernism has received scant attention in poorer countries of the world), or whether it simply reflects adolescent rebellion and opposition to the establishment by those deprived of power (as Berman implies). Feminist critiques, alternatively, can be applied to both modernist and postmodernist thought.

FEMINIST CRITIQUE

Feminism suggests that science is dominated by, and reflects the position, of men, specifically, white, wealthy Western men. They suggest that there needs to be a re-negotiation of the role and structure of institutions and the production of knowledge. Here, there is a re-negotiation of power relations within society so that how we come to know the world is more reflective of the people living in it. Feminist critiques of cyberspace seek to demonstrate the ways in which power relations within this new space are developing and explore whether a socially just virtual society is emerging. While one set of critiques have been examining gender roles and whether the imbalances that pervade real-world societies are perpetuated in virtual society, another set has been suggesting ways in which cyberspace might develop and the promises offered to groups who are marginalised and oppressed.

Kramarae[96] argues that, from hardware engineers to software programmers, men dominate cyberspatial technological development. To her this means that at some level both the technology and the software used are likely to reflect this group's desires and intentions to the exclusion of others. It is therefore probably unsurprising to know that in 1994, 73% of Internet use was by men.[97] Shade[98] portrays a bleaker picture, estimating only 10–15% of Internet usage as being by women and over 90% of American computer scientists being male. The Dutch free-net site *Digital City* had 15% female users, a 6% increase from 1994.[99] The WWW surveys of the Georgia Institute of Technology have consistently showed a large imbalance in male to female users, although the picture is improving (Figure 3.1).

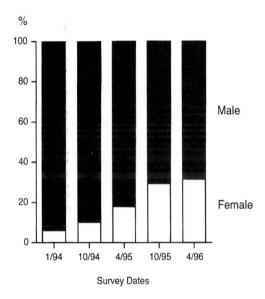

Figure 3.1 *Internet Usage by Females and Males (Georgia Surveys). Source: Based on http://www.cc.gatech.edu/grvu/ user.surveys/*

Kramarae[100] is concerned by such an imbalance in use and in design. She fears that women are in cyberspace 'but in the same basic ways they have been in the rest of men's technology creations, not as primary decision makers but primarily as tools or concepts to be used in the creations of men'. She suggests that we are not doing enough in the early stages of education to 'genderise' computer studies. Problems tend to exist at two levels. First, girls and women do not have the same access to computers and cyberspace that boys and men have. Second, that databases, bulletin boards and newsgroups are almost universally aimed at, and dominated by, male issues and male discussants. There are very few forums germane to the feminist student and scholar.[101] Similarly, computer games are nearly all universally concerned with contact sports, war or fighting, with lots of blood and combat.[102] In these games women are either victims or slender, beautiful killing machines. Further, as Borsook[103] notes, magazines such as *Wired* and *PC Magazine* are nearly universally written by men, for men and are read mainly by men. Kramarae contends that 'cyberspace, like earthspace, is not developing as a viable place for women'.[104]

Kramarae's fears are largely borne out by studies that look at gender differences of life on-line. For example, Herring,[105] on examining the interchanges on academic computer news lists, found a number of differences between male and female posters. Men's messages tended to be longer, issue orientated, more assertive, challenge making, sarcastic and self-promoting. Women's messages tended to be shorter, personally orientated, less assertive, apologetic and supportive. We[106] shows how these findings correspond well to traditional theories about men's and women's communication. For example, Lakoff[107] has argued that women are taught a different language to men. Girls are taught to be passive and boys to be more assertive.

In contrast to these findings, Witmer and Katzman[108] found that women's messages contained more emoticons and more challenges, and that women flamed more than men. They suggest that this might be because of the relative anonymity of cyberspace and because the women on these discussion groups are well used to making their voices heard in the male-dominated worlds of high-tech and academia. As a result, they suggest that these results might not be applicable to the female population as a whole. Bellman *et al.*[109] provide evidence that cyberspace can have a liberating effect. They found that when allowed to post anonymously Latin American women were more likely to express their opinion and join in debates than in face-to-face meetings. We[110] similarly reports that women and men reported that they found it easier to communicate on-line than face-to-face. Women found it easier to get their voice heard and found men more receptive to their ideas and more open in their attitudes. However, there was a flip side to this in the form of increased harassment, abuse and unwanted attention from some sections of male population.

For theorists such as Haraway, Plant and Light,[111] these spaces, while designed and maintained by men, offer women new opportunities to undermine the world-view and material reality of the patriarchal system. As described in Chapter 4, they believe that these systems allow women the opportunity to reconstruct their identities and to challenge dominant ideas and dualisms that structure lives. It is argued that cyberspatial technologies, because of their decentralised political and legal control, rather than being used to consolidate the power of the dominant male society can be used to increase the socio-political status of more marginal groups (including women). Hall[112] terms this approach, where social dualisms are challenged, as liberal cyberfeminism. At the centre of these arguments is the belief that women do not have to become the victims of this new technology. Rather, 'if women are willing to become proactive users expressing a point of view about how they want to interact with new technologies, then they can use technology for empowerment'.[113]

In the main, this empowerment comes from using cyberspatial technologies to re-negotiate essentialist dualisms, gain information and knowledge, develop stronger political networks and take part in participatory democracy.[114] Within this liberal framework, women will be freed of gender relations and sexual hierarchies because the physical differences that underpin social relations in the non-virtual world will be eliminated or at least radically subverted within a space where the body is of no importance: the mental will no longer be limited by the physical.[115] Hall thus suggests that liberal feminists envisage a time when oppression will be replaced by equality, binaries with plurality, categories with fluidity, separation with unity. MacKinnon thus argues that virtual spaces such as MUDs offer an opportunity for social reordering, as the social construction of women relative to the social construction of men can be re-negotiated in a space beyond embodiment.

As discussed in the next chapter, it is not clear whether any re-negotiation of the body is happening. While some suggest that gender-swapping is opening the eyes of men to life as a woman and the oppression women face daily in negotiating their lives, others suggest that cyberspatial technologies are in fact reinforcing current representations of women through the prevalence of pornography and the retention of stereotypical gender roles. Women in cyberspace still attract the unwanted attention of men, are still sexually harassed and receive abusive messages and are still expected to adopt the same gender roles as in real space. Clerc[116] suggests that the pattern still exists because men communicate on-line for status whereas women communicate to develop and maintain relationships. Further, the dominant group in cyberspace and the group who are deciding upon appropriate on-line behaviour are men.[117] At present, men have decided that flaming and individualism are okay. The fear for some feminists is, and there is some evidence that it is happening, that women will try out cyberspace but will leave after unsolicited attention or abuse or only post self-censored messages for fear of reprisal.[118] In fact, one person Brail[119] spoke to stated that 'I think (the Internet) is the last bastion of real ugly sexism because it's unmoderated and faceless'. One response has been to create women-only spaces and the development of a radical feminist position which rather than wanting a change in existing structures wishes to see these structures replaced.[120] As such, whether women do become empowered through cyberspace only time will tell. Clearly, there will have to be a number of significant developments, which radically subvert power relations that are currently being transferred on-line. There can be little doubt, however, that at present cyberspace is dominated and largely controlled by men.

RE-APPROACHING CYBERSPACE

Separately, each of these approaches seems limited and limiting. Utopianism/futurism blindly predicts the saviour of humankind through technological development. Analysis tends to focus on how cyberspace will revolutionise the way we live and documenting how such changes might occur. Little regard is given to wider social or economic considerations concerning how technologies are re-appropriated and used by society or how technologies fit into the economic landscape. Technological determinism suggests that the way we live our lives is purely dictated by technology in simple cause and effect relationships. Analysis focuses upon how society might adapt to cyberspace rather than on how we might use cyberspace to our benefit.[121] Within both utopist and technological determinist viewpoints, technology and society are seen as separate and uncomplicated; there is no complex interplay between the two. This is clearly too simplistic. Technology and society are intimately entwined and inseparable. Technologies do not give rise to themselves but are the product of human endeavour and bound within historical structures.

The approaches of social constructivism and political economy both recognise that technology and society are inseparable. Both approaches, however, are narrow in their focus and views. For social constructivists, cyberspace is mediated and understood through culture. They are only interested in micro-level social processes used in shaping and re-appropriating the interactions between different actors and institutions that socially construct cyberspatial development and use. As such, they reject the influence of broader social and economic structures of capitalism and the power of political-economic forces. Political economists, in contrast, only focus upon these larger political-economic structures, failing to acknowledge the role of social processes in determining how a technology is developed and appropriated.

Postmodernists suggest that we are in a time of rapid change where the modernist approaches of utopianism, technological determinism, political economy and social constructivism are inappropriate in understanding and explaining technology and its relationship to society. They suggest that we are living in times of fragmentation, decentring, disorientation and disenchantment where individuals are unstable, multiple and diffuse. Technologies, such as cyberspatial technologies, are agents of change, leading to new forms of relations, expressions and society, and a move towards a 'mode of information' away from the 'mode of capital'. It is clear that fixed notions of the self are unwarranted and that identity is fluid; however, the intersections of virtual culture and broader political-economic concerns are as yet relatively under-theorised. Similarly, it is clear that we are in a time of great economic and commercial restructuring, and that information is becoming more important. However, at present, there is little evidence to suggest that the 'mode of capital' is weakening. Rather, cyberspatial technologies are being developed by transnational and entrepreneurial companies with the aim of opening up new markets to be exploited for profit. Similarly, information is being used to streamline operations and optimise efficiency in all aspects of business from record keeping to marketing. It seems that any global restructuring is occurring to accommodate shifts in opportunity and is not the result of a move away from capital as the driving force of the global economy. Cyberspace, therefore, reinforces and reproduces many hegemonic structures rather than challenging them.

Poststructuralists' desire to focus upon textuality, narrative, discourse and language in order to de-construct the meanings in our actions provides too narrow a focus, closing off our analysis from wider considerations and the knowledge to be gained from more empirical analysis. Poststructuralism's focus upon the micro and its aversion to grand narratives means that it seems unsuited to trying to understand concepts such as capitalism. Capital and the political economy are clearly implicated in cyberspatial development. Cyberspace does not exist in a capital vacuum. Essentially, we have to go further than just gaining an understanding of cyberspatial interaction and development. Incorporating the ideas of language and culture is important if we are to achieve a balanced perspective but on their own they do not provide enough substantive evidence of the ways in which cyberspace is being produced and consumed.

Similarly, feminist approaches seem too narrow in focus, concentrating too strongly upon the gender relations underlying cyberspatial usage and development. As such, in the main, cultural ideologies are given more credence than political-economic ideologies. While an understanding of gender relations is important for understanding the ways in which cyberspace is adopted and appropriated, the focus needs to be expanded to centre upon power relations *per se* both with cultural and political-economic ideologies and how these are expressed at the local and global scale.

Given these limitations, it seems appropriate to develop a new approach in order to understand more fully cyberspace and its social, cultural, political and economic implications. My suggestion is that we need to construct a broad research base to try to understand and explain the experiences, behaviour and knowledge of cyberspatial users, and the mechanisms and processes that underlie cyberspatial use and development. Combining aspects of postmodernism and feminism with social constructivism and political economy gives a well-balanced approach, which acknowledges that the virtual overlies and intersects with the 'real' in a symbiotic relationship. Here, the combined power of cultural and political-economic ideologies to shape human life is recognised while the grand narrative aspects of social constructivism and political economy are rejected. Instead, I am forwarding a position which seeks to deconstruct the complex ways in which the local and global, sociocultural and politico-economic intersect and are played out, a framework in which the fragmentation, decentring and restructuring of society can be read and interpreted.

This approach thus seeks to build upon that of Graham and Marvin,[122] whereby they combine social constructivism and political economy in order to try to explain the geography of telecommunications. They argue that these approaches are suitable for combination because they both recognise that technologies are applied within rather than from outside society. However, both are flawed when used independently as political economy neglects social processes and thus overplays the significance of capitalist structures, and social constructivism by solely concentrating on social processes, neglects wider political and economic forces that create power imbalances and help shape local conditions.[123] It is thus clear that the relationships between technology and society can no longer be framed within strict economic and political terms or in strict social and cultural terms but must encompass both.[124] Essentially, cyberspatial use and development is socially constructed at the local scale and mediated by a broader, more regional/global political economy: there is a recursive relationship between local, social/cultural and regional/global, political/economic processes. Here, technological developments, uptake and usage are locally constructed through the interplay between individuals and institutions, and bound within historical systems: technology is not just given. These local constructions are, however, bound into larger political and economic contexts and affected by factors such as investment, policy, marginalisation, local economic conditions and status (levels of unemployment, poverty etc.), and the opportunity to exploit and break into both local and global markets.

However, unlike the approach of Graham and Marvin, this new integrated approach adopts a more critical stance and rejects some of the modernist underpinnings of their approach, particularly the notion of grand narratives, universal truths and causality. As such, the integration of a postmodernist perspective seeks to acknowledge a rejection of modernist values and adoption of an approach that seeks 'readings' not 'observations', 'interpretations' not 'findings', 'intertextual relations' rather than 'causality', and the recognition of difference and a recognition that society is rapidly progressing through a series of rapid transitions as traditional modernist ideas concerning space, time, reality, nature are undermined and reconfigured. Whereas Graham and Marvin plot the changes that telecommunications are making to the urban landscape, I am more interested in how cyberspace reconfigures and transforms society into a new, postmodern world. Within this context, it is possible to integrate notions of power relations and dominant ideologies and to acknowledge that identity and community are fluid, multiple and contested. In the next chapter, we explore this new approach, in relation to the social and cultural aspects of cyberspace with particular reference to the way in which cyberspace raises key questions relating to identity and community.

CYBERSPACE, CULTURE AND SOCIETY

CHAPTER 4

CYBERSPACE, CULTURE AND SOCIETY

> New technologies alter the structure of our interests: the things we think about. They
> alter the character of our symbols: the things we think with. And they alter the nature
> of community: the arena in which thoughts develop.[1]

For many social commentators cyberspatial technologies represent a catalyst for a broad
and extensive change in culture.[2] For them, information and communication technologies represent the third major media revolution, after the Roman alphabet and the
printing press, which is profoundly affecting culture and society.[3] As such, it is suggested that electronic technology stands as the most demanding denominator of current
culture.[4] At both the individual and collective levels, cyberspace is facilitating the deep
restructuring of society, challenging traditional notions of identity and community. As
Guattari[5] states:

> today's information and communication machines do not merely convey represen-
> tational contents, but also contribute to the fabrication of new assemblages of enun-
> ciation, individual and collective.

For Poster,[6] the key question is what forms of cultural articulation is cyberspace
going to promote and discourage. He suggests that cyberspace technologies do enrich
existing forms of consumer culture, but also depart from traditional mass media and
culture industries in a number of ways.[7] Firstly, cyberspace is not a broadcast medium
with few producers and many consumers, but rather a decentralised communication
system where individuals are both the consumers and the producers. Secondly,
cyberspace is interactive; users can choose what information they receive and send.
Thirdly, cyberspatial technologies provide extensions of biological abilities, allowing
machines to do what the body once did.[8] It is these factors that facilitate the challenge
to the traditional notions of identity and community by providing new social spaces of
interchange and cultural transmission. Indeed, Thu Nguyen and Alexander[9] argue that,
combined, these three factors produce cultural mutation and considerable cultural
promise.[10] Similarly, Schroeder[11] envisages the emergence of a society in which
cyberspatial communications become all-important; where technology and science
transform the structure and meaning of society and culture. Escobar[12] terms the

resultant emerging culture as 'cyberculture', and Jones[13] names its associated society as 'cybersociety'.

LIFE IN A VIRTUAL WORLD

> People in virtual communities use words on screens to exchange pleasantries and argue, engage in intellectual discourse, conduct commerce, exchange knowledge, share emotional support, make plans, brainstorm, gossip, feud, fall in love, find friends and lose them, play games, flirt, create a little high art and a lot of idle talk. People in virtual communities do just about everything that people do in real life but we leave our bodies behind. You can't kiss anybody and nobody can punch you on the nose, but a lot can happen within those boundaries. To the millions who have been drawn into it, the richness and vitality of computer-linked cultures is attractive, even addictive.

The above quotation by Howard Rheingold,[14] one of the leading proponents of cyberspace adoption, is a good illustration of how some people view cyberspatial interaction. Virtual worlds are seen to offer all that the real world has to offer with a few little extras and some of the more unpleasant features removed. More and more studies are now starting to chart what life in a virtual world is like. The focus ranges from the consequences relating to identity, to the use of language, social interaction and whether virtual communities exist. In general, these studies focus upon the social and cultural world of MUDs, discussion groups and bulletin boards. The majority of these studies tend to conclude that there is a rich vibrancy of life on-line. For example, Baym[15] has interviewed and documented the interchanges of users participating in the rec.arts.tv.soaps (r.a.t.s.) Usenet newsgroup. She contends that the people who participate in this group have created a dynamic and rich community. Just as in real-world communities, there are behavioural norms, differing personalities, shared significance and allegiances. For her the Internet fosters the growth of distinct cultures grounded in communicative practice. Baym[16] suggests that:

> community is generated through the interplay between preexisting structures and the participants' strategic appropriation and exploitation of the resources and rules those structures offer in ongoing interaction.

Correll[17] details an ethnographic study of an on-line lesbian cafe. She used a three-way methodology to study an on-line community and the processes at play. First she observed the daily traffic between cafe patrons, occasionally asking patrons to explain various actions or conversations. Next, she interviewed twelve patrons using a semi-structured interview via private e-mail. Last, she met in person with eight of the patrons who had decided to meet face-to-face, interviewing these individuals in two groups of four. Correll describes how patrons have constructed an elaborate virtual cafe in which to contextualise their interactions. She suggests that this shared setting creates a common sense of reality constructed purely through verbal descriptions. In essence, the locale needed for community has moved from the real to the virtual, but place and setting is still of importance. For her, the transference of the locale into the virtual is the secret to the community working. Without the shared reality of the bar, she suggests that the community itself might have dissolved. The locale constructed and maintained, however, was safer than the real bar scene 'where the games are for real'.[18] The glass screen of the computer was providing a window into a world where the patrons could explore their ideas and thoughts without fear of physical or mental retribution; true identities were hidden and patrons could participate without being visible members. Correll explains that one of the primary roles of the lesbian cafe is to act as a surrogate community for those who tend to be marginalised from traditional communities, while providing many of the same functions. She discovered four types of patron who constitute the community: the regulars, who chat in familiar, smooth conversational style; the 'newbies', who have just joined the cafe and are trying to learn the protocols, gain trust and develop friendships; the 'lurkers', who tend to just observe interactions and occasionally post notes; and the 'bashers' (mainly men), who send abusive posts. Correll suggests that her findings challenge the traditional notion of community by demonstrating that a community can be created in alternative spaces.

Others such as Bruckman and Resnick, Mnookin, Reid, and Turkle,[19] rather than concentrating on mailing list groups, document life within MUD environments, focusing particularly upon the nature of communication, and the formation and development of on-line communities. Within MUDs social interaction takes place within a textual virtual environment described by the computer and created by a programmer or by individual participants (in contrast to Correll's study, where the concept of a cafe environment was created by mutual consent). When you log on to a MUD you receive a textual introduction. For example, if you decide to connect to JaysHouse MOO[20], you are greeted with the following message:

Underground
This is a dark, cramped space. It appears to be very crowded in here; you keep bumping into what feels like drainage pipes, alligators, and other people (apparently sleeping). One useful thing that you've discovered in your bumbling about is a manhole cover above you. Poof is here, shedding industriously.

By pushing up the manhole cover you enter the world of JaysHouse. Here, you can move about, explore the world, alter the rooms and chat to the other people you encounter. Interaction is based within the context of the imaginary setting and not rooted in the context of a specific subject (e.g. soap operas). MUDs provide an artificial place to interact and several commentators have observed that users treat these places as if they were real. As such, like real-world encounters, conversations are commonly based within the context of the environment they are spoken in. As such, interactions are framed by physical setting and the context of social relations and roles that participants perform. A surprising amount of exploration and interaction can take place with very few commands, many of which are generic across different MUDs (see Table 4.1).

Table 4.1   *Getting Started in MUDs (Basic Commands in JaysHouse MOO)*

Purpose	Full command	Abbreviated command	What you type	What appears
To talk	Say	”	Say hello	Guest says hello
Do actions	Emote	:	Emote reaches out	Guest reaches out
Find out who else is on-line	@who		@who	List of people on-line, plus how long they have been on-line and how long since they typed anything
Find out where another player is	@where		@where (name)	Name is in the Lounge
Contact someone who is not in the same room	Page	p	Page (name) This is my first page	Name senses that guest is looking for them in Long-distance Communication. E pages, 'This is my first page.'†
Look at people or objects	Look	l	Look at house	(description) The house is a big rambling . . .

Examine objects	Examine	e	Examine map	List of commands to interact with map further, e.g. Obvious verbs:
				    r*ead map
				    er*ase map
				    etc.

Manipulate objects	Get Hand Drop		Get (object) Hand (object) to (name) Drop (object)	You pick up object You hand object to name You drop object
Move east/west	East/West	e/w	East or West	Description of new place
Move north/south	North/South	n/s	North or South	Description of new place
Move up/down	Up/Down	u/d	Up or Down	Description of new place
Link several moves together	Go		Go e n u	Description of place three moves along
Create description of character	@describe		@describe me as ' – your description here – '	Use look command to see new description
Change gender	@gender		@gender (your choice)	Use look command to see new gender
Change name	@rename		@rename (new name)	
Leave MUD	@quit		@quit	

†The last column of the 'Contact someone . . .' row in Table 4.1 states 'E pages'. E is a gender-neutral pronoun. It means that your character is neither male nor female.

To many researchers, MUDs offer us the opportunity to study identity and the way in which communities form and develop over time. They suggest that through studying virtual worlds we might also learn important lessons regarding identity and communities in the real world. Turkle,[21] for example, has extensively studied the relationship between real life and virtual life of a number of people who regularly use MUDs. She found that people use MUDs for a variety of reasons – some for play, others for emotional support lacking in real life. She reports that for those seeking emotional support MUDs act in two ways. In the first instance, MUDs act as a place for self-reflection, a constructive environment to work through or act out real-world problems. In the second instance the virtual environment acts as an emotional escape, a substitute for real life which often deepens real-life anxiety.

In relation to community, Bruckman and Resnick[22] argue that in MUDs, where users can build a virtual world rather than just interact with a pre-designed world, people find outlets for self-expression, there is increased engagement and interaction between users, diversity is encouraged and there is an enhanced sense of community. For some commentators[23] this sense of community has found expression in the way that, just as in real-world space, the inhabitants of MUDs are now seeking to formalise the new, parallel world they inhabit by formulating social and legal order. For example, LambdaMOO has started a process of democratisation as the inhabitants try to create a social order and lay down the social rules of life in a virtual world.[24] At first, the owners of LambdaMOO regulated the space and had ultimate control over the inhabitants. Now a system of petition has been introduced whereby people can vote over issues of concern and formalise social rules. Issues can range from whether someone should be denied access for anti-social behaviour to whether there should be a formal law. In addition, the petition system is used to arbitrate over personal and group disputes. Mnookin[25] suggests that these disputes are usually based around two themes, the nature of property rights and the extent to which free speech is a right. The protagonists are usually aligned into one of two camps, the formalisers and the resisters. The formalisers want to see the process of social order forwarded with the introduction of enforceable laws as they increasingly come to see the MOO as society. Correspondingly, the resistors want to see the LambdaMOO remain the way it is and reject any notion of formalisation. They see the MOO as a game, a bit of fun, and want the others to 'lighten up'. To many commentators, LamdaMOO illustrates that there are significant social processes at play in virtual worlds.

DISEMBODIMENT, RECONFIGURING THE BODY AND IDENTITY

Castells[26] argues that, as a result of the transformation of society into a postmodern era characterised by the global flow of wealth, power and images, 'the search for identity, collective or individual, ascribed or constructed, becomes the fundamental source of social meaning'. He suggests that people are increasingly organising their identity not around what they do, but what they are, or think they are. Cyberspatial technologies are seen as an important medium because they allow us to explore who we are and because they are changing who we are. As such, there are two emerging theories concerning the relationship between cyberspace and identity, and both centre on changing conceptualisations of the body. In the first, cyberspace is seen as a disembodying experience with transcendental and liberating effects. The second position conceptualises interactions with cyberspace as aiding the merging of nature with technology as humans and computers coalesce through a process of cyborging. These theories are by no means mutually exclusive, and both argue that cyberspatial technologies have significant implications concerning identity and how we come to understand identity. Both theories draw on notions of Foucault's theory of 'technologies of the self'.[27] Within this theory, Foucault suggests that certain technological devices change the social construction of personal identity. Cyberspace is deemed to be such a 'technology of the self'.[28] Poster[29] argues that cyberspace promotes the individual as an unstable identity, an individual bound within a continuous process of multiple identity formation: 'the self is reconstituted as a fluid and polymorphous entity'.[30] Here, 'the boundaries of the self are defined less by the skin than by the feedback loops'.[31] Cyberspatial technologies thus alter the conditions under which self-identity is constructed.

DISEMBODIMENT

As noted in Chapter 1, for many, cyberspaces form a new social space where reality and virtuality merge, where the physical and material are transcended. Arguments centre on the ideas of disembodiment and transcendence. Many of the contentions are extremely utopian, centring on post-human life and the migration into the machine. In this scenario, embodiment is often represented as an unfortunate barrier to interactions; for serious cyberspace enthusiasts 'an organic body just gets in the way'.[32] Here, the body is often referred to as 'meat'[33] or 'data trash'[34] and 'the dream . . . is to leave the 'meat' behind and to become distilled in a clean, pure, uncontaminated relationship with computer technology'.[35] Free of our bodies we can transcend our own mortality and discover true understanding and new philosophies. Moravec, for example, insists that we are entering a 'postbiological' world where we will be able to download our memory into the computer or a robotic host,[36] and Virilio[37] argues that all of the qualities of the body are being transferred to the machine:

> we are forgetting our body, we are losing it. This is an accident of the body, a decorporation. The body is torn and disintegrated.

Morse suggests that such a potential transition is fuelled by the desire to disengage from the human condition.[38]

At a less utopian level, although still centring on the ideas of disembodiment, cyberspaces are seen to form protective spaces free of the constraints of the body. A place where 'the self is constructed and the rules of social interaction are built, not received'.[39] Here you are accepted for what you say and do, rather than your physicality, status or material wealth. Rheingold[40] explains that:

we reduce and encode our identities as words on a screen, decode and unpack the identities of others. The way we use these words, . . . is what determines our identities in cyberspace . . . The physical world . . . is a place where identity and position of the people you communicate with are well known, fixed, and highly visual. In cyberspace, everybody is in the dark. We can only exchange words with each other – no glances or shrugs or ironic smiles. Even the nuances of voice and intonation are stripped away.

In cyberspace, nobody need know your race, disability or gender. You can hide behind, and view, the same situations, using different masks. Your body is irrelevant and invisible.[41] As Kane[42] notes, 'unless you choose to disclose it, no one knows whether you are male, female, tall, short, a redhead or blond, black, white, Asian, Latino, in a wheelchair or not'. Unlike real-world meetings, individual representation on the Net is not based upon biology, birth or social circumstance, but is a 'highly manipulable, completely disembodied intellectual fabrication'.[43] Cyberspatial interaction, it seems, provides an unrestricted freedom of expression that is far less hierarchical and formal than real-world interaction.[44]

The appeal of cyberspace is based upon this anonymity and the opportunity of escapism. It is anonymity that creates the opportunities to invent alternative identities and to engage with untried forms of interaction.[45] Correll[46] comments that cyberspace gives the user more time to carefully construct their personae, delicately crafting emotions and appearances and giving a control not experienced in face-to-face conversations. In addition, interactions in cyberspace carry less responsibility and, Aycock and Buchignani[47] suggest, no more personal consequence than reading a book. For Lanier[48] these factors 'give us a sense of being able to be who we are without limitation'. These sentiments are borne out in Stephanie Fletcher's novel *e-mail://a.love.story.//*, a frank account of life on a bulletin board. In this book, the characters revel in their anonymity, the lack of responsibility and ability to manipulate their characters and explore alternative identities.

Thu Nguyen and Alexander[49] further state that cyberspace appeals to the young because it represents an escape from a world that does not, and does not want to, understand or provide for them. On-line they can explore their feelings and identity, and communicate with like-minded individuals. This freedom to explore identity and feelings has led utopian commentators such as Timothy Leary to suggest that we will slowly forsake personal interaction and face-to-face meetings in favour of socialising via the computer:

> Face-to-face interactions will be reserved for special, intimate, precious, sacramentalized events. Flesh encounters will be rare and thrilling. In the future each of us will be linked in thrilling cyber-exchanges with many others whom we may never meet in person and who do not speak our phonetic-literal language. Most of our important creations will take place in ScreenLand. Taking off our cyberwear to confront another with naked eyeballs will be a precious personal appearance. And the quality of our 'personal appearances' will be raised to a level of mythic drama.[50]

In cyberspace, therefore, it is suggested that identity becomes fluid, ephemeral and empowering because people can choose how they are represented.[51] Users literally become the authors of their lives. Further, identity becomes multiple and decentred as different aspects of our lives are disengaged and happen in different worlds, sometimes at the same time. Turkle[52] suggests that it is like moving from a uni-task (Dos) to multi-task (Windows) environment. We can have several windows open at once all running separate programs within the same machine. Such a conceptualisation fits well with current psycho-analytical (Lacan) and postmodern theories of identity. Within these theories, rather than the self being some permanent structure of the mind or fixed within some genetic code, self is thought of as a discourse where identity is constructed through multiple experi-ences. Identity is thus fragmented, decentred and fluid, changing with time and situa-tions, and indeed different for different occasions. With the growth in information industries, and the opportunity to interact in a number of different environments (includ-ing cyberspatial ones) commentators now suggest that we rapidly cycle through different identities so that this progress of fragmenting and multiplicity multiplies. The self thus becomes a series of roles that can be mixed and matched.

As Pile and Thrift[53] note in relation to real space, mapping identity, given its fluid, multiple and fragmented nature, is fraught with difficulties. This is multiplied when time–space itself becomes fluid as traditional relationships between power, knowledge and people become unstable and reconfigured and the body in which identity is grounded takes on less (or no) importance. As such, untangling cyberspatial identity is complex. Recent studies have, though, highlighted the ways in which people are constructing their cyberspatial identities. For example, there are a number of well-documented cases of people constructing multiple, fluid on-line lives based around experiments with gender. In one example, a middle-aged, male psychiatrist pretended to be a compassionate, dis-abled, older woman who tapped out her messages using a headstick.[54] Using this persona, the psychiatrist developed several, deeply personal relationships, mainly with women. Some of these women shared their deepest troubles and he (Julia) gave advice. In another example, Slouka[55] describes how Avram had been conversing with Janie using a chat facility. They had fallen in love, and had been conducting a cyberspatial affair including talking each other through masturbation. There was one catch – Avram was pretending to be Allison, a persona he had created. Some report that these on-line personas can become very powerful to the extent that being denied the ability to log-on under a designated 'nickname' can leave a person frustrated and bewildered as their identifier of recognition has been stripped, denying them access to social networks that might have been sustained for some period of time.[56] In a space where your name is your sole identifier being denied the ability to use it can lead to an identity crisis. However, while these studies naively map on-line identities they do not as yet tease out the complex relationships of life on-line and have also failed to map the ways in which they intersect with real-world lives. Further, they tend to concentrate on agency at the expense of structure. The importance of this undertaking cannot be understated as it is only with more detailed analysis that we will be able to start to understand life on-line.

Not all commentators are enamoured with the idea of life in a virtual world and question some of the claims made regarding identity. For example, Robins[57] argues that cyberspaces represent:

a familiar old appeal to an imaginative space in which we can occupy new identities and create new experiences to transcend the limitations of our mundane lives. It is the aesthetic of fantasy-gaming; the fag-end of Romantic sensibility.

While we might experiment with 'new identities, mobile identities, exploratory identities', they are invariably banal identities, and identities removed from the realities of everyday life.[58] Cyberspace as viewed by utopists, for Robins, is a space where the imagination is dead, where old dreams are foisted upon new technology. In this context, cyberspace provides nothing beyond a new space, a new medium. There is no denying that cyberspace makes an interesting arena to study identity, but the medium does not fundamentally challenge how self-identity is constructed – we still use the same rules of engagement, the same consensual protocols that we use in everyday life. While identities are fluid, contested and multiple, on-line identities are shallow and distract from life in the real world. Admittedly given the nature of cyberspace it is easier to go through a journey of self-discovery but it is a journey removed or distant from where the self predominantly presides. Cyberspace does provide a more protective space to 'play' with our fantasies, our othernesses (e.g. gender), but it is only a protective space; we can 'play' these fantasies by cross-dressing, by inhabiting the different social spaces that make up the social fabric of communities we *have* to live in.

Further, while it is clear that we do construct on-line social spaces whose rules are built not received it is also evident that the vast majority of social spaces on the Internet bear a remarkable resemblance to real-world locales. As such, many on-line interactions are in fact situated in real-world protocols, undermining the potential liberating effects of being on-line. In other words, on-line spaces are situated; not only are they like real-world spaces but they are often in the image of real-world spaces. Foucault[59] constantly reminds us that it is practice and not belief that shapes our lives. The real question therefore does not relate to disembodiment but rather to 'what extent the embodied spaces in real life become replicated on-line' – to what extent do the practices and structures (organisation and regulation of space, time, movement) which shape our lives off-line also shape our lives on-line? As noted in Chapter 3, women are not finding cyberspace to be free of sexual harassment, unwanted approaches and blatant sexism and their lives on-line are being shaped through the same practices that regulate their lives in real space. Indeed, Hall suggests that, on-line, gender, rather than being erased, is being intensified discursively. In Foucaultian terms, on-line women (in general) still remain 'docile bodies' – bodies that are regulated by, and subjected to, men. Rather than gendered identities becoming re-negotiated in cyberspace, cyberspaces are becoming clearly demarcated through heightened sexism and the creation of protective women-only spaces. Clearly, the roles of the body in interaction on-line and off-line are different but to what extent are our real bodies being metaphorically re-created as virtual bodies in cyberspace? While Haraway[60] has argued that 'bodies are maps of meaning and power' in real space, does the text simulate bodies in cyberspace so that the spaces become embodied or is it a fallacy to suggest that we can become disembodied when on-line?

It is difficult to accept the argument that on-line identities are *completely* separate from identities within 'embodied' real space; going on-line does not 'flatline' a person, immobilising the body and suspending everyday consciousness (as argued by Thu Nguyen and Alexander[61]). In other words, you do not suddenly turn into 'somebody' different like some modern day Jekyll and Hyde. Whereas Jekyll had no recollection of Hyde and vice versa, we are aware of our lives on and off the screen and our actions are mediated with reference to both: spaces might be distinct (different windows) and identity might be fluid and fragmented but it is also situated – our lives in one window are contextualised in relation to life in others. Indeed, Sobchack[62] reminds us that we do not just have bodies, but that we are our bodies. Bodies cannot be transcended; rather, they are a fundamental constituent of us, of being.

Sobchack argues that cyberspaces are spaces that are entered and interacted within from the site of the body: it is the fingers that type or move a joystick, it is the whole body that enters a virtual reality space, not just the eyes and the brain. For her, the ideas of disembodiment are largely misnomers. As Woodward[63] suggests, 'the possibility of an invulnerable and thus immortal body is our greatest technological illusion – that is to say, *delusion*'. The body is always present when we interact, whether it be face-to-face, or via the computer. It does not disappear or relax into coma. As, first, Stone[64] and, second, Argyle and Shields[65] express it:

> It is important to remember that virtual community originates in, and must return to, the physical. No reconfigured virtual body, no matter how beautiful, will slow the death of a cyberpunk with AIDS. Even in the age of the technosocial subject, life is lived through bodies.

> There is no loss of body in and through virtual reality technologies. While we may 'lose ourselves' in a good book or in the trance-like state of online interaction, we know that this is a change of consciousness: something in the mind, not the body.

Evidence for the embodied nature of cyberspace perversely comes from studies that show that many people do not take the opportunity to play with their identity on-line. The number of MUD users remains small and the majority of news list members remain 'lurkers' (readers but not posters). Kawakami[66] reports that 83% of list members had never contributed and two-thirds of those that had spoken had done so fewer than three times. Studies indicate that the reasons why people are staying silent in on-line 'disembodied spaces' are the same as those for people who are reserved in real 'embodied spaces'. For example, Kawakami suggests that 'lurkers' outnumber contributors for six main reasons:

1 Reluctance to speak to people whom they do not know.
2 Resistance to participate in a group that had been formed and developed without them.
3 Lack of expertise to participate and a fear of being evaluated by others.
4 Difficulty of deciding to what extent they should disclose of themselves to others.
5 Worry about expressing themselves clearly.
6 A fear of receiving criticism from others.

For these people, identity and self-expression are being little explored because they are treating cyberspace as an embodied space, a space with traditional power relations. Since much of the research is conducted on-line, and the majority of lurkers remain silent, then the conclusion that cyberspace is liberating because of its disembodying nature is not surprising. Those people who have the same reservations listed above are unlikely to reply to requests to take part in research.

RECONFIGURING THE BODY

For others, cyberspace represents the continued merging of technology and nature. Here, identity is being recontested as the divisions, which we have traditionally used to structure our understanding of the world, dissolve and blur. Proponents of this theory suggest that it is increasingly difficult to separate nature from technology and support their claims through the development of a cyborg discourse. 'Nature and culture are reworked; the one can no longer be the resource for appropriation or incorporation for the other'.[67] A cyborg is a human–machine hybrid where technology replaces or supplements flesh.[68] The idea of a cyborg body has been popularised in much science fiction writing and in films such as *Star Wars* (e.g. Darth Vader), *Robocop* and *Terminator*. At present, technologies such as cosmetic surgery, biotechnology, genetic engineering and cyberspatial systems are increasingly making us cyborg entities:

> In cyberculture, the body is a permeable membrane, its integrity violated and its sanctity challenged by titanium alloy knee joints, myoelectric arms, synthetic bones and blood vessels, breast and penile prostheses, cochlear implants, and artificial hips.[69]

While these technologies all physically alter our bodies, cyberspatial technologies (particularly virtual reality) completely immerse the body within technology and also provide new extensions to our bodies through features such as datagloves, and headsets, with visionaries such as Laurel[70] predicting some future merging between virtual reality technologies and humans. This theme is well developed in the science fiction writings of authors such as Gibson.[71] The characters in his novels are predominantly cyborgs, frequently living lives immersed in technology with bodies that combine flesh with technology.

Cyborg discourse, is predominantly poststructuralist in nature, denying any reality to the body that is not constructed through culture[72] and hence language. Here, the exchange of flesh for machine produces 'rewritings of the body's social and cultural form that are directly related to the reconstitution of social identities'.[73] As such, theorists are interested in how these technologies do and will affect the 'self', humanness and identity.[74] For some, the cyborg body, as with cyberspace's transcendental qualities, represents 'liberation from the confines of gender and other stereotypes, by rendering cultural categories indeterminate and fluid'.[75] As such, the cyborg body represents new opportunities for women and feminist politics. In particular, Haraway[76] has argued that we are all cyborgs; chimeras – the 'fabricated hybrids of machine and organism'.[77] As cyborgs, she suggests that women have an opportunity to reappropriate, contest and enforce new social relations through the recoding of the self and the body. Until recently, she contends, 'female embodiment seemed to be given, organic, necessary',[78] geared towards mothering and its extensions. However, as a cyborg, embodiment is fluid, partial and dynamic, not given but waiting to be ascribed meaning. Here, the dominant patriarchal dualisms that underlie and structure our society can be challenged and replaced by a new philosophical basis that re-balances the position of women within society. Haraway's cyborg discourse also challenges other forms of feminist theory, which have tried to invert the dualisms and have largely rejected technology and science. She suggests that by reappropriating technologies, they will ultimately be empowering for women. Her manifesto, however, is extremely short on practical politics for women wanting to embrace the cyborg ideology and change things at the grass-roots level in the real world, away from the niceties of the written page.

Cyborg-rendering technologies have opened a whole can of ethical worms. The body is being transformed into a site for a series of ideological skirmishes (body politics) relating to abortion rights, foetal tissue use, AIDS treatment, assisted suicide, euthanasia, surrogate mothering, genetic engineering, cloning, sex changes, cosmetic surgery and disability issues. Where once the body was given, god-like, unchanging and fated, it is now chosen, moulded and contested. Dery,[79] rather than viewing this as a challenge to Cartesian dualisms, sees this as the triumph of the mechanistic view of the body rooted in these dualisms; immaterial mind/material world. Here the body is seen as just a machine, a commodity for sale. To some, this commodification is the logical conclusion of a market economy. The evidence they cite is the growing world market in human organs and products: kidneys, livers, hearts, blood, ova, semen etc. To Dery, nowhere is this dualism more dramatic than the disembodying experiences of immersion technologies such as television, gaming and virtual reality where disconnecting involves the 'reincorporation of the wandering mind within a vacant body. . . . [Here,] we are becoming alienated from our increasingly irrelevant bodies'.[80] Rather than challenging the dominant patriarchal, philosophical ideas concerning the body, as Haraway, Balsamo and Plant envisage, viewed within this context cyberspatial technologies are helping to reinforce existing viewpoints. Here, rather than the technologies being reappropriated for feminist politics, they are being used to fortify the ideas of body beautiful (re-touching digital photos), body loathing (dieting, cosmetic surgery), women as objects of beauty, desire and passivity (nearly all women in games and cyberspace are thin, beautiful and passive) and women as cheap, semi-skilled workers (clerical, data entry, component assemblers). Rather than freeing women, cyborging technologies further enslaves them into stereotypical roles and mean little to women who are already 'man-made' in mind and body.[81]

Moreover, it has been argued that while recognising that we are increasingly becoming cyborgs, the machine does not lead to a full rewriting of self-identity. Rather, the merging and meshing of machines leads to a subtle rewriting of the body that is contested and historically grounded (the experiences gained in our old bodies continue to shape self-identity). Indeed, as Sobchack[82] argues, while she is undeniably a cyborg (she uses a prosthetic leg), she has not forgotten that her identity is grounded in her lived-in body, a body she has no intention of trying to escape from. Jamison[83] thus argues that within the cyborg discourse the human body is no longer a place but a collection of parts. The body thus becomes secondary and replaceable in relation to the mind. Jamison contends that such a split is problematic, as it is through their bodies that women negotiate their social relationships. As such, Jamison suggests that we are being seduced by the notion of cyborging and its possible consequences rather than working fully through the implications of cyborg technology upon how people are received and judged. Cyborging might be further enslaving women to conceptions of body beautiful and body loathing.

VIRTUAL COMMUNITY

Just as there are changes relating to identity, some academics argue that cyberspace is fostering new forms of community. Researchers suggest that cyberspace allows the formation of 'virtual (on-line) communities' that are free of the constraints of place and based upon new modes of interaction and new forms of social relationships.[84] Indeed, Poster[85] contends that the Internet's ability to simulate communities far outstrips, in importance, its other functions as a marketing, advertising and information dissemination device. The Internet through its interactivity and relative speed offers users a freedom of expression and personal contact, allowing a sharing of ideas and thoughts regardless of geographical distance and time zones.[86] It is argued that cyberspace does support new forms of social relations, and, like radio and television before it, it will produce a different society.[87]

For utopists such as Howard Rheingold, computer-mediated communication represent the opportunity to recover the meaning and experience of community that is rapidly dissolving from our everyday lives. Rheingold[88] argues that much of our public space, and hence social fabric, is disappearing. The places where we used to meet, talk and swap information are being reclaimed for other purposes; the cafe is replaced by the impersonal mall. For Rheingold the Internet represents a new space in which to form new forms of communities based upon our interests and affinity, rather than coincidence of location.[89] Here, individuals will be able to shape their own community through real choices about who they interact with: 'we will be able to forge our own places from among the many that exist, not by creating new places but by simply choosing from the menu of those available'.[90] Turkle[91] suggests that on-line communities form an attempt to re-tribalise in a new space. In this context, community is seen as a network of social relations and not necessarily a concept that is tied to place. In traditional conceptions of community, place is considered of importance along with common ties and social interaction.[92] *The community*, however, is characterised by factors such as personal intimacy, moral commitment and social cohesion. Indeed, Luke[93] suggests that any notion of a community in geographic space is a false one. To him, communities are now little more than geographically defined and administered land units, which consist of atomised individuals who share little common historical consciousness or beliefs. For commentators such as Rheingold, cyberspace does allow the development of *the community* without the locale; people can form into strong, cohesive and supportive groupings. Indeed, Rheingold's grand vision is a 'global civil society' with a shared consciousness: community will no longer be local but global.

Rheingold's arguments seem in line with theorists such as Habermas[94] and Sennett,[95] who suggest that the notion of community is in transition as the public arena merges with the private and personality overrides opinion. Sennett, for example, suggests that our notion of community has evolved from *Gemeinschaft*, where community relationships are tied to social status, public arenas and bounded, local territory, towards *Gesellschaft*, where community relationships are individualistic, impersonal, private and based on 'like-minded' individuals.[96] Rheingold, however, suggests that *Gemeinschaft* and *Gesellschaft* aspects of community can be brought together so that we have individualistic, like-minded people forming public-based communities. Whereas Sennett feels that the material (the locale) and symbolical dimensions of community are increasingly being conflated in geographic space, Rheingold feels that they can be rejoined in cyberspace. If this is the case, then Rheingold little speculates upon whether cyberspace will rapidly progress the degeneration of communities in geographic space as people search out public forums based upon individual personalities.

There is a growing body of empirical work that has started to examine ideas pertaining to community formation and regulation. For McLaughlin *et al.*[97] the fact that there are commonly agreed protocols, the advent of distinctive referent language (abbreviations, jargon, symbols) and the formation of strong social networks suggest that on-line communities, in one form or another, do exist. Rafaeli and Sudweeks[98] suggest that people would not invest so much time and effort into computer-mediated communication without gaining some sense of social cohesion or sense of community from their virtual actions. They suggest that the form and depth of interaction mean that these communities are neither pseudo nor imagined. As noted earlier, Baym, Correll and Reid[99] all provide evidence of well-formed on-line communities.

For Reid,[100] a virtual environment 'binds users into a common culture whose specialised meanings allow the sharing of imagined realities'. Similarly, Arygle[101] argues that interaction through computer-mediated communication can lead to relationships with immense social meaning. She documents from experience that only when a list member died, however, did she begin to realise the depth of these meanings and how the group supported each other and grieved as a community. Weise[102] similarly documents how the Newslist she logged onto every night became her 'extended family'. Bromberg[103] suggests that MUDs, far from being just a 'game' or another form of communication, serve four useful social functions. On one level, MUDs offer an antidote to loneliness, providing solace through communication. Secondly, MUDs allow users to experiment with identities and personae. Thirdly, MUDs allow users to explore their erotic sides by providing a new site for sexual encounters. Lastly, MUDs allow users to become the masters and controllers of their environment.

Fernback and Thompson[104] pose the question as to whether on-line communities are little more than postmodern simulacra. While it is clear that many commentators suggest that interactions via computer-mediated communication do form on-line communities, others are beginning to question the nature of this community and if it can be called a community at all. For example, Robins[105], suggests that the use of the Internet does not mean that we will be able to recover the meaning and the experience of community, which commentators such as the optimist Howard Rheingold feel are dissolving in real space. It is a misnomer to directly equate communication with communion and community.[106] For example, while some people would claim to be part of a virtual community the vast majority of cyberspace users are transient, moving between different spaces. While some virtual communities seem to have rules and protocols very similar to those of real communities, they do not possess the same kinds of responsibility. How deep and bonding are virtual relationships in comparison to real-world relationships? What is the nature of the commitment and how strong is the sense of responsibility?[107] Rheingold[108] himself questions whether 'relationships and commitments as we know them [are] even possible in a place where identities are fluid'. In communities in 'real space', community members must and do live together. It is not simply a case of logging on and, when we feel like it, logging off. The Internet, however, allows interaction where we can disengage with little or no consequence – if you do not like what the neighbours have to say, you can just turn the machine off, or uproot and connect to somewhere else, or enter a flaming match where the fear of physical reprisal is minimal. Whereas personal conflict is often dealt with using diplomacy in real places, flame wars are not uncommon in cyberspace – the screen depersonalises contact. As Sardar[109] argues:

> Communities are shaped by a sense of belonging to a place, a geographical location, by shared values, by common struggles, by tradition and history of a location – not by joining a group of people with common interests. On this logic, the accountants of the world will instantly be transformed into a community the moment they start a newsgroup. . . . Real community generates context. It generates issues which arise with relations to time and space, history and contemporary circumstances, and require responsible judgements. . . . A cyberspace community is self-selecting, exactly what a real community is not; it is contingent and transient. In essence a real community is where . . . you have to worry about other people because they will always be there. In cyberspace you can shut people out at a click of a button and go elsewhere. One therefore has no responsibility of any kind. . . . Cyberspace is to community what Rubber Rita is to woman.

Gray[110] expresses similar sentiments:

> We are who we are because of the places in which we grow up, the accents and friends we acquire by chance, the burdens we have not chosen but somehow learn to cope with. *Real* communities are always local – places in which people have to put down some roots and are willing to put up with the burdens of living together. The *fantasy* of virtual communities is that we can enjoy the benefits of community without its burdens, without the daily effort to keep delicate human connections intact. Real

communities can bear those burdens because they are embedded in particular places and evoke enduring loyalties. In cyberspace, however, there is nowhere that a sense of place can grow, and no way in which the solidarities that sustain human beings through difficult times can be forged. [My emphasis.]

For McLaughlin *et al.*,[111] then, virtual communities are at best pseudo-communities and Ogden[112] suggests that they are more accurately called 'transcendent' or 'meta' communities. Dialogue only exists between relatively few news/mailing list members (typically less than 10%) and yet is read by a larger unknown set of participants, who may or may not be considered community members; conversations are less inhibited, non-conforming and relatively free of personal consequences; and, despite exchanges, the correspondence is predominantly between virtual strangers – when the machine is turned off the only things known are those given, those written, the person essentially remains a stranger. In essence, for McLaughlin *et al.*[113] text-based communication systems do not facilitate the development of *meaningful* interpersonal ties, but rather form pseudo-communities based on superficial exchanges. There is a limit to how intimate a computer-mediated relationship can become without face-to-face contact;[114] these are, after all, artificial, safe worlds providing a certain sense of sanctuary; they are places to escape the realities of everyday life.

For Robins[115] 'there is an invocation of community, but not the production of society'. Cyberspatial technologies are not going to provide a quick technological fix to the communities that we live in on a daily basis. Providing alternative communities does not negate the problems of the ones we do actually live in. In fact they are likely to add to their further demise. Cyberspace in this light is seen as providing an escape hatch; if you do not like reality, just try to ignore it by logging on. Rather than placing our efforts into trying to escape our problems we should be channelling our efforts into finding solutions to the erosion of community spirit and cohesion in the Western world. Heim[116] also fears that as the number of Internet users rises, the spirit of community diminishes, relationships become between many and are no longer purely personal. Here, we will start to chart the division between virtual communities (*Gemeinschaft*) and virtual society (*Gelleschaft*) as discussed by Sennett, and the dissolution of meaningful public forums as they increasingly become over-noisy, and, as Habermas has noted in geographic space, based upon personality rather than 'voice'. Hollifield and McCain[117] express concern that socially constructed network communities are breaking down for this precise reason. They suggest that with more and more commercial and public users gaining access to the Internet, normative values built between groups of largely homogenous individuals are starting to break down through increased diversity. Aycock,[118] for example, suggests that such a breakdown has occurred, with discussion between individuals dominated by an aesthetic of anarchy and disparate voices leading to a high signal-to-noise ratio.[119] Indeed, Parks and Floyd[120] have found that only 60% of their respondents had formed new acquaintances, friendships or other personal relationships with someone they had met for the first time via an Internet group. Of this group 35% had supplemented their on-line communication with telephone conversations, 28% with surface mail and 33% had met face-to-face. As such, they conclude that relationships that start on on-line often move into other media to be sustained.

There are two ironies here. First, there is a notion that we will be able to form coherent and stable communities in a space that allows people to play with identity; fluid and multiple identity 'militates against community'.[121] Second, communities based upon interests and not location might well reduce diversity and narrow spheres of influence, as like will only be communicating with like.[122] As such, rather than providing a better alternative to real-world communities cyberspace leads to dysfunctional on-line communities while simultaneously weakening communities in real space. McCellan[123] comments that:

> rather than providing a replacement for the crumbling public realm, virtual communities are actually contributing to its decline. They're another thing keeping people indoors and off the streets. Just as TV produces couch potatoes, so on-line culture creates mouse potatoes, people who hide from real life and spend their whole life goofing off in cyberspace.

Lajoie[124] thus fears that cyberspace might replace real-world face-to-face interactions and further reduce the public sphere of life. For him meeting on-line is no substitute for real-world encounters and he fears that we are increasingly being reduced to the 'status of atomized entities ill equipped for collective politics or public life'. As Davis[125] explains, the danger is that society will become even more polarised and segmented than at present. Beamish[126] thus suggests that on-line spaces should be used as 'third spaces' where members of real-world communities can discuss issues and arrange face-to-face meetings. On-line communities would therefore just be the virtual manifestation of the local community. These community networks, however, should not be based solely upon social contacts but should also include, as in real communities, business and commercial establishments.

Aoki[127] contends that much of the rhetoric concerning virtual communities seems to automatically assume that computer-mediated communication is a desirable outcome and that people, once given the opportunity, will flock on-line. However, as he notes in relation to Japan, computer-mediated communication, while becoming popular in the US, is viewed with more scepticism and suspicion by the Japanese. He suggests four reasons for this. First, Japanese people place a high value upon face-to-face communication and the opportunity to read between the lines based upon voice tone, facial expression and posture. Second, Japanese people have to pay for their telephone connections and this has discouraged installing a modem at home. Third, there has been the development of a negative stereotypical image of the unsociable home computer user. Last, using the conventional keyboard to type Japanese is difficult and has to be learnt. He suspects that virtual communities are less likely to form in Japan and when they do they will be used to supplement face-to-face interaction rather than replace it.

Virtual Culture, Real-World Communities: Hackers and Cyberpunks

While it is argued that cyberspace is fostering the formation of new subcultures and communities on-line, it has also been suggested that it is performing the same off-line. The original off-line, computer-based subculture involved hackers. Hackers are now firmly popularised within the media as deviant, (often) adolescent delinquents masquerading as computer junkies. These individuals are classified as 'rebels with a modem', a threat to industrial and national security.[128] The term hackers, though, was originally used in the 1950s and 1960s to denote early budding computer proteges who believed in decentralised, multiple-access systems and the right to know.[129] They were the sort of people who invented the Internet and rose to create the first wave of personal computing. Many formed and met at the first computer clubs, tinkering with machines and playing with code. With the rise of the personal computer, accompanied by distributed, public-access systems, some individuals/groups took to roaming cyberspace and exploring other people's computers. During the 1980s this group rose to prominence as the new American counterculture, the modern-day reactionaries against authority, filling the role of the sixties student dropout and the seventies punk.[130] Hacking took on a more political tone and became more subversive, challenging authority with blatant cultural resistance. With the rise in public malaise and distrust, and the State's crackdown upon hacking, which became a criminal offence, the hacker subculture has dissipated, mutated and moved on from its college-kid base into the broader realms of cyberpunk. This is not to say that hacking is no more. The amount of hacking has increased but is now more likely to be practised by disgruntled workers seeking revenge against their employers.[131] Gilboa[132] reports that current estimates place the number of active hackers at approximately 35 000 and growing by 10% per year.

Dery, Schroeder and Rushkoff[133] all describe a cyberpunk movement within Western culture. The term cyberpunk was originally coined to describe the science fiction literature of writers such as Gibson and Sterling[134] (themselves inspired by the punk bands and attitudes of the late 1970s), who portray a dystopian future of post-human life-forms and a society formed around cyberspatial technologies, massive urbanisation and militarised corporations.[135] By the late 1980s, the term cyberpunk had been uprooted from its strict definition of a science fiction genre and reappropriated by the mainstream (like cyberspace) to refer to a diverse set of cultural forms based around futuristic ideas of computing and communication, and became associated with cybercafes, nightclubs, rave, ambient and industrial music, smart or designer drugs, science fiction writing and calls for cultural and political change. The merging of the cyber, the technical, with punk immediately conjures an alternative, a challenge to the norm, self-marginalisation from the mainstream and social resistance.[136] For certain sections of today's society cyberspatial images of the future hold resonance and they structure their lifestyles into a particular subculture, which aims to live out and bring about selected aspects of cyberspace's promise.[137] Dery suggests that cyberpunk consists of a number of related subcultures including Deadhead hackers, ravers, technopagans, and New Age technophiles.[138] He describes technopaganism as:

> the convergence of neopaganism (the umbrella term for a host of contemporary polytheistic nature religions) and the New Age with digital technology and fringe computer culture. . . . Psychologically, technopaganism represents an attempt to come to existential terms with the philosophical changes wrought by the twentieth century science . . . and to find a place for the sacred in our ever more secular, technological society.[139]

Linking 1990s cyberculture and 1960s counterculture, technopaganism seeks to legitimise 'spiritual beliefs in scientific terms'.[140] Here, although Dery discusses technopaganism and New Age as one, because of their common relationship to science and technology and their reverence of the Earth and spiritual beliefs, he recognises that these groups see themselves as polar opposites, neopagans representing 'the earthy and the airy' and the New Agers 'the chthonic and the celestial'.[141] Several groups, such as TOPY, and BBSs are dedicated to spreading the technopagan word and host experiments with 'magick', moving their neopagan, spiritual beliefs away from nature and towards the new site of the computer. These beliefs have also fed directly into the music and lyrics of contemporary music genres, notably rave (rapid percussion, rapped lyrics, samples and simple, synthesised melodies), ambient (moody, atmospheric and relaxing instrumentals) and industrial (hard, edgy rock underlain by heavy, tribal percussion). Within these genres, it is probably fair to say that ambient music has the strongest links to the spiritual movement within technopaganism. 'Industrial' music, as created by bands such as Nine Inch Nails and Front 242, are more inspired by the visions of cyberpunk writers such as Gibson and Sterling. Rather than connecting in on the spiritual and neopaganism, they tap in to the dystopian visions of the future, political consciousness and the cyborging of man and machine. However, raves are mainly populated by youths seeking a good time, not youths taking part in some neopagan gathering and endorsing particular philosophical or political beliefs. Similarly, the music is largely written by those who like to rave, rather than by any new prophets. Admittedly, some bands such as The Shamen do espouse technopagan philosophy and others subscribe to other cyberpunk elements but these are few and far between. Artists have also used cyberspatial visions of cyborging, disembodiment and robotic machines capable of their own thoughts as inspiration for their work. Through pictures, sculptures (fixed and moving) and body art they explore possible futures and the material and philosophical consequences of cyberspatial technologies.

Linked to the notions of cyberspace, cyberpunk rhetoric often describes a parallel place – Cyberia. Cyberia is the next dimensional home for consciousness:[142]

> Cyberia is the place a businessperson goes when involved in a phone conversation, the place a shamanic warrior goes when travelling out of body, the place an 'acid house' dancer goes when experiencing the bliss of a techno-acid trance. Cyberia, is the place alluded to by the mystical teachings of every science, and the wildest speculations of every imagination.

Cyberia, for Rushkoff and many cyberpunk subcultures (cyberians), is about the hardwiring of a global brain, a new way to think and exist; it is a paradigm for life. Cyberspace is just one aspect of this vision; it is one space within the multidimensional spaces that compose Cyberia. Cyberians aim to highlight and challenge current social relations – 'the cyberian vision is a heretical negation of the rules by which Western society has chosen to organise itself'.[143] One of the cyberians' beliefs is that reality will conform to their hallucinations, that it is mapped within the realms of consciousness. To understand and re-choose reality, they advocate a move from traditional, rational science to trying to gain some deeper comprehension through exploring the unmapped parts of our consciousness. One way to do this is take hallucinatory drugs; another is to dive into cyberspace and explore, chart and create the electronic highways and its supposed 'alternative' reality. Here 'information becomes texture . . . almost an experience'.[144] The real enlightenment, and counterpoint for the cyberpunk/cyberian movement, is when the psychedelic and technical are combined. Although the Internet is providing this function, at present, it is envisaged that virtual reality will provide the perfect space to explore these ideas. For McKenna,[145] virtual reality will be the site of our greatest philosophical discoveries. Cyberians arguing for a changing social climate point to the evidence that renaissance periods always have a resurgence of archaic elements (spiritual, tribal, psychedelic, pagan) along with new technologies (cyberspace) and new mathematics (in this case fractals). For them, we are about to enter a new world order characterised by higher consciousness. In this consciousness the 'tripper' gets to see things in an unprejudiced manner, in new ways, in creative ways, attacking problems from new angles. Rushkoff suggests that it is no surprise that many of the US's most successful cyberspatial computer scientists are those with west coast, counterculture, 1960s lifestyles. They were the ones who first learned to tap into this consciousness. This is the reason why many 'respectable' companies now employ psychedelically-influenced developers, with relaxed, informal workplaces, where drug use is tolerated rather than condoned. At present, these groups are fairly small outside of the States and based around major cities such as London and Amsterdam. In the US, the phenomenon is mainly confined to the West Coast centred on San Francisco (notably those areas that were most influential in the sixties drug culture – a culture which also focused upon the transcendence and philosophical insights).

At a theoretical level, there seems to be a double recursive relationship between cyberpunk fiction writers such as Gibson and rock/punk music and with postmodern theorists. Many cyberpunk writers quite explicitly declare that the music of bands such as The Velvet Underground and the Sex Pistols directly feed into their writings. For example, Gibson names and bases characters within *Neuromancer* upon Chrissie Hynde (Molly) lead singer with The Pretenders, and Robert Quine (hacker Bobby Quine), guitarist with Richard Hell and the Voidoids. His term for prostitutes, 'meat puppets', was taken from the Arizona punk trio with the same name.[146] Gibson has described how the music he listened to while writing the novel inspired the content and the atmosphere. Other writers, such as Shiner, Shirley and Sterling, all testify to similarly linking punk and rock into their writing and confessing a deep desire to be musicians and pop stars (Shirley, for example, has been in several punk bands). Sterling draws direct parallels to the punk movements of the late 1970s, suggesting that cyberpunk writers wanted to achieve a 'garage-band aesthetic', to strip science fiction of its polished finish. He argues that cyberpunk has drawn the two overlapping worlds of pop culture and science fiction literature together to form a new culture, of which cyberpunk is the literary incarnation. Bands such as Nine Inch Nails and Front 242, as discussed, have been inspired by these science fiction writings and fed them back into a new form of post-punk, weaving the strains of punk with technological, artificial sounds – they form the musical incarnation. These bands in turn inspire real-world cyberpunks, recording the music that hackers listen to while glued to the screen.[147] For Sterling,[148] 'cyberpunk is very much a pop phenomenon . . . the realm where the computer hacker and rocker overlap'. Ironically, many of the cyberpunk writings are an implicit plea for the authentic sound of instruments and a cry against the postmodern tendency to imitation, reproduction and the false sounds of electronic boxes.[149]

A similar, although much more recent, recursive relationship exists with postmodern theorists. Here, cyberpunk has been taken up as a resource for understanding contemporary social and cultural changes.[150] Theorists such as Jameson[151] and Davis[152] draw upon Gibson's writing to explain changes in today's society, while Gibson himself uses Davis's descriptions of public space and surveillance in Los Angeles as the basis for his 1993 novel *Virtual Light*.[153] Academics such as Tomas and Stone[154] openly turn to Gibson to credit his foresight and acknowledge his influence in shaping the 'information society'. They suggest that recent developments in both computing and society can be seen as an attempt to put Gibson's visions into practice. Whereas cyberpunk writers recursively draw from punk/rock music the characters, the tempo and the atmosphere of unrest, they recursively draw from postmodern theorists a more global feeling of transformation, of fragmentation and of changing social relations. As we have seen in this chapter, the ties between postmodernism and cyberspace and its effects on society and culture are well developed. For example, Fitting[155] states that 'cyberpunk should be seen as "the apotheosis of the postmodern"'. These ties can be further illustrated in reference to Maffesoli's concept of postmodern neo-tribes.

Both on-line and off-line, Maffesoli's concept of the neo-tribes can be used to describe the development of these communities and the formation of a postmodern society. Maffesoli[156] describes neo-tribes as groups that form and reform on the basis of temporary modes of identification. In this context, the Internet is allowing people to gather together and seek self-identification and to 'bathe in the affectual ambience'[157] in their search for community and belonging. Maffesoli argues that in defining and explaining everyday life, traditional modernist classifiers such as class are no longer of importance. Instead, we associate upon the basis of common experience. Thus, postmodern neo-tribes differ from *Gemeinschaft* communities in that they are actively achieved, rather than being born into.[158] Halfacree and Kitchin[159] explore the concept of neo-tribalism in relation to the diverse genre of popular music and their associated lifestyles, but the concept can easily be extended to the Internet. Here, our choice of mailing or discussion list, or the acceptance of a cyberpunk lifestyle, represents a cultural expression that is increasingly significant in defining who one is.[160] On the Internet, we join emerging communities whose qualities are ephemeral, transient and always in flux. Many of these communities are not stable and some constantly struggle to survive because the self-consciousness of the community they engender is often self-destructive as its limitations become apparent.[161] Maffesoli[162] contends that for these imagined communities to survive they need to materialise 'on the ground', to produce a distinct space where the routines and behaviour of the neo-tribe members can become part of everyday life. If cyberpunk is not to go the same way as punk, and just be part of a passing fad, it needs to reach a critical mass and become ingrained in, and the basis for, everyday lives – as 'rave' culture has now become in the UK, with its own language, clothes and attitudes (although rave is associated with Cyberia, I am sure that not all ravers would want to be, or even consider themselves to be, cyberpunks or cyberians). The transition of cyberpunk into a dominant stable subculture seems unlikely outside the US West Coast, where cyberian lifestyles have gained acceptance. However, this movement might feed into a series of neo-tribes metamorphosing around the original ideals, which may eventually stabilise. On-line communities, however, have no material to be grounded in – it is always an imagined space. Correll, Reid and Bromberg,[163] however, suggest that by creating a place, an artificial setting to contextualise interactions, these imagined communities can become well developed, more stable and more likely to stand the test of time; the machine code becomes the material.

Critics of the cyberpunk/cyberian movement suggest that it is hard to imagine it as little more than a fringe counterculture, linking consciousness-altering drugs, political ideals and music with high technology. Fitting[164] suggests that these groups are at best images of punk, 'a fashion emptied of any oppositional content'. Although their writings often show a dystopian future of urban decay, much of the text is hyperbole, lightweight and utopian. McKenna,[165] for example, believes that exploring Cyberia will allow us to achieve the most profound event in planetary ecology, the freeing of life from the chrysalis of matter. The general thesis is that by taking our minds to a higher dimension we will open up a whole new world of possibilities. There is no discussion about whether people want to abandon current lifestyles for an existence in Cyberia, or whether a sustained lifestyle in Cyberia is plausible. What about food, drink, production and consumption? Can we all go? It seems highly probable that, while the music (e.g. rave) and smart drugs will continue to remain part of mainstream youth culture, any technological components linking the music to cyberspace will remain small and confined to areas such as the US west coast. Society, in the main, is too deeply entrenched within the current culture of consumption for there to be a radical shift in the way we live our lives. To those outside of the movement, the lifestyle and the music seem intangible and arouse suspicion, scepticism and cynicism.

The cyberpunk movement has many parallels with the 1960s counterculture and seems destined to follow the same route. The lifestyle is just not realistic, let alone sustainable for the majority of the world's inhabitants. Even in America where the political Right is reasonably tolerant of the cyberpunk/cyberian movement, it is difficult to imagine that much of society would want to embrace it, and there would be a general resistance to any large-scale growth in a drugs-related, 'mind-altering' culture. In areas where one might expect liberal attitudes, such as education, cyberian academics are largely regarded as maverick and to some extent subversive, the classic example being the late Timothy Leary. In many computing companies the lifestyle is tolerated but not approved of because many of the significant research and development breakthroughs seem to come from those embracing cyberian values.

It is fair to say that the dreams of cyberians are the daydreams of the relatively privileged. The readers of magazines such as *Mondo 2000* and *Wired*, and technopagan groups, are predominantly information/communication professionals with incomes that are well above average, and most of them are 'sufficiently insulated from the grimmer social realities inside their high tech comfort zones to contemplate the power of positive hedonism'.[166] Within this population, groups such as technopagans and New Agers see cyberspace as a sociocultural and spiritual 'empowerment zone'. To others, the cyberian dreams are pure escapism, devoid of social consciousness and designed as rich people's toys, rather than being a reasoned, realistic response to the problems facing humankind. Dery describes these opposites as the transcendental versus the political – the 'change consciousness, change life' versus the 'change the world'. He suggests that cyberians, by placing their faith in the 'magical possibilities of a computer-generated world[,] are abandoning all hope of political change in the world'.[167] For him, cyberpunk subcultures are essentially naive, self-serving and 'defiantly antirational', and 'believe they can alter the external world by mere thinking'.[168] Cyberians have created a siren song combining nineties technophilia with sixties transcendentalism aimed at seducing the public imagination. He points to Kirn's warning:

> what the [cyberians] appear fated to learn from their ventures into pure electronic consciousness is that ultimate detachment is not the same as freedom, escape is no substitute for liberation and rapture isn't happiness. The sound-and-light show at the end of time, longed for by these turned-on nerds, seems bound to disappoint.[169]

One of the paradoxes is that many of the proponents of cyberian values, such as Timothy Leary, revere and constantly refer to Gibson's *Neuromancer*, a book that paints the future world as a dark, amoral, despotic, violent place ruled by large, all-powerful corporations. The irony of this utopian, technological re-interpretation of *Neuromancer* and its cyberpunk trilogy companions *Count Zero* and *Mona Lisa Overdrive* is not lost on Gibson himself:

> I was delighted when scientists and corporate technicians started to read me, but I soon realised that all the critical pessimistic left-wing stuff just goes over their heads. The social and political naivete of modern corporate boffins is frightening, they read me and just take bits, all the cute technology, and miss about fifteen levels of irony.[170]

VIRTUAL REVOLUTION OR POSTMODERN EVOLUTION?

While many would argue that cyberspace presents a revolution, or the opportunity for a revolution in the way that society works, clearly others are more sceptical. Rather than representing a cultural revolution, the sceptics suggest that cyberspace is merely a natural, postmodern evolution in technology, which, although having significant cultural repercussions, does not represent a radical reconfiguration. These two positions have been developed throughout this chapter. For example, Aycock suggests that cyberspace is a 'technology of the self', which will radically alter the ways in which identity is constructed. On-line identities become much more fluid and malleable because of the disembodying nature of the medium. Further, cyberspatial technologies help to blur the boundaries between nature and technology, allowing a re-negotiation of gender roles. Similarly, Poster suggests that cyberspace is going to radically alter our conceptions of community and the nature of our communities. In contrast to these virtual revolutions, Robins suggests that cyberspace is merely a new space for social interaction and represents a postmodern evolution. While cyberspace, because of the level of anonymity, does allow people to play with their identity, he suggests that the processes of identity formation differ little from real-world experiences. This is because, at present, we still use the same rules of engagement, and on-line spaces are still embodied and regulated in the same ways as are spaces off-line. Life on-line is thus currently situated within real-life contexts. Sobchack furthers that we cannot deny our bodies and, despite the hopes of cyborg feminists, cyberspatial technologies are being used to reinforce real-life conceptions of women. Similarly, McLaughlin *et al.* contend that on-line communities are at best pseudo-communities because they are built upon superficial exchanges, little responsibility and escapism. While virtual communities do allow individuals to converse, they do not negate the fact that we do live and work in real-world communities. The growth in off-line cyberian communities is paradoxically evidence that virtual communities still need to be 'grounded'.

It should hopefully be clear that I favour the position of postmodern evolutionists. As has been argued throughout the book so far, cyberspace needs to analysed within the 'real', to be contextualised within the micro and macro, social, economic, political and cultural contexts within which we live. In other words, we need to recognise that cyberspace, far from being detached and governed by completely different rules, exists in a symbiotic relationship with the non-virtual world. Cyberspaces are situated and embodied spaces; they are simulations or extensions rather than substitutions. Cyberspaces and the rules of engagement within them do bear a remarkable resemblance to real-world spaces and protocols.

A combined approach that mixes elements of postmodernism with social constructivist and political economy allows an examination of cyberspace's effect upon society and culture within the context of the 'real'. Such an approach explicitly recognises that identity and community are fluid and contested but that cyberspatial interaction and appropriation are also socially constructed within the 'real' and bound within broader societal structures. Cyberspace is not an egalitarian space. Even once on-line, some people have more freedom to explore and control cyberspaces. As we will see in Chapter 5, it is a highly regulated space that is bound up in real-world social, political and economic structures. In other words, life on-line is not completely divorced from non-virtual life but is highly situated within it. On-line spaces are not completely disembodied but rather are highly embodied, with real-world discrimination and abuse reproducing itself in a new space. In this context, cyberspatial studies would be interested in the social and cultural processes operating at the intersections between virtual and non-virtual worlds, the interplay and historical context involved between individuals and institutions, and how cyberspatial developments and interactions are situated within broader political and economic structures and mechanisms. As such, studies, through careful deconstruction of sociocultural and political–economic processes at both the local and global scales, would seek to understand how cyberspatial technologies are designed, used and applied at both an individual and a collective level.

Such an approach recognises that the ability to play with and explore identity is one of the factors that feeds into cyberspatial usage, and that cyberspatial technologies do have important implications for how we view and understand the processes of cyborging. Similarly, the approach appreciates that one of the appeals of cyberspace is that people can interact and form themselves into groups of common interest. However, the approach also recognises that identity within virtual worlds is not divorced from that offline and that the processes of cyborging are envisaged in the real world. Further, while some virtual communities are recreational and social, many are contextualised within local (and national) politics (e.g. PENs and free-nets) and serve public utility, and others are academic and commercial. To understand their use and growth, these communities must be placed within the context of the micro-scale, local, social processes but also within the broader scale political processes within city hall and those feeding down from national and international policies. Similarly, commercial and economic conditions feed into how PENs and free-nets are appropriated and used. The broader political and economic processes that impinge upon cyberspace are discussed in the next chapter.

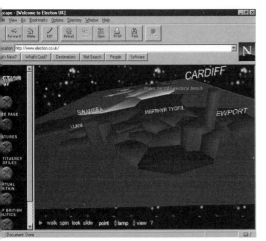

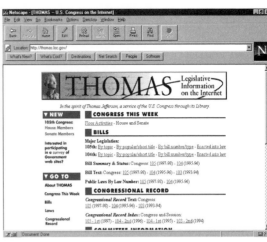

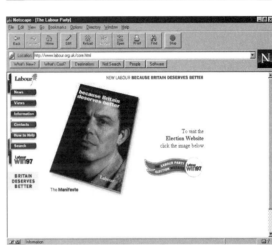

CHAPTER 5

CYBERSPACE, POLITICS AND POLITY

CYBERSPACE, POLITICS AND POLITY

The National Information Infrastructure (NII) that is now being built will have enormous impacts, both obvious and subtle. If properly designed and implemented, it can promote widespread prosperity, decentralize power, revitalize democracy, strengthen or even create communities, and make this a better world in which to live. If poorly designed and implemented, it can do just the opposite. . . . Markets do not exist to empower individuals, create vibrant communities, strengthen democracy, promote intergroup respect, end violence, or serve the millions of other things that humans need for a good life.[1]

For many analysts, cyberspace has large-scale political implications that will directly and explicitly impinge upon how we live our everyday lives. It is argued that as cyberspatial technologies become more widespread, their capacity as an effective mass-communication device and their ability to hold vast amounts of easily transferable data will increasingly draw them centre stage. Visions concerning the political consequences of the cyberspatial age are both utopian, with cyberspace providing a more democratic forum for debate and decision making, and dystopian, with cyberspace providing a suitable environment for deviancy and an *1984*-style regime where control is mediated through information, knowledge and 'all-seeing eyes'. In this chapter, we explore how cyberspace will impinge upon political life and polity through an examination of issues relating to democracy, ownership and regulation, access and exclusion, privacy and confidentiality, and ethics and deviancy.

DEMOCRACY AND POLITY

Commentators are nearly all universally agreed that cyberspatial technologies have wide-scale implications for politics and polity. In one form or another, they are set to transform political structures and organisations, political campaigning, lobbying strategies, and voting patterns.[2] Cyberspace is viewed as opening 'qualitatively new political opportunities because it opens new loci of speech'.[3] This has led academics to two separate but equally radical conclusions. The first is that representative government could potentially be replaced by direct government. We would all be able to propose, debate and vote upon governmental issues rather than an elected official doing so on our behalf. The second is that the role of place-based political mobilisation will rapidly diminish.[4] Instead, political opinion concerning specific topics will be mobilised globally by interested organisations as party-based politics fragment and people's perspectives narrow. For example, groups such as Tibet Information Network, Greenpeace and Amnesty International all use the Web to disseminate information and raise political awareness at an international rather than just a local scale. Browsers of these pages are given specific information concerning particular issues and how to effect political action. Indeed, for Poster,[5] global communication networks challenge the notion of nation states. Technologies such as cyberspace defy the character of power employed by modern governments by undermining the concept of territoriality. Cyberspace knows no borders. This has wide-ranging implications given that boundaries are seen as central to current political theories:

> Whatever is political staunchly demands a recognition of boundaries. These include the encircling walls of the polis, the segregation of governmental powers, and political sovereignty. Without boundaries, the political atrophies and becomes quietly obsolescent.[6]

Lake[7] thus suggests that the geopolitical conditions of the 1990s are best described as spatial confusion. Indeed, Thu Nguyen and Alexander[8] argue that although nations still exist they are progressively losing control over their people because cyberspace is undermining polities through the availability of information. They describe how nations and organisations keep political control through gatekeepers (people who control and regulate information). They argue that cyberspace allows people to by-pass the gatekeepers and directly access information.[9] This by-passing represents a 'major shift in the nature of embodied power' away from central individuals who 'hold' power:[10]

> In cyberspacetime, the social realm is engulfing and overwhelming the political realm. The social is decomposing the body politic. Decay of politics is proceeding as quickly as the matrix is growing. . . . The forces impelling political atrophy are far too strong.[11]

Thus, for them, the Internet is a 'conversational, demassified, non-representational democracy that transcends nation-state'.[12] It represents the communication system needed to underlie the continued differentiation and complexity of society. As society fractures, the more information the social systems need. Cyberspace is providing for that need and, as such, is an active agent of change – an agent that is challenging the traditional notions concerning power, knowledge and information through the altering of conventional power relations. This challenge, they contend, through demassification and atrophy of the polity, will eventually lead to chaos through weakened polities unable to contain disruptions. In short, there will be a basic conflict between the coming Internet society and modernist democratic institutions. They explain that modern politics is grounded in geographical units and communities, and the assumption that individuals have concrete identities and interests. However, cyberspace renders place meaningless, identities fluid and reality multiple. Cyberspace will thus gradually undermine the current pyramid structure of authority and participation, leading to a flatter, more egalitarian society.[13] As such, democracy based upon geographical units is seen as withering and destined to suffer the same misfortunes as the monarchy.

In contrast to the position of Thu Nguyen and Alexander, it can be argued that although the Internet may seem to challenge traditional notions of political power, it is only a microcosm of real-life social relations. Internet services in many instances, such as free-nets and many commercial web sites, rather than challenging convention actually work to reproduce and reinforce existing hegemonic structures.[14] For example, local government in the USA is increasingly experimenting with community-orientated, participatory democracy within their cities through the use of free-net systems. These public electronic networks (PENs) allow citizens free access to e-mail civic leaders and take part in on-line conferences relating to local issues.[15] PENs such as Santa Monica PEN and Cleveland Free-net have grown in use and popularity, and hundreds of community organisations use them to maintain and disseminate information. Santa Monica's PEN was developed as a unique experiment in cyberdemocracy in an effort to create an electronic city hall, and was developed and owned by the city's government.[16] Using this system registered users can access city information, complete some transactions, send e-mail to departments, elected officials or other PEN users and participate in public conferences from their own PCs or those strategically placed in public areas, such as libraries, around the city. By 1992, the Santa Monica PEN had 4505 registered users (5% of the total population representing 10% of households).[17] Similarly, the South African government has been using the Internet as an open forum for debate and suggestions regarding the drafting of the country's new constitution. In this context, the Internet strengthens the civic, public dimensions of cities/nations by providing a free access, public space for debate and interaction.[18] Cyberspace is thus potentially providing a new Habermasian public space for open dialogue between all individuals, including those who are currently disenfranchised.[19] Indeed, the homeless, a normally poorly organised group, successfully used Santa Monica's PEN to lobby for shower facilities. Here, cyberspace is going to bring us a democratic renaissance based on the notion that an abundance of available data and information is liberating ('instant information creates involvement in depth'[20]), that cyberspace allows greater access to officials, and that cyberspace undermines the traditional media bases of democratic institutions such as broadcasters by allowing individuals to be both sender and receiver,[21] thus permitting a more eclectic range of views be disseminated. Most Western governments and political parties have recognised the power of the Internet to disseminate information and political ideology, and have set up their own web pages and e-mail addresses.

In this context, rather than radically overhauling existing structures, the Internet is seen at best as just another tool to help conduct the everyday, democratic functioning of a government, allowing people to express their opinions. The traditional place-based political system is not under threat. People can, and will continue to, lobby in conventional ways. Similarly, representative government will not disappear but will become more accountable through a process of socialisation; that is, more two-way dialogue between politician and citizen. Schemes such as *City Talks* (aimed at improving public debate), *City Consultations* (aimed at making the decision process more transparent) and *Digital City* (information and discussion centre), all Dutch initiatives, have explored the socialisation of democracy with limited degrees of success.[22] It was clear that all three initiatives just extended and improved existing structures rather than socialising democracy.

This may not be surprising. Government requires an understanding of complex and interrelated issues. Most people do not understand, and do not want to understand, the detailed arguments needed to be able to vote on a *number* of substantive issues. A direct government would be largely inquorate, anarchic (it would have no leadership, no centre and no organisational structure) and only used by those of strong political persuasion. For example, both the *City Talks* and *Digital City* initiatives tended to be dominated by those who already had access to public debate with a bias towards well-spoken, educated and politically interested individuals, creating a space for the (new) technological elite and 'techno-freaks' rather than the ordinary citizen.[23] Cyberspace is thus more likely to be used instrumentally as a technological tool to improve existing political structures, rationalising governmental organisation, improving policy processes, opening up consultation and improving the role of the citizen as voter.

From this point-of-view, it is clear that a global database and an e-mail system is not going to radically overhaul existing democratic structures but rather streamline them and make them more transparent and accountable. At the most, electoral mechanisms might become electronic, with voters polling their opinions on a selected range of issues rather than just once every four or five years. At present, it is not practical to repeat the sluggish, expensive, manual process of polling too often, but votes cast electronically can be counted instantly.[24] As Lyon[25] points out, however, in the absence of a coherent equal access policy, it is difficult to see an electronic democracy translated into reality. This is especially true given that cyberspaces are increasingly becoming public spaces with private owners and regulators. Here, companies run a fine line trying to balance the need for many customers – so seeming welcoming, accessible and inclusive – with wanting to stay firmly in control.[26] For example, companies such as AOL and Prodigy portray themselves as family service providers, providing on-line public space where postings are actively policed, and those of a sexually explicit nature are weeded out. Perhaps a more realistic analysis is that cyberspace might help towards greater democratic accountability at both the local scale, specifically relating to local issues, and at the global scale, particularly relating to specific interests/concerns by mobilising support and protest.

REGULATION, OWNERSHIP AND CONTROL

The traditional form of regulation within cyberspace has been through an informal set of customary laws. On-line interactions have been policed through the consensus actions of those accessing and interacting in cyberspace.[27] For example, it is expected that those people interacting in MUDs respect each other's characters and recognise the unwritten rules of engagement; it is expected that those taking part in newsgroups will stay within generally agreed community protocols ('netiquette'). If participants of MUDs or newsgroups transgress the bounds of customary laws then they must accept community administered 'punishment'. Every MUD and newsgroup has a set of protocols which its members are expected to abide by. These protocols are often available from FAQ (frequently asked questions) files. These are generally common across MUDs and newsgroups. For example, customary laws relating to newsgroups include sticking to the topic of the group, no advertising or commercial postings, no or limited cross-posting, sending private mail or mail of little interest to the rest of the group to the individual, not to the list, and no excessive flaming. One of the most well-known instances of netiquette is 'spamming'. Spamming involves sending the same message to many lists. This practice is discouraged, because it needlessly multiplies traffic, occupying valuable bandwidth. Community administered 'punishments' consist of other users mail bombing or mass flaming the offender's mail account[28] or a vigilante programmer deleting offending messages from a list on behalf of everyone else.[29] Kollock and Smith[30] suggest that these customary laws are an attempt to manage the virtual commons with users on-line seeking to balance individual and collective rationality.

Within this liberal position, those surfing the web become responsible for choosing what they download. In the case of children, parents are responsible for making sure that software such as Net Nanny or SurfWatch, which denies access to certain sites, is installed and used. As such, customary law proponents argue that no formalised laws are needed to regulate cyberspace interaction. Such a strategy guarantees first amendment rights (free speech) to adults and means that cyberspatial interaction does not need to be limited to the lowest common denominator (e.g. small children or the values of the most conservative people using the Internet).[31] They argue that obscene material has to be sought by the user – it does not just appear on the screen. With regard to problems such as harassment, people can use 'kill files' to delete unwanted mail before reading or 'gag' the comments of users in MUDs.

There are three reasons why customary law is currently under attack. The first is that customary laws represents the 'law of the land' or 'mob rule' and are not necessarily just. For example, if somebody is being victimised in cyberspace, through sexual harassment, their mail being intercepted or people impersonating them, then these customary laws have little effect. This is because there are 'offences' that customary law is generally unable to deal with (see Table 5.1). Customary law concerns violation of group concerns, not individual concerns. In particular, there is no appeal for the 'victim' of customary law. There are those in cyberspace who do have more power than others, either because they are the system administrator or because they possess better programming skills. As such, while customary law is useful in enforcing a basic netiquette, users are 'tried and convicted' without appeal and by 'mob rule'. Further, those who are the victim of the offences in Table 5.1 do not have recourse to any legal protection, with the offender going unpunished. This has led Johnson[32] to ask whether the emerging cyberlaw will provide 'due process'; that is, respect the principles of fairness.

Table 5.1 *Offences in Cyberspace that Customary Law Does Not Address*

Mechanism	Meaning	Examples
Harrassment	Forced reception of unwanted information	Flaming
Silencing	Interfering with current or future transmission of information. Destroying past archives of transmission	Cancelling current messages. Deleting stored messages from a public database
Capture	Controlling transmission	Posting offensive messages under another user's name
Interference	Obstructing ability to receive information	Mail-bombs and mass flaming. The controller of a system denying access to part of or all of a MUD

Source: Maltz (1996)

Secondly, customary law only addresses community interaction and does not address deviant and criminal activity. In fact, customary law positively condones the propagation of what would be offences in the non-virtual world by suggesting that if you are unhappy with the material available in cyberspace, then you should not log on, avoid these sites or purchase software that polices cyberspatial interactions. By placing responsibility into the hands of the user the activities of deviant users are tolerated. To many people this is an unacceptable situation, especially when the activities in cyberspace do directly impinge upon life in the real world. As such, lobby groups have now been formed calling for cyberspace to be morally 'cleaned up', much like the 'wild west' frontier it is so commonly compared with.

Thirdly, customary laws were written in a time when the Internet was largely publicly-owned and regulated by 'friendly' sys-ops. The Internet has now been largely privatised and is owned and run by large transnational corporations. Private ownership sits uncomfortably with customary law, and many Internet service providers have introduced their own regulatory controls, which largely formalise customary laws while also addressing deviant practices. Many of these companies also favour an unformalised system of law and governance. They suggest that cyberspace might be best regulated and 'policed' by industry leaders and administrators, possibly in conjunction with users. On-line providers would thus be responsible for creating a market-led legality built upon trust and the ability of users to transfer business elsewhere if they are not happy with the ethical code of the provider. In other words, cyberlaw should develop along lines of market forces and an industry-regulatory model.[33] Proponents of this suggestion argue that people are reluctant to empower governments by handing over issues such as privacy. Market competition means that companies will compete to demonstrate that they are the most trustworthy, so privacy is ensured by market demand. For example, AOL has recently issued a privacy policy informing its members about the collection, storage, use and disclosure of individual information.[34] Information is divided into three types: member identity information (e.g. name, address), navigational and transactional (e.g. on-line areas visited, on-line purchases), and private communications (e.g. private e-mail, chat conversations). AOL will not disclose personal information except where legally required. Additionally, some argue that since many services are provided privately (i.e. you have to subscribe and the contents are not accessible to all Internet users), customers of these services should negotiate the contents themselves rather than having the content dictated by an external regulator (government).

Market-led regulation also has its critics. Shapiro[35] is extremely worried by what he sees as the inherent conflict between private ownership and freedom of speech. He states that:

> Speech in cyberspace will not be free if we allow big business to control every square inch of the Net. The public needs a place of its own.[36]

For him, cyberspace should be challenging the dominant and exclusionary spaces that we currently live in rather than perpetuating these spaces by having nice, compartmentalised, sanitised cyberspaces. Just as the pickets, leaflet givers and demonstrators are largely excluded from the private malls, he suggests that under private ownership these groups will be marginalised within cyberspace. He suspects that people will be re-routed or led away from public forums that are essential to an informed citizenry and to a pluralistic democracy. Cyberspace, like real space, will be cleansed of dissenters and public debate. Under a market-led system of regulation, the extent to which the customer would have legal recourse in the event of a dispute between themselves and the provider would be limited, as the company is defendant, judge and jury. For example, Shapiro reports that Prodigy is a company that actively restricts dissenting speech.[37] In 1990 it raised its charges for those posting large amounts of e-mail. Some of the more prolific posters protested that they were being penalised for speaking frequently and sent e-mail to Prodigy's on-line advertisers threatening a boycott. Prodigy, however, intercepted, read and destroyed these messages and dismissed dissenting members from the service. These members had no legal recourse and no way to picket Prodigy's services. In a *New York Times* opinion piece, Prodigy was adamant that it will continue to restrict speech as it sees fit. In many cases people do not want to change their service provider because they have built up complex social networks and created an identifiable address. The fear of such market-led regulation is that we will be given the impression of control, of freedom to express views and opinions but ultimately it is an impression – the mediators will have control, dictating access and censorship. As such, market-led legality does have some major problems.

The alternative to customary and market-led regulation is formalised laws introduced by the government and lawfully enforced by a publicly accountable agency such as the police. The call for such a system of laws is coming from business users and those users unhappy with the loose framework of customary laws. In particular, businesses want their commercial interests protected and want issues relating to ownership and copyright clarified. Lobby groups are more concerned with issues of deviancy, ethics, censorship and privacy. Legal questions are now starting to be addressed, and there have been a number of recent developments and test cases. For example, in the US Jake Baker was successfully convicted of threatening to commit rape in posted e-mails; some federal courts have held that bulletin board owners are criminally liable if the system violates obscenity statutes of a given State; Robert and Carleen Thomas were convicted of transmitting obscene material over a computer network; and the Communications Decency Act (CDA) (February 1996) passed and then repealed through the courts (preliminary injunction against the Act, June 1996; CDA overturned on appeal, June 1997).[38] The CDA sought to criminalise indecency on the Internet and carried a maximum fine of $250 000 and two years in prison. The bill sought to criminalise a wide range of speech and content, including:

- speech that harasses, annoys or alarms
- materials deemed obscene or harmful to minors
- information relating to terrorist acts or explosive materials
- sexual solicitation of a minor by computer
- online transmission of child pornography

The CDA came under repeated attack and was overturned because it infringed First and Fifth Amendment rights. The case of Robert and Carleen Thomas is interesting because they were convicted in Tennessee although their bulletin board is based in California, with the court ruling that they were responsible for information from their machine travelling through other jurisdictions. There are clearly many problems of applying current laws that apply to printed works to cyberspace. One irony of attempting such an application is that the telecommunication networks that carry many cyberspatial communications are classed as common carriers, which means that companies must transmit all messages regardless of content.[39] Further, systems such as Usenet will be difficult to regulate because there are no identifiable agents to direct actions against, many discussions are unregulated and many individuals use anonymous usernames.[40] Some analysts suggest that removing anonymous remailers would have benefits.[41] Firstly, it would aid in identifying those who are being antisocial. Secondly, it would allow people to assess the truthfulness of a sender's opinion. However, removing anonymity would penalise people who use anonymous remailers for good purpose (e.g. the victim of child abuse receiving support through a newsgroup; a Chinese dissident revealing conditions within China)[42] and would undermine the positive effects of disrupting social hierarchies (e.g. opinions being accepted on the basis of opinion rather than social status).

A number of questions concerning property rights and ownership, especially in relation to intellectual property rights and copyright, are now being asked. For example, on a bulletin board who 'owns' the messages? The system operator? The poster? How do we determine responsibility for libellous postings? How do we assess the damages for libel on a system that is truly global? A New York court has recently ruled that Prodigy could be sued for libel because it acts as a publisher and is therefore liable for posters' messages.[43] This perversely gives Prodigy the right to censor people's mail. Additionally, how do we assess the basis for copyright use costs? The assumption of copyright law is that creators would benefit by licensing their work for a fee, thus securing incentives for further creation.[44] Traditional copyright laws are being extended to cyberspace. Both in the USA and Europe, recent legislation has aimed to protect intellectual property rights. In September 1995, the US National Information Infrastructure Task Force (IITF) Working Group on Intellectual Property Rights issued its White Paper on Intellectual Property and the National Information Infrastructure.[45] In July of the same year the European Commission issued its Green Paper on Copyright and Related Rights in the Information Society. The governments of Canada and Australia have issued similar documents. Japan and the World Intellectual Property Organization (WIPO) have both been concentrating on trying to develop a workable multimedia rights clearance system.[46]

Poster and Elkin-Koren,[47] however, both argue that it is absurd to try to apply traditional copyright laws to digital media. Cyberspace does not have the same one-to-many properties as traditional media such as print or television. For example, in cyberspace distribution does not involve the dissemination of copies but the creation of new copies and reprocessing by a machine.[48] Under current legislation this reprocessing would be an infringement of copyright law. In particular, it raises the question of first sale doctrine whereby the owner of copyright only has the exclusive right of copyright for the initial distribution of a particular copy. Further, in Web-based publishing information on the pages need not actually be copied.[49] Page-creators instead use a process of inlining where inlined material is taken from its original source each time it is used. Although it is expected that page-creators will seek permission for inlined material the legal position of those failing to do so is unclear. For Samuelson, these law reforms (particularly in the US) not only reinforce traditional copyright laws but have also been skewed in favour of the publishers' interests and are detrimental to the public interest.[50] As such, traditional copyright laws have been extended beyond those applicable to printed material, making some practices that are legal with print media illegal with digital media (e.g. decompilation, or the splitting of text and images into smaller component parts for separate use – the equivalent in the music world would be sampling). An alternative solution to digital copyright is not clear when everything in the cultural market-place – words, images, music, lyrics, logos, voices, photographs, film footage – is property owned by someone, somewhere.[51] Many of the Hollywood take-overs in recent years have been by companies seeking to cash in on the re-runs of the back-catalogue. Similarly, entrepreneurs are now buying up and hoarding every scrap of culturally produced material in the hope of making a profit in the 'information revolution'. For example, Bill Gates's new company Continuum Productions Corp. is seeking to buy the digital rights to millions of images to form a virtual database.[52] For these companies, it is increasingly clear that an agreed global copyright policy must be adopted. This leads Elkin-Koren[53] to suggest that a thorough re-examination of copyright laws, particularly relating to what constitutes a copy and detecting whether unauthorised copies were made, is needed at a global scale. However, Barratt[54] suggests that this will be easily solvable with the introduction of encryption methods – people will be able to view the documents but not download them without permission. Although this generally runs against the open ethos of the Internet it would provide those concerned about copyright a way of protecting their current rights in a digital form.

Proponents of customary law reject the process of formalising legal frameworks to regulate cyberspace. They suggest that because life in the virtual world does not directly parallel life in the real world and each virtual world differs, then each MUD community should be responsible for regulating itself. That is, it is untenable to apply real-world laws when virtual life and the consequences of virtual actions are so distinct. They would prefer to see a process of virtual democratisation whereby power is wrested free from the system owner and placed into the hands of the community, who would regulate grievances through a community-based virtual law programme. One particular example of a MUD that has undergone a process of democratisation has been LambdaMOO. Within this MUD power has been distributed away from those who own the system to those who use the system. After the infamous MOO 'rape' incident,[55] the owner and creator of LambdaMOO, Pavel Curtis, decided to introduce a system of petition whereby the inhabitants could operate a system of self-governance. If inhabitants were unhappy about an individual's behaviour or wanted the protocols governing on-line behaviour altered they could campaign on an issue and, after a set time (two weeks), there would be a vote on whether to carry the motion. An independent arbitrator was appointed to monitor the process and announce the outcome and punishment. Palme[56] furthers that customary laws are more suited to virtual worlds because they can develop rapidly to suit changing circumstances. More formalised laws, however, would quickly become antiquated and might do more harm than benefit in the long term.

There is clearly a long way to go in deciding upon how cyberspace might be regulated and we are currently witnessing a playing out of potential futures. Within this future, it is clear that while customary law will be of importance in regulating interaction within specific contexts, it will be subsumed into a more formal framework. Ogden[57] and Roszak[58] suggest that we are at the point in time where we need to decide whether to act to secure access and rights through formalised law or to let multimedia conglomerates take over and mediate the network. Arguments about regulation are tied into the power struggle over how the Internet will develop. Miller[59] has reviewed the political–economic strategy camps of those in Washington seeking to guide Internet development in the US. These camps can easily be applied to lobbying groups throughout other Western nations. First he describes the *market libertarians*. These people believe that the free market-place is the best engine for a successful cyberspatial future. They suggest that government should only sponsor basic science and early stage research and development, rather than using taxpayers' money. However, they also regard transnational companies as undesirable because they corner markets, stifle competition and reduce potential benefits to customers. They would like to see a cyberspatial future driven by market demand, consisting of many small, decentralised, competitive businesses relying on in-house research and development and entrepreneurial spirit, providing customers with choice and value for money, and with little government involvement.

The *corporate conservatives*, similarly, would like to see a cyberspatial future driven by market demand. However, in contrast to the libertarians, they feel that transnationals and a few select start-up companies are best positioned to bring major projects such as the US National Information Infrastructure (NII) to fruition. They would like to see government deregulation, although they would also like government subsidisation for production costs and to develop new markets. In effect, they want the government to help in the early stages and then to 'get out of the way' to allow the free-market to expand and control development, allowing the early pioneers to dominate the market.

Mixed-market libertarians try to find a balance between private enterprise and collective, social good. They are willing to accept that private companies will be the dominant force in shaping cyberspatial futures but believe that government should regulate the market to stop groups with low-income and marginal, social status being sidelined and excluded from technological developments. Here, government provides special subsidies and support for these groups so that they can join the market with a level of 'effective demand', attracting profit-seeking firms.

Progressive communitarians share many of the concerns of mixed-market liberals but take a stronger view of regulation, arguing that cyberspace's future should be guided through the public sector acting in the public's interest rather than leaving public interest in the hands of self-interested corporations. They therefore advocate that key cyberspatial technologies, such as backbone Internet connections, should be publicly owned. Standards and quality of the system should also be monitored by public and non-profit sectors to ensure quality of service. In order to achieve these aims they suggest that cyberspace should be built from the bottom up, through the development of community networks. These networks should be regulated through democratic civil groups and institutions. They also envisage a universal system of access, as with the telephone network, where anybody can gain access and interact with other users and services.

The last group Miller terms *state socialists*. This group wants to see technologies such as the Internet being predominantly owned, regulated and developed by national government. They see the development of the Internet as too important to be left in the hands of for-profit corporations, who are ultimately seeking commercial gain. For them, commercial gain is at odds with the potential public social service that they envisage cyberspace should be appropriated for. Although the telecommunication networks of many countries used to be state-owned and run, in recent years many of these services have been privatised to compete more competitively in the world market-place. In practice, re-nationalising these industries, or even sections within them, would be costly and difficult. However, within these countries government policy is still likely to be orientated quite strongly towards providing the universal services that nationalised industries were first created to protect.

Within these futures it is clear that regulation will consist of two tiers. The dominant tier will consist of formalised laws or market-led rules, depending on which political–

economic camp is the victor, and the second tier will consist of customary laws that will still contextualise basic interaction. The main problem of such a system is that the laws of one country do not apply to all. For example, Janower seriously questions the ability of the US Government to prosecute foreign operators of on-line casinos or other deviant enterprises. One solution, forwarded by Oberding and Norderhaug,[60] might be the formulation of an international convention similar to the Laws of the Sea and Admiralty Law. As such, there would be an internationally recognised set of laws which would allow those in one country to prosecute offenders living elsewhere. An alternative would be the creation of commercial norms that are standard across cyberspatial commercial interest.

At present, the corporate conservatives seem most likely to direct future developments. This is particularly the case in the US, where the Clinton Administration is promoting a strategy where for-profit firms will develop the Internet. As such, the US government is trying to balance public and private interests by sponsoring a system of self-regulation where possible so that the development of cyberspace does not become strangled by legal red tape. So far, they have only intervened in concerns of regulation where the interests of the public are considered most at risk, such as issues of decency, and to examine issues of property which might stifle commercial investment. Otherwise, they have left cyberspace to be regulated through market-led 'rules' and have largely avoided many issues, such as the 'victims' of market-led regulation and customary law. It is hoped that existing statutes concerning libel and discrimination will be naturally extended to virtual worlds. Whether this is realistic given the differing nature of communication in cyberspace is open to debate. However, the US government is conscious that it does not want to stifle early growth with excessive legislation. Most other Western governments are following a similar tactic.

ACCESS AND EXCLUSION

> Just because the spaces with which we are now concerned are electronic it is not the case that they are democratic, egalitarian, or accessible, and it is not the case that we can forgo asking in particular about substance and dominance.[61]

Related to ownership and regulation are issues of access and exclusion. Cyberspace is promoted as a space for all. Looking beyond the egalitarian hyperbole, however, it is clear that cyberspace usage is fragmented along traditional spatial and social divisions and it is not universally accessible. In fact, far from creating a more egalitarian society, some commentators have suggested that cyberspace is going to reinforce and create new inequalities, bringing about a world that is more unequal and socially fragmented.[62] Fernback and Thompson[63] report that unless the three basic barriers to widespread cyberspace use are removed, cyberspace will remain an elitist space. Cyberspace must be affordable, it must be intellectually accessible, and time must be available to interact with it.

Some groups are undoubtedly excluded from the 'global information superhighway' or at best have very limited access. Cyberspace is a space dominated by white, middle-class males from Western nations who can converse in English and are generally in their late teens or early twenties. Graham and Marvin[64] contend that while cyberspace might seem an empowering or liberating space for disadvantaged groups, such as disabled people, minorities and the poor, it is a space requiring certain skills, which are often difficult for these groups to acquire. Without the necessary skills to use a computer, and the financial parity to buy a machine or pay for a service provider, these groups are effectively excluded from the Internet. Financial parity is of particular importance. Usage is currently dominated by those of middle to upper level income. Access to a computer at home and work is highly correlated with household income and socioeconomic grouping.[65] As Golding[66] states:

> Entrance to the new media playground is relatively cheap for the well to do, a small adjustment in existing spending patterns is simply accommodated. For the poor the price is a sharp calculation of opportunity cost, access to communication goods jostling uncomfortably with the mundane arithmetic of food, housing and clothing.

For Miller,[67] deregulation of the market accentuates this social division by allowing companies to target the most affluent sections of society.

While the skills to operate a computer and access the Internet might be denied to disadvantaged groups, the population as a whole is largely computer-ignorant.[68] We are told that we, as a society, are becoming more computer literate, yet most computer users are not experts on the machines they operate – they just carry out the tasks assigned to them and do little exploration of the packages. Many on-line interactions are not intuitive: you have to learn how to log on and have the courage to experiment. As Badgett and Sandler[69] note, 'learning your way round IRC is a lot like learning another language, finding your way around a new town, or playing blind man's bluff'. Those who are not computer literate are obviously at a disadvantage. Software houses, as yet, do not seem to have appreciated that most programs are not intuitive – they are large and complex and involve a certain understanding of the likely consequences of an action. A large proportion of our population does feel alienated by computers and the constant stream of updates serves to mystify further. We are becoming increasingly reliant on the 'computer experts' that each facility now has to employ to guide us through the rapid developments and sort out our daily queries. As Roszak argues:

> 'The rest of us' keep hearing about the spectacular benefits of desktop publishing, multimedia, interactivity; but whenever we thumb our way through the documentation, we realize that we are way out of our technological depth. And whenever we look at the price tag, we know we are out of our financial league.[70]

We are hailing the 'golden age of information' and yet most people who access the Net are academics, college students and business people. Until the population as a whole becomes more computer literate the utopian visions of cyberspace will remain that – just visions.

Access is also denied or limited through the availability and cost of suitable technology and connections. Mitchell[71] reports that the bandwidth-disadvantaged are the new have-nots within Western society. He suggests that if the value of real estate is dependent upon location, then the value of a network connection is determined by bandwidth. Accessibility becomes redefined as a poor, slow network connection so that the 'friction of distance' is replaced by the 'bondage of bandwidth'. Whereas unprofitable telephone services are largely cross-subsidised as a public service, it is unclear whether high bandwidth connections will be given the same treatment. If not, he argues, bandwidth costs will lead to information hotspots, mainly focused around key universities, high capacity data sources (e.g. a telecommunications company) and telecottages in rural areas. This will mean that those with poor links will become increasingly marginalised from the information economy. Cyberspatial adoption is not equally distributed, even within Western countries. For example, Moss and Townsend[72] report that 50% of all US Internet hosts are located in just five states. This inequality is replicated at the county and district level (see Figure 5.1). Moreover, those who fail to pay their bills will be blacklisted and cut off from the service. The irony is that while the Internet has largely been created with public money, its current design largely limits access to those with the suitable private incomes. Further, the new corporate owners are seeking ways in which to incorporate charge-back mechanisms to recuperate investments. As such, further barriers are being erected to a public, democratised system linking all.

Cyberspace also accentuates the division between developed, rich nations and poorer developing nations. In developing nations Internet access is limited mainly through expense. Where there are connections they are likely to be industry or university related. As Hess[73] describes:

> Cyberspace is an elite space, a playground for the privileged . . . There is a global glass ceiling, and for many in the world a large part of . . . technoculture lies well above it.

Lajoie[74] identifies some perverse irony in the situation developing, arguing that cyberspace effectively renders the new technology 'slaves' out of sight and mind. The 'slaves' are the workers in developing countries who are exploitatively employed to make and construct high tech components and machines. Although producing the enabling technology, these groups are effectively excluded from Internet usage through prohibitive expense and the availability of the machines they make, which are exported for use in developed nations. High-level industrial and economic development is, according to Interrogate the Internet,[75] a prerequisite before access to Internet services is meaningful. Citing the example of Jamaica, they state that Internet access is not really for everyone, as access to e-mail, for example, will not remedy the problems of shanty towns without running water. Dyrkton[76] similarly questions whether a computer network connected to the Internet is necessary to Jamaica's lifestyle and needs, especially when what the country really needs is better housing, infrastructure and a stable economy. He fears that Jamaica is ill-prepared for the computer age, which requires

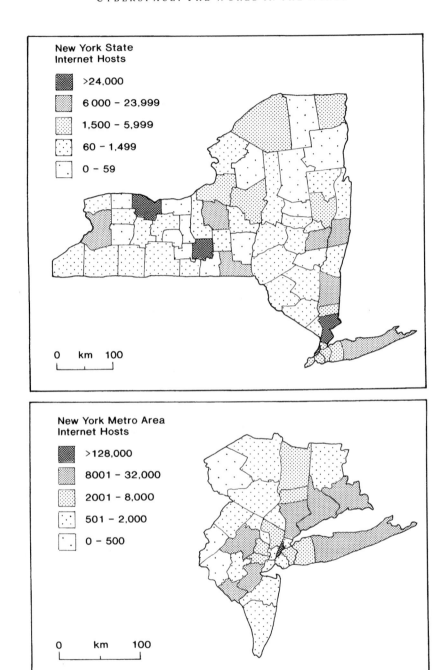

Figure 5.1 *Distribution of Internet Connections at County and State levels. Source: Based on Moss and Townsend (1996)*

technological support and software literacy, and a move towards computing might polarise the national literacy problem and create an elite of computer literates. He concludes by stating: 'In Jamaica the breeze of the computer fan empties itself into an abyss of unrelenting everyday life'.[77] For Abiodun,[78] in contrast, technological development is seen as a way to close the gap between developed and developing countries by providing an economic catalyst. He strongly suggests that developing nations should invest heavily in technology, infrastructure and training or be left further behind.

To other commentators, however, the adoption of cyberspatial technologies leads to the further Westernisation of society. Not all nations are at ease with the Westernising tendencies of the Internet and the aims of a global village. They would rather retain their identities, cultures and senses of place. The Internet is, though, Western in origin and its (and virtual reality's) development is firmly contextualised within a Western, male, patriarchal, and Christian cultural history.[79] Much of the hype surrounding it speaks of a global village or community, espousing the McLuhan vision of thirty years ago:

> with electricity we extend our central nervous system globally, instantly relating every human experience. . . . This is the new global village.[80]

It is envisaged that through global communication the differences between cultures and societies will be transcended. For Waters,[81] for example, the current process of globalisation is reliant on the symbolic exchanges, that is communication and symbiosis between different cultures. We will come together and work towards mutual trust and understanding, creating a world that is 'smaller' and more democratic.[82] However, this community is one that is undoubtedly envisaged as Western and, more specifically, American. English is the Internet's first language. The USA currently dominates developments, innovations and Internet usage. Some see this as the continued drive to Westernise the world:

> Cyberspace did not appear . . . from nowhere. . . . It is the conscious reflection of the deepest desires, aspirations, experiential yearning and spiritual angst of Western man, it is resolutely designed as a new market, and is an emphatic product of the culture, worldview and technology of Western civilization. . . . Cyberspace, then, is the 'American dream' writ large; it marks the dawn of a new 'American civilization'. . . . Cyberspace is particularly geared up towards the erasure of all non-Western histories.[83]

Similarly, for Peet,[84] global communication media, such as the Internet, are increasingly producing a homogeneous, global, Western consciousness and culture. Moreover, the spaces and representations within virtual reality portray a highly specific view of the world that is predominantly Western, resting on conventions such as Cartesian space, objective realism and linear perspective.[85] It seems that cyberspatial adoption in non-Western countries needs to find a critical balance between combating social problems, investing for the future and surrendering their culture.

PRIVACY AND CONFIDENTIALITY

> Imagine a place where trespassers leave no footprints, where goods can be stolen an
> infinite number of times and yet remain in the possession of their original owners,
> where businesses you never heard of can own the history of your personal affairs, . . .
> where everyone is as virtual as the shadows in Plato's cave. Such a place already exists
> . . . cyberspace.[86]

In recent years, a number of commentators have started to question the implications of
cyberspatial technologies for individual and collective privacy and confidentiality, high-
lighting the emergence of a sophisticated 'surveillance society'.[87] The risks to privacy
range from personal infringements to 'big brother' scenarios. At a personal level, e-mail
messages are easily intercepted, read, copied and redistributed – 'e-mail privacy is an
oxymoron'.[88] The system operator generally has the power to access all files on the
server. E-mail privacy can also be compromised by those external to the system in four
other ways (in descending order of likelihood): choosing bad passwords, importing
corrupt software by valid users, entering through misconfigured software and entering
through a flawed operating system.[89] Given recent cases concerning freedom of speech,
organisations are now caught in a position whereby they have to balance privacy with
policing the transfer of obscene material. As noted, organisations such as Prodigy have
used this position to justify the censoring of mail and many companies argue that
mailboxes and their contents are company property.

At a larger scale, the great fear is that the Internet 'may well simply turn into an
extension of social control through the control of information',[90] replacing capital as a
dominating shaper of everyday lives:

> Information has become the lubricant for a swiftly emerging social structure that is
> wholly dependent on the potential, malleability, and exchangeability of data. [Wit-
> ness] . . . the recent merger-mania between broadcast, telephone and computer
> companies.[91]

Whereas capital was power, information will be power. For many, the transition from
the mode of capital to the mode of information is in full progress. Increasingly large
portions of our individual details have been converted into digital form, residing in
various databases.[92] Our details are on display to anybody with access to the right
computers. Agencies from the police, to the military, to the government and industry
are all actively collecting and exchanging data. For example, most government agencies
in Western societies enter details of applications and payments into database systems;[93]
transactions such as buying goods using a credit card are continuously recorded, as are
the number and type of goods you buy;[94] educational and health records are increasingly being recorded digitally; and there is a growing geodemographic industry[95]
which identifies the characteristics of suitable areas for advertising and marketing based
upon census and other corporate database variables. As such, Critical Art Ensemble
argues that the virtual body is being complemented with a data body.[96] They construct

a conspiracy style thesis, which suggests that this data body serves the needs of corporations and police states.

Geodemographic databases can be highly sophisticated, dividing nations into characteristics based upon their postcodes. For example, the UK based CACI has devised ACORN, which divides all postcodes in the country into 39 categories. The descriptions of each category typically include information concerning house size, area characteristics, likely earnings profile, car ownership etc. Other companies can then purchase this information and through the use of relational databases combine it with their own or other purchased data. As a result, in the USA, for example, it is possible to purchase digital information from companies such as TRW, Equifax and Trans Union, which reveals facts concerning birth, family, address, telephone number, social security and salary history, credit transactions, mortgage, bankruptcy, tax and legal records, education and health records.[97] Information comes from a variety of sources, some surprising and some dubious. Chapman[98] recalls a story whereby over a period of a year a young boy filled out several promotional cards, each with a fictional name but with the same address, at a Baskin-Robins[99] store in order to receive free ice cream on all the invented birthdays. Ten years later the house received several notices of prosecution for failing to register for the draft. Baskin-Robins had been selling their database to the Pentagon (a practice now discontinued).

Some 'data merchants' have found niche markets collecting data and recording it electronically for sale to groups such as potential employers relating to legal claims, arrests but not convictions (using local press reports), disputes between tenants and landlords, and insurance claims.[100] This information can be used to construct extremely accurate personal profiles concerning everything from finances to what a person eats, drinks and wears, as well as revealing intimate personal details. As the advent of digital and pay-per-view television unfolds, what we watch and when can be added to these profiles.

For the most part the individuals to whom this data refers have little control over its use or who it is passed on to, and in many cases no knowledge of its existence.[101] In short, it is increasingly difficult to take part in everyday life without leaving a digital trace: 'life in cyberspace generates electronic trails as inevitably as soft ground retains footprints'.[102] What were once private transactions are increasingly becoming less so. Further, we are willing to part with our information without recourse to violence or trickery by simply filling out the form or passing over the credit card. For Poster,[103] this smacks of some 'super-panopticon', a gigantic and sleek surveillance machine:

> The phone cables and electric circuitry that minutely crisscross and envelop our world are the extremities of the super-panopticon, transforming our acts into an extensive discourse of surveillance, our private behaviours into public announcements, our individual deeds into collective language. Individuals are plugged into the circuits of their own panoptic control, making a mockery of theories of social action, such as Weber's, which privilege consciousness as the basis of self-interpretation, and liberals generally, who locate meaning in the intimate, subjective recesses behind the shield of the skin. The individual subject is interpellated by the super-panopticon through the discourses of databases that have very little if anything to do with 'modern' conceptions of rational autonomy.

This suggests that we are on the brink of moving into a Gibsonian dystopian future, where the access to information is all-important, that Orwell's *1984* is arriving later than expected but is just around the corner. Ross reports that 70% of corporations are now using electronic surveillance (and other means) to monitor employee performance, checking on such things as the number of keystrokes, and the amount of time spent socialising, eating and even going to the toilet.[104] Such practices have led some to argue that the office is the new 'Western' sweatshop of the twentieth century.[105]

In contrast, electronic databases also ensure that we are paid correctly, that we receive the correct government benefits, that crime protection is improved, our health monitored more effectively and that we have the convenience of paying for goods using plastic debit and credit cards.[106] Clearly, surveillance or monitoring systems have benefits as well as costs. The secret is to make sure that the benefits become dominant, so that these systems are not used in a criminal or constricting manner but rather to increase efficiency and provide individual and collective benefits. It is, however, easy to see how the costs could be stifling and controlling, especially in a non-democratic, totalitarian state. Even within democratic states, privacy and confidentiality are obviously being compromised. The records and actions of every individual is, in the developed world, being rapidly digitised, cross-referenced and increasingly used to 'police' and control society. For Roszak,[107] legal safeguards are largely ineffective, full of loopholes and constantly chasing new technological developments in an effort to keep pace with the new ways in which public life is being compromised. He fears that the Internet is too large and dynamic to be effectively regulated. A number of controls are, though, being added to the system, not to protect the privacy rights of individuals, but, as Roszak fears, to try to monitor, police and regulate the system. In France all cryptography is to be licensed, with the government entitled to a key.[108] In the UK, police have set up 'sting' bulletin boards to catch electronic criminals. The Obscene Publications Act has been extended to cover the Internet – the transmission of pornographic images using UK phone lines is a new prosecutable offence. There are reports of US authorities using 'sniffer' programs to trace those logging onto bulletin boards that post illegal images and information (e.g. about paedophilia).[109] This has led Barlow[110] to state that:

> trusting the government with your privacy is like having a Peeping Tom install your window blinds.

However, it is difficult to see a solution to the compromising of privacy when data is considered so valuable and stopping its collection near impossible. Surveillance and monitoring are nothing new. For centuries we have kept and maintained records. Records are a fundamental element for maintaining the 'cohesion and coordination of the economic and social order'.[111] The difference now, though, is that computers, in combination with telecommunications, qualitatively alter the nature of surveillance by routinising, broadening and deepening it[112] through the increased transferability, replicability and availability of these records to sources they were not intended for.

Digital is different to paper and analogue. For example, digital integration and cross-checking is allowing companies to draw up blacklists of potential 'bad' customers. This information can be resold to companies who control access to credit, goods and services.[113] Digital information is a commodity.

ETHICS AND DEVIANCY

Shade[114] details how there have always been fears and moral consternation associated with new technologies. Parents were outraged at the telephone's appropriation as a courting device; 'dirty pictures' quickly followed the advent of the camera; television eroded family values. Similarly, there has been moral consternation at the uncensored nature of much of the Internet. Cyberspace is seen to be a space where some of the more distasteful facets of contemporary society can proliferate and flourish.[115] Here, images and messages of sex and abuse, and racial and ethnic hatred can be found, and groups such as paedophiles and Nazis have quickly moved into the electronic format, where they can communicate easily and reproduce endlessly their messages and images. For example, people can subscribe to a large number of sexually-orientated Usenet mailing lists, including alt.sex.bondage, alt.sex.bestiality, alt.sex.fetish.amputee and alt.sex.spanking. Discussions on these lists can vary in style and content but can be very sexually explicit, including debates on certain sexual practices and practical advice for other subscribers.[116]

The alt.sex mailing lists are extremely popular; for the month of October 1993, there were an estimated 3.3 million readers worldwide.[117] Shade reports that many alt.sex readers defend the newsgroups by arguing that they only deal with consensual sex and if readers do not like what they are reading, they should not subscribe to the list. Some argue[118] that the alt.sex hierarchy is a place where college students can learn about sexuality and safe sex. Similarly, a number of dedicated BBSs have come on-line allowing users to chat in real-time about various sexual topics. Event Horizons for example, has 64 telephone lines and 25 000 users. Others are specifically gay or lesbian. Some adult BBSs feature photo libraries (for example Nixpix is a free BBS that claims to have 10 000 subscribers, providing global access to pornographic photographs). Most of the images on these boards are soft-core material but there are pointers to private e-mails offering more hard-core images.[119]

Cyberspace, it is therefore argued, is creating a new space of deviancy, a space that provides a social context that the socially alienated can occupy and where they can play out their fantasies. Sardar[120] estimates that 10–20% of cyberspatial users are the 'genuinely psychotic' who occupy this new space of deviancy:

> There *are* a lot of people on the Internet – all hyperventilating, hyperabusing, and hyperself-abusing, sitting alone in front of their computer screens 'chatting' to people they have never met and are unlikely to ever meet.

He is seriously worried about their mental state and the possible real-world ramifications that these sorts of interchanges are going to lead to. Durkin and Bryant,[121] for example, suggest that cyberspace 'may revolutionize crime and the parameters of deviant sexual behaviour' and quote a Massachusetts prosecutor, who stated that 'instead of hanging around the playground looking for the loneliest kid, potential child molesters merely have to log on'.[122] For Durkin and Bryant, cyberspace provides more than just a consensual space of sexuality:

> the computer can be conceptualized as a mechanism of metamorphosis, or a kind of deviant 'dream machine'. Deviant sexual fantasies that might well have remained simply the musings of an imaginative mind may now be operationalized and implemented. Like the genie in the bottle, the computer can transform deviant sexual reverie into deviant reality by feeding and enriching the individual's fantasies, aiding him or her in identifying others with analogous sexual predilections, assisting in the coalescence of like-minded sexual deviants, and contributing to the constitution of an opportunity structure for the actualization of the fantasised behaviour.

In other words, cyberspace is providing the catalyst for a whole range of real-world deviant behaviour that would have just remained fantasy, by providing a space where fantasies can grow and are more likely to be realised.

Such has been the public outcry that some major Internet providers (e.g. CompuServe) are blocking access to pornographic sites and there has been a growth in 'blocking' software to protect minors (e.g. Net Nanny). For some analysts, however, although these measures 'protect' subscribers, they do not alter the fact that these images and messages, often outlawed and strictly policed in a non-electronic format, remain relatively unpoliced on the Internet. However, the problems of policing are compounded because of the distributed nature of cyberspace, where borders are largely meaningless. Although the content of a site might break the censorship laws of one country, it might be perfectly legal in another. The information on a site in an uncensored country is, though, readily accessible to citizens of the country where censorship is enforced.

For Calcutt,[123] though, the panic over pornography is worry over a 'phantom epidemic'. For him, the publicity surrounding this issue is out of all proportion to the limited availability of this 'new horror'. This inflated concern has led to a general culture of fear, which has then fed off itself to create a perpetual cycle. Dery[124] similarly rejects the 'perception of the Internet as an electronic Sodom awash in hard-core porn and overrun by predatory paedophiles' as unfounded. Calcutt forwards a conspiratorial notion that a computer porn panic is being used as a corrosive catalyst that seeks to push Internet and non-Internet users into the protective embrace of authority. Here, public fear is being falsely aroused and then used to direct attitudes, behaviour and policy in relation to cyberspace. This is formally and informally leading to unneeded controls and regulation. The evidence that these controls are based upon, he suggests, is flimsy and unsubstantiated. He cites a recent UK Home Office report,[125] which backed a pro-censorship position based on suspect evidence that was admitted to be anecdotal, and which failed to mention any opposing evidence, thereby painting a very selective picture.[126] Again, Dery paints a similar scenario, referring to a debate on NPR's *Talk of the*

Nation where the National Law Center for Children and Families claimed that the Internet was 'full' of hard-core pictures involving violence, torture and animals, citing evidence from two dubious studies.[127] Calcutt argues that much of the evidence is unsubstantiated hearsay and gossip and is used in the self-interest of moral entrepreneurs. He contends that only a small number of young people have full access to the Internet and that the images they are most likely to find are the soft-porn pictures adorning any top-shelf and touted in school playgrounds. Anything more hard-core is encrypted by pornographers, who do not want to be traced, and Usenet postings are on many sites screened. For example, all Usenet postings in the UK are screened at their point of entry, University of Kent, for anything overtly pornographic. For him, then, the pornographic panic is a myth. He also dismisses the idea that witnessing pornographic images during adolescence is going to turn the viewer into a potential rapist or a victim of paedophilia as extremely simplistic, reducing a complex social and psychological condition to a simple cause and effect relationship. Further, DeLoach reports that the large pornographic publishers such as Playboy are quick to point out that the material on the Internet is just 'recycled old stuff'.[128] As such, we are just witnessing the changing of a medium rather than the fostering of new exploitation, particularly of children. To these commentators computer porn is just being used to bring an unregulated space back into line with all other media. Not unsurprisingly, however, the media hype and hyperbole has been drawn to pornography on the Internet and the possibilities of technosex.

For Rheingold,[129] technosex is potentially revolutionary, allowing you to experience eroticism and deep emotional communication with somebody without the fear of pregnancy or sexually transmitted diseases. In fact, he concludes that the disembodying tendencies of cyberspace might represent the ultimate sexual revolution. Technosex can be divided into sexual conversations, usually accompanied by mutual masturbation, between people communicating via a chat facility, and sexual fantasies played out with a virtual partner, a construction of the computer. Dery describes the appeal of technosex as a 'seductive alternative in an age . . . yearning for untainted love'.[130] Kane[131] reports that up to 50 000 people partake daily in technosexual activities, using up to 700 real-time chat lines. They are partaking in what Branwyn[132] terms 'text sex', on-line sex play involving seduction and, ultimately, a mutual sexual act between people (normally strangers). Branwyn describes three types of text sex. The first involves a straight conversation between two people leading to mutual masturbation (in some instances photographs are digitally transferred). The second involves several people constructing a communal, orgy fantasy. Thirdly, there is what Branwyn calls 'teleoperated compusex' involving two sets of couples, where one couple acts out the instructions meted out by the other (e.g. 'Ken, I want you to position Beth so that she is . . .'). Real-time 'text sex' is not just confined to BBSs but is also increasingly occurring in MUDs as part of the everyday adventures within these worlds. Here, sexual activities are conducted within character. 'Text sex' is literally just talking each other through sexual fantasies and masturbation. In Branwyn's first two instances, there is no person to cuddle up to afterwards, no person to wake up beside. Argyle[133] reports, from personal experience, that 'hotchatting' leaves the two 'lovers' with all the emotions and physical arousal of a sexual act. However, she also notes that once it is over the sense of aloneness is heightened and the event is ultimately unfulfilling: to 'break the connection seems more painful than fulfilling'. In Stephanie Fletcher's novel, *E-mail://a.love.story./*, for example, although the characters rejoice that the 'text sex' is better than the real thing, most come to realise that it is no long-term substitute for a real-world relationship, giving only short-term novelty value. Unless taken forward through telephone conversations and real-life meetings, hotchatters feel little lasting emotion when a cyberspatial relationship ends. The appeal is based upon anonymity, little responsibility and the ability to play with personality. As Mandel[134] argues, 'sex per se does not occur at all in virtual communities. Writing and communicating about sex does occur a lot, but that is not the same thing'.

'Text sex' seems as if it is just one step down from phone sex, except the chat is not a commercial service and both 'partners' are getting a sexual 'kick' of some form[135]. Clearly those involved in both hotchatting and contributing to newsgroups feel safe from any real-world repercussions or embarrassment relating to their interactions.[136] 'Text sex' also raises a number of other issues. For example, what are the legalities of paying someone to 'hotchat' with you? Is this some form of prostitution? Should it be treated in the same way as phone-sex?[137] If one of the discussants had a 'real-world' partner, would 'hotchats' constitute some sort of on-line indiscretion, and if the 'hotchats' were regular would this constitute an affair? It would be interesting to know whether hotchatting could be used as the main vehicle for obtaining a divorce. A question that seems to be overlooked is why people are 'hot-chatting' in the first place. Why are people seeking sexual encounters that by some accounts are ultimately facile and unfulfilling – chasing romance by sitting alone at a computer screen? All encounters are not just for fun and one suspects that a great many are actually heart-felt searches for a suitable partner. Dery's suggestion that it is a safe-sex way to 'get it on' seems a little too weak – you can practise safe sex with 'real' partners without having to resort to a condom consisting of a glass screen. Like personal ads and dating agencies, this may be just a new place to seek out a suitable partner or a place to explore ideas that the person is to afraid to explore in real-life. Correll's study of an on-line lesbian bar described in Chapter 4 gives some useful insights into why these women seek solace and sex via the Internet.[138]

'Interactive' virtual sex programs are already on the market. *Virtual Valerie*, for example, is a best selling CD-ROM title billed as 'your cybernetic fantasy'.[139] The most interactive such programs get, however, is to allow you to design your 'ideal' partner and construct a story-line by choosing from multiple options what your 'partner' does next. They are often a blend of still images mixed with stored video clips.[140] For most, however, it is virtual reality that holds the true erotic appeal of full interactivity, of a sexual encounter through the use of computer controlled body suits. Here, sex would be between person and computer or between two people separated by vast distances and mediated through the computer[141] (as popularised in the film *Lawnmower Man*, where two individuals make love via virtual reality headsets and bodysuits suspended in giant gyroscopes). For Dery, this foray into virtual reality sex will be enlightening, allowing us to explore all the sexual fantasies we can conjure – we could experiment with gender, ethnicity, redesign our images (equally, more controversial sexual practices such as bestiality and paedophilia could be experimented with):

> Most of us will limit ourselves to the occasional steamy romp with Raquel Welch or Robert Redford, while the irretrievably perverse will take part in threesomes with, say the arch conservative crusader Phyllis Schafly and the Devil-worshipping debauchee Aleister Crowley. Many personalities will be available only as simulations, of course, and efforts to re-create the love-making techniques of Cleopatra, Casanova, Marilyn Monroe, or JFK will doubtless give rise to a new market for the skills of historians.[142]

For some, however, the concept of virtual sex with a virtual partner holds problems. For example, as with top-shelf pornography, virtual reality is seen to perpetuate the well-documented objectification of (women's) bodies.[143] Further, Kramarae[144] fears that sex will become just like another sport and become limited and limiting: 'virtual reality will become the emotional condom of the 21st century'.[145] In addition, she fears that the virtual sex, like telephone sex before it, will become a male-dominated activity where men are led to believe that they have complete control over women, producing a relationship that is devoid of responsibilities and the demands of reciprocity. Here, virtual sex is seen as encouraging notions of power over, detachment from and objectivity towards the female body,[146] and promoting sex as primarily a doing activity rather than an intimate, caring experience. Again, the fear is that men will approach real-world encounters with the same attitudes as those developed on-line:

> The female sex machine serves not only as a shiny surface on which male visions of femininity may be etched but as a mirror whose reflection reinforces the masculine sense of self.[147]

In relation to virtual reality sex, these fantasies and arguments are for the foreseeable future going to remain largely conceptual and the source of much overexcited speculation. For example, Rheingold[148] reports that it will not be until at least the early-to-mid twenty-first century that true 'teledildonic' (virtual reality sex) will come on-line. Any system would require massive supercomputing power and enormous bandwidth to control bodysuits consisting of millions of sensors and effectors. Even then, a multitude of other issues come to the fore, such as testing, temperature, taste, smell and the fact that all the technology needed will hardly be discreet![149]

Other commentators have expressed concern over what they see as the colonisation of cyberspace by other undesirable industries. For example, Janower[150] charts the emergence of on-line casinos and gambling houses. The first on-line casino, Internet Casino Inc. (ICI), opened its electronic doors in August of 1995 with 18 different games, access to the National Indian Lottery and plans to launch a sports book. This has been followed by Interactive Gaming & Communications Corp., which run a sports book and casino, with bets phoned into Antigua on a toll-free satellite link, and several other competitors. Most of these companies operate from non-US territory to avoid prosecution. For example, ICI operates out of the Caicos Islands and WagerNet out of Belize. Bets can be placed through companies offering secure Internet payment or through an offshore account. The size of bets rises from a nickel to thousands of dollars. Janower suggests that by allowing this industry to go on-line we have allowed an addictive and exploitative industry to reproduce itself in a more powerful form. On-line gambling houses have reduced costs and increased profit margins, and the gamblers do not have to leave home to place their bets. For example, ICI typically 'cuts' 24% of each dollar waged against 8–16% in a typical casino. The ICI site has become popular, with over 40 000 registered users and 7 million visits per month by early 1996. This, Janower fears, might lead to heightened crime, increasing numbers of compulsive gamblers and cannibalised spending in other areas of the economy. At present, she argues, the government is unprepared and legislation inadequate for on-line gambling. Currently, these on-line gambling houses are controlled by self-imposed regulations and are not scrutinised by government regulators. Additionally, some question the security of financial transactions across the Internet and problems of hacking. The on-line gambling houses are unregulated and might be open to abuse.

In addition, to being heralded as the new space of deviant enterprise, cyberspace has been trumpeted as a new space of white-collar crime. Here, cyberspace is creating a new space where embezzlements can be camouflaged, fraudulent payments made and reports and inventories falsified. For example, Sardar[151] reports that cybercrime is going to be the crime of the future. He suggests that much of the estimated $750 billion organised crime and $400 million drug trafficking revenue finds its way into cyberspace, where it is legitimised in thousands of transactions. Fraudulent crimes need not be large-scale organised crime. Customs and Excise are concerned that people will increasingly seek to avoid paying local or national taxes by buying goods elsewhere and having them mail-delivered. The scale of this potential problem is highlighted by the fact that $3 billion are lost through unpaid lost local sales tax through cross-state trade in the US.[152] Cyberspace also has its unique crimes of hacking. Hackers work their way into other people's computers and accounts, some for fun, others for profit, downloading confidential information to sell on or to use for blackmail or thieving goods by redirecting them or ordering without payment, or altering files or programs as a form of sabotage. Martin[153] reports that cybercrime is encapsulated as the seven Es – Error, Embezzlement, Ego, Eavesdropping, Espionage, Enmity and Extortion – and costs the US at least $2 billion in direct costs every year. At particular risk are banks and insurance companies, which electronically track and transfer huge sums of money every day. As a result, several countries have introduced criminal laws making hacking a punishable offence. For example, hacking is a criminal offence in the UK under the Computer Misuse Act 1990.

POLITICAL FUTURES

There can be no doubt that cyberspace does raise a number of serious questions concerning politics and polity. It is imperative that individual citizens, academics and representatives of both government and industry actively engage in exploring these questions if we are to ensure the success of cyberspatial technologies and reap the potential benefits they offer. It is suggested that the best way for us to assess the political changes that are occurring and their effect on polity is to use the approach outlined in Chapter 3, namely combining postmodernism with aspects of social constructivism and political economy. This approach appreciates that the local, political organisation and mechanisms are socially constructed by the interplay between individuals, institutions and technologies, while acknowledging that these constructions are bound within a historical context and the wider political agenda of nations and businesses. As such, the political implications of cyberspace need to be contextualised into wider economic concerns relating to ownership, control and regulation and into social concerns relating to voter behaviour, political mobilisation and cultural ideologies concerning what is determined to be deviant. In our studies of on-line politics and polity, then, we need to deconstruct the recursive relationship between on- and off-line political spaces. Such an approach thus tries to find an acceptable balance between the individual and institutions in understanding the political implications of cyberspace.

Adopting this approach, it is apparent that the hype centring on the reorganisation of political structures clearly overplays the decentralised, open-access nature of the Internet. It is unlikely that place-based, representative politics will be replaced in the short or long term for a number of reasons. Firstly, although cyberspace does lead to highly permeable borders, susceptible to information transfer, sovereignty is still highly guarded in 'real' space, across which tangible trade is highly regulated. Admittedly, industries such as finance have largely transcended the nation state, and corporations are now largely globalised, but nation-states will continue to exist as necessary organisational structures, fuelled by deeply entrenched historical prerogatives. The assessment of Thu Nguyen and Alexander[154] that cyberspace will lead to chaos through weakened polities seems excessively bleak. People off-line still have to live in the local, and will continue to be represented by the current democratic systems based within discrete geographical units.

Secondly, direct government as a concept is impractical and unlikely to work. Government is an extremely complicated system requiring complex systems of consultation, debate and understanding. In practice, most people will not want to understand these debates and partake in the political process, replacing elected, representative figures. Evidence so far reveals that participatory democracy attracts well-spoken, highly educated individuals who are politically motivated and normally interested in only one or two issues. A direct system would therefore be largely unworkable through inquoriency and anarchy, with no centre, leadership or organisational structure.

Thirdly, the Internet is touted as a political modifier because of its ease in disseminating information. However, the Internet can be seen as just a different source of information and a new way to send an opinion. More information than we could possibly refine and digest is already available in print, in libraries, daily newspapers, government reports – all freely available through the post. There is a misconception that more information will lead to better understanding. However, better quality information

leads to better understanding, but only if it is suitably analysed, digested, contextualised and critically assimilated. More does not necessarily equal better. Most of
the 'information' on the Internet is trivial, personal and local, and that of any consequence can also be found in print, often in extended formats. Sardar[155] refers to the
Internet as a 'grotesque soup of information', most of which is a deafening noise, half of
which is equivalent to graffiti on a toilet wall. Further, on-line Federal government
information that may be useful for forming political opinion (in the US at least) has
been made chargeable – what was freely available in print becomes privatised and
costly; for-profit vendors distribute government data and information.[156] Digital information that has commercial worth as well as public utility will be used as a commodity
in a market-place – it is not going to appear on the Net as public domain. The philosophy here is, why give away when you can sell?

A more realistic scenario is that rather than challenging convention the Internet will
at best serve to reproduce and reinforce existing political structures, and more likely (in
the short term at least) have negligible political effects. Teleconferencing, e-mail lobbying and a global database are not going to radically overhaul existing democratic
structures. This is not to say that there will be no effects. Cyberspatial interaction might
well lead to politicians becoming more immediately accountable through a process of
socialisation. At both the local and global scales, political enterprise may become more
issue led, with the Internet becoming a public forum in which to foster support and
maximise lobbying. This will probably be the Internet's political forte – political lobbying and political canvassing.

Cyberspace, with the exception of free-nets, PENs and academic networks, is increasingly becoming a private concern as it is taken over and run by transnational companies offering value-added services in highly regulated spaces. Fiscal realities mean that
there is no going back from this position. Obviously, this raises a whole series of important
questions relating to regulation, access, property rights, freedom of speech, privacy and
confidentiality. In the short term, at least, however, industry will find it difficult to deflect
the decentralised, open system momentum gained in recent years. As such, it seems to me
at least, that the most likely future is that resembling the telephone system, consisting of a
regulated, decentralised system where individuals have freedom of expression and statutory rights. Here, there will be a balance between private and public interests. Within this
scenario the potential threat of exclusion and marginalisation, and to privacy and confidentiality, is real, and a rigid, consistent set of statutory rights, protective laws and an
overseeing body need to be set in place to protect both consumer and creator rights. As
such, there will need to be a balance struck between market-led rules, formalised laws and
customary laws. At present, this balance is skewed towards market-led and customary
laws, with formalised laws being fashioned in an *ad hoc* manner as governments try to allow
cyberspace to expand and flourish without being stifled with excessive legal red tape.
However, cyberspace predominantly regulated through market forces raises a number of
other questions concerning access, privacy and deviancy.

At present, cyberspace is a restricted space. It is clear that cyberspace is not, at
present, an egalitarian space, open to all. In fact, cyberspace is accentuating social and

spatial divisions by creating information haves and have-nots to accompany fiscal differences. Given current social organisation this situation will not be easily solvable unless computer prices fall dramatically to the equivalent cost of a television. As such, we must work to ensure that access to this new space is guaranteed for all, rather than it becoming an elite space, accessible to the privileged few with the fiscal power to ensure access. Governments should therefore be encouraged to use public spaces such as libraries as open-access sites, and to provide affordable training and skills. The question concerning the exclusion of the developing world is trickier because of the complicating factors of much more pressing social and economic needs and the inherent Westernising tendencies of cyberspatial technologies.

There is no doubting that the rise in the surveillance society is real. Increasingly, our lives are captured through digital imprints stored in relational databases that can be sold and cross-referenced. In the main, we have no control over this information's use, and in many cases no knowledge of its existence. As a result, our private lives are becoming more public as niche market companies collect, store and sell our details. The implications of this are obviously disturbing, destroying our notion of privacy and confidentiality. However, there is a flip side to this view. Electronic storage and monitoring ensure that we receive the correct benefits, that our health is monitored more effectively, that we can shop more conveniently, that crime detection and protection are improved. Clearly, there are benefits and costs. However, there is no way around the need for surveillance and monitoring. Society would grind to a standstill without it. Our goal for the future must be to make sure that the benefits outweigh the costs by protecting the rights of citizens through effective data protection laws. Formalised laws, then, must accompany market-led rules and customary laws.

Although the arguments concerning the protection of the public from institutions and the State are becoming popular, arguments concerning the protection of the public from the public are more heated. Censorship and freedom of expression have long been contentious issues. As Shade pointed out, there has always been fear and moral consternation concerning new technologies. Cyberspace has been no exception, with commentators quick to seize upon its more deviant practices. There is no denying that cyberspace does provide a new deviant space, that there is overt racism and pornography on the Internet, that hotchatting is increasing in popularity, and that cybercrime is proliferating. However, many of the fears are over-inflated and blown out of all proportion by the popular press seeking headlines or by politicians and moral crusaders seeking votes and popularity. Freedom of expression is what attracts many people to cyberspace and while the 'innocent' do need to be protected we need to be careful of stifling and killing the life-blood of the system. How to proceed is a thorny question that has received heated debate from both the pro- and anti-censorship lobbies. Perhaps the best way forward is to let the system progress as it seems to be doing into a two-tier system, consisting of a largely unregulated, public space overlain by a highly regulated, value-added service provider space allowing access to certain sections and 'protecting' consumers. Admittedly, this system is tolerant of racism and sexual perversions but it also allows choice and protection. The unregulated space would be policed largely by customary law but would also be regulated by more formalised laws designed to police criminal behaviour such as money laundering and hard-core pornography.

Given these arguments, I think it is fair to argue that while cyberspace does raise a number of substantive issues relating to future politics and polity, in the main it will be reappropriated for the good as long as future developments are accompanied by efficient and effective laws that protect the rights of the consumer, accompanied by a satisfactory regulatory environment that monitors service providers. As such, the threat of a new wild-west frontier, with few laws, no protection and a general atmosphere of deviancy and crime, will be tamed, colonised and ordered, just like its historical predecessor. This will be largely through a process of market-led self-regulation accompanied by a set of more formalised laws. As noted throughout the chapter, a number of new laws concerning copyright, security and deviancy on-line have already been passed and it is likely that more will follow. However, we must endeavour to make sure that these laws are aimed at benefiting the consumer and not at further empowering private enterprise or governments.

CHAPTER 6

CYBERSPACE, THE INFORMATION ECONOMY AND URBAN–REGIONAL RESTRUCTURING

CHAPTER 6

CYBERSPACE, THE INFORMATION ECONOMY AND URBAN–REGIONAL RESTRUCTURING

Rooted in the communications technology of the electronic, one can say without doubt that the so-called New World Order will be digital.[1]

Thanks to technology, the world is going bonkers. And it's going to get more bonkers – bonkers squared in a few years with bonkers cubed on the way.[2]

The analysis and hype surrounding cyberspatial technologies have mainly focused on their social, cultural and political implications. It is hypothesised by some, however, that these technologies, in conjunction with other telecommunication media, also have far-reaching consequences concerning employment patterns, economic performance and urban–regional development. In particular, the intranet connections of transnational companies are significantly reshaping the economic and social landscape, accelerating recent trends such as globalisation, office automation, regional and suburban back-offices and the slow rise in telework. It is argued that these trends have led to significant organisational and employment restructuring and urban–regional reconfiguration as companies, cities and regions seek to gain competitive advantage. This chapter explores how cyberspatial technologies are changing the global economic landscape and restructuring urban–regional infrastructure. Cyberspatial technologies are prevalent in telematic (computer-based telecommunication) infrastructures, which consist of local area networks (LANs – site specific), metropolitan area networks (MANs – intra-urban) and wide area networks (WANs – inter-urban) consisting of dedicated international corporate networks (intranet) and public, global telecommunication networks (Internet), all capable of transmitting multimedia data (voice, image and text) through one medium.[3]

THE INFORMATION ECONOMY

As discussed in Chapter 3, to some, knowledge and information are in the process of replacing labour and capital as the central variables of the Western economy: the processes of production, consumption and management are becoming increasingly reliant on 'knowledge generation, information exchanges and information handling'.[4] In this new economy, information is digital-based, wired and decentralised, as opposed to the old economy where information was paper-based, centralised and isolated.[5] Digital-based information is gaining value, allowing businesses to reorganise and merge to form multi-functional, multi-product corporations spreading across all continents, and enabling the formation of increasingly competitive markets. Information has gained value due to the need for companies to increase productivity, reduce costs, be innovative and be forerunners within a market sector.[6] This has led some to suggest that information and communication technologies are forming the cornerstone of the new economy.[7] Not only that, but they are seen as fundamental 'agents of change' in the resulting restructuring of society, infrastructure and the economic landscape. Three interrelated aspects of structural change are highlighted:

- the growing contribution of information-related activities to wealth generation and employment;
- the increasing centrality of new information technology, as a form of capital, in management, production and consumption processes;
- higher levels of specialisation based upon the commodification of information, involving particularly the privatisation of public information and the externalisation of 'in house' information services.[8]

Such is the impact, that some commentators have drawn parallels that suggest that the telematic infrastructure currently being created will be as important for today's economy as the railways were for the age of industrialisation, and automobiles in the post-war boom,[9] forming the basis of the next long wave of economic development (fifth Kondratieff cycle).[10] Here, information is a commodity to be bought and sold, the basis of new emerging entertainment and service industries, and the foundation to maximise production and management of private enterprise. In this context, information and communication technologies alter the economy because they allow the swift transfer of information stored as digital media, and allow sites of production and consumption to become spatially and temporally fluid. The information economy is thus the embodiment of the 'mode of information', the economic basis of the 'information society', the cornerstone of the post-industrial world.

At the forefront of this emerging discussion has been a series of works proclaiming the arrival of an information economy, accompanied by a parallel information society. Almost universally utopian, these texts explore life in an information age. In particular, Alfin Toffler's[11] thesis has gained prominence. Toffler develops a model whereby society is seen to advance or progress through a series of technological 'waves'. The first 'wave' was the agricultural revolution, allowing increased agricultural production, stimulating economic growth and increasing the ability to support a larger population. The second 'wave' was the industrial revolution, leading to increased and more diversified production and consumption, and the development of both capitalist and democratic structures. The third 'wave' is the current, and is the 'information revolution'. This third 'wave' represents a shift from the industrial era to what Bell[12] terms the postindustrial era. Just as manufacturing replaced agriculture as the dominant economic basis of society in the shift from the first to the second wave, service industries are becoming the dominant basis of economies, replacing manufacturing. For Bell the postindustrial era characterised by the generation of knowledge as a source of productivity and growth, a shift from goods production to service delivery and growth in the importance of information-rich jobs such as managerial, professional and technical positions.

For Bell, at the centre of this shift to a postindustrial – or, as he later renamed it, information – society are the computer and telecommunication industries. These industries are providing the basis for rapid development, explicitly changing the economic and social landscape by accelerating the rise of information-intensive industries. These industries include banking, credit agencies, insurance, business and legal services, and government. At all levels within these sectors, managerial, professional and technical, information and communication technologies are becoming more pervasive.[13] This process is also occurring in other service sectors, such as retailing and manufacturing, where information is increasingly being used to gain competitive advantage and to streamline operations. This expansion and diversity of information-related occupations is illustrated by Hepworth's taxonomy of information employment (Table 6.1).

Governments have not been slow to pick up on the predicted benefits of an information economy. As noted in Chapter 2, one of the main goals of Clinton and Gore's NII

Table 6.1   Taxonomy of Information Occupations

Information producers	Information processors
Scientific and technical E.g. chemists and engineers	*Administrative and managerial* E.g. production managers and senior civil servants
Market search and coordination E.g. salesmen and buyers	*Process control and supervisory* E.g. factory foremen and officer supervisors
Information gatherers E.g. surveyors and quality inspectors	*Clerical and related* E.g. clerks and bank tellers
Consultative services E.g. accountants and lawyers	
Health-related consultative services E.g. doctors	
Information distributors	**Information infrastructure**
Educators E.g. teachers and university lecturers	*Information machine workers* E.g. computer operators and printing pressmen
Public information disseminators E.g librarians and archivists	*Postal and telecommunications* E.g. mail carriers and telegraph operators
Communication workers E.g. newspapers editors and television directors	

Source: Hepworth (1990)

initiative is to gain a competitive edge, thrusting the USA ahead as the global market leader in the information economy, creating new jobs and a new source of wealth. The European Union has also recently published its long-term strategy to develop a strong position in the information economy. The Bangemann report[14] proposed ten initiatives concerning possible applications and growth markets for new information technologies (Table 6.2).

The Bangemann proposals are fairly universal and give a good indication of how information and communication technologies are being, and could be, used within the emerging information economy. As Table 6.2 indicates, cyberspatial technologies are creating new commercial markets relating to teleworking, health care, administration, road traffic management and home life (city information highways are intended as a means for home-shopping, home-banking, interactive television, etc.), utilising high

Table 6.2 *Potential Applications of Telematic/Cyberspatial Technologies in the New Information Economy*

1.	Teleworking
2.	Distance learning
3.	Networks for universities and research centres
4.	Remote processing services for small businesses
5.	Road traffic management
6.	Air traffic control
7.	Health care networks
8.	Electronic tendering
9.	Trans-European administration network
10.	City information highways

Source: Bangemann Report (1994)

speed information processing and transfer of multimedia data. Other niche, commercial markets are emerging relating to Internet service providers, entertainment/leisure services, on-line marketing, advertising and design, and visual exploration (virtual reality).

There is no doubt that the type and range of individual services on the Internet are maturing fast and hold considerable economic promise. In general, these services can be divided into narrowband and broadband services.[15] Examples of narrowband services include electronic newspapers, electronic encyclopaedias, bulletin boards, utility metering, home banking, advertising and business data transfer. Examples of broadband services include videoconferencing, home shopping, video-on-demand, high definition television and medical services. It is assumed that, with time, new services will be added, and those currently offered improved, providing real choice and benefits to the consumer while forming the basis for an expanding industry of information compilers, service providers, telecommunication suppliers and personal computing producers and retailers.

The result of these government initiatives, the rapid adoption of telematic services and the expanding range of applications has been a fresh spate of utopian hype and predictions. For example, Makridakis[16] now predicts that the information age will have reached maturity by the year 2015. By this time, shopping, services, work, education and entertainment will all be conducted through information and communication technologies, and interfaced by the computer. Correspondingly, transnational companies will have evolved from the hierarchical organisations that they are today, to take on a new, flat, horizontal structure to fully capitalise on the globalising tendencies of cyberspatial connections.

Utopian writers such as Toffler and Makridakis all look to the (information) future with enthusiasm, imagining a world of super-abundance, contentment and social harmony. In this new future, the problems of today such as war, famine and oppression will have been eliminated. This has led Martin[17] to predict a time of better health, education and entertainment, improved communications and information supply, and cleaner and more efficient industry. As Stonier[18] preaches:

> for the first time in history, the rate at which we solve problems will exceed the rate at which they appear. This will leave us to get on with the real business of the next century. To take care of each other. To fathom what it means to be human. To explore intelligence. To move out into space.

As Robins and Webster[19] point out, many of these utopian writers are under no illusions as to the state of the world today and a decade ago when many of these predictions were first forecast. Although they seem blinkered and selective, writers such as Toffler are fully aware of the poverty, war and oppression that many people face daily (although Stonier is under the impression that the 'industrial economy eliminated slavery, famine and pestilence'[20]). However, their belief is that, such is the potential magnitude of the coming (computer) technologies, these problems will be cast aside as we progress forward in a giant social and economic leap. Those that suggest other less favourable futures are roundly regarded as 'luddites', 'future haters' and 'technophobic', halting and even potentially jeopardising future prosperity and survival by querying the unquestioning adoption of advanced, computer technologies.[21]

In general, however, although there have undoubtedly been massive changes in the global economy and organisation brought about by information and communication technologies, much of the early promise as prophesied by utopian visionaries such as Toffler and Naisbett[22] has not materialised. This is not to say that there has been no shift to an economy ever more reliant on information, but rather that while this shift has been rapid in historical terms, it has been much slower than first predicted. Kumar explains that recent postindustrial theory has come to appreciate that Toffler's utopian, postindustrial society is currently unrealistic.[23] If the predictions of analysts from the 1970s had been correct we would be living in a time of intelligent computers capable of understanding and speaking fluently natural languages, able to understand speech and read handwriting easily, and be surrounded by intelligent robots and smart environments. While these advances are undoubtedly on their way, their mass-market arrival does not seem imminent. Computer power may have increased considerably and prices have dropped dramatically but computers by and large are still mainly used for record keeping, word processing and data processing.[24] Moreover, the utopian lifestyle to accompany these changes seems ever more distant as social and spatial divisions continue to deepen. However, recent postindustrialists are still insistent that Western industrialised societies have crossed the divide into a new postindustrial era. They suggest that, despite setbacks, the information society has been ushered in.

To illustrate the growing importance of information and cyberspatial/telematic technologies within this new society, analysts point to a number of recent trends, namely the globalising of trade and culture, changing working practices with the rise in office automation, back-offices and the growth of teleworking, and the growing appreciation of the competitive advantage to be gained by employing information and communication technologies. These trends, they argue, have led to wholesale organisational and employment restructuring and urban–regional reconfiguration in developed countries and in an increasing number of developing nations.

RECENT TRENDS

GLOBALISATION OF TRADE

For many, since the 1970s the world has been involved in a vast restructuring process of the capitalist base that underlies and constitutes much of the world's social system. The emergence of new informational technologies is seen to be at the heart of this restructuring, leading to a new mode of sociotechnical organization, which Castells terms the 'informational mode of development'. He characterises this mode as the action of knowledge upon knowledge as the main source of productivity. Accompanied by deregulatory changes, which introduced new competition, investment, a desire to expand to capture a larger market share and a series of significant technological advances,[25] cyberspatial technologies are seen to be facilitating the internationalisation of production (worldwide integration of production, warehousing, finance and marketing),[26] international networking, cross-cultural contacts, the internationalisation of financial markets, and increased international cooperation, joint ventures, strategic alliances and mergers.[27] Such a system is global because the core activities, production, consumption and circulation, and their components are now organised at the global scale, and traditional economic policies that work within the confines of political boundaries are increasingly becoming ineffectual.[28] Informational technologies are thus leading to a new socioeconomic–technical matrix that is transforming the old industrial economy and leading to a new urban–regional complex as the global economic landscape is resculpted. This has led Langdale to argue that without adequate information flows the new global economy will fail to operate effectively.[29] As such, a telematic infrastructure is vital. The rate and extent of globalisation is illustrated by this passage from Luke:

> ordinary consumers and workers in America depend upon oil lifted in Saudi Arabia, fast food from Canadian-owned franchise operations, credit cards from Hong Kong owned banks, automobiles built in Mexico by Japanese firms transplanting their

output as American cars, groceries produced in Central America, South Africa or South East Asia sold in British owned store chains, newspapers held by Australian multinationals but publishing in New York, televisions fabricated in Taiwan by American companies to show programs made in British Columbia by Japanese owned studios headquartered in Los Angeles, and information gathered by British wire services in Eastern Europe for broadcast on 24-hour cable news networks centered in Atlanta. [. . .] these zones of production and consumption [are] becoming far more centered in global flows than national space.[30]

As discussed in Chapter 1, it is the collapsing of space and time through instantaneous communications that is seen as fundamental for rapid, corporate globalisation.[31] Here, informational technologies are being used to increase the scale of production, as driven by the logic of accumulation, and to increase the scale of consumption, as driven by the logic of commodification.[32] Castells characterises this as shift from a 'space of places' to a 'space of flows', where a specific locale is not vital to fulfil a corporation's goals. Here:

> The new industrial space and the new service economy organize their operations around the dynamics of their information-generating units, while connecting their different functions to disparate space assigned to each task to be performed; the overall process is then reintegrated through communications systems.[33]

In other words, transnational companies take on a new, greater power through the effective management of their structure, using information transfer to gain competitive advantage over smaller operations. Rather than a company having a series of largely autonomous sites/plants serving a specific region, these operations can be effectively linked to form one giant system incorporating R&D, marketing, finance, production, and coordination of distribution – although material goods, because of prohibitive transport costs, remain largely regional. For example, IBM products are designed, marketed and sold on a worldwide basis, heavily relying on a comprehensive, integrated intranet system to integrate information from several, global sites concerned with manufacture, R&D, sales, ordering, scheduling and distribution.[34] These networks can be large and complex. For example, by 1988 Citicorp, one of the world's largest banks, had developed a hierarchical intranet network connecting 145 cities in 74 countries, allowing it to trade $200 billion daily in foreign exchange markets.[35] To illustrate this, Figure 6.1 displays the corporate network of Hewlett-Packard and the various links between different operations at several global sites. Obviously, this global integration has benefits for companies, reducing duplication, streamlining operations, decreasing uncertainty and lowering marginal costs.[36] As a result, Myers reports that the top 500 transnational companies now generate 30% of gross global product, 70% of global trade and 80% of international investment flows.[37] Within this networked system Castells[38] reports that labour is not becoming globally mobile but rather that labour is becoming a global resource and is becoming increasingly interdependent. Explicitly tied into this process of globalisation is the trend towards office automation and the shift to distributed, back-office operations.

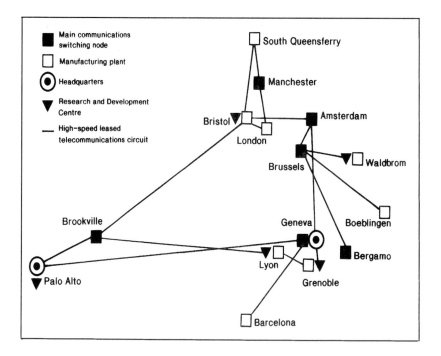

Figure 6.1 *Hewlett Packard's telematic network. Source: Based on Graham and Marvin (1996)*

OFFICE AUTOMATION AND BACK-OFFICES

In recent years there has been an increasing trend in office automation as manual office work is replaced by automated computer processing operations. Such a process of automation, accompanied by the ability to transmit and receive digital information, has led to the growth in back-office operations as companies use the Internet, and in particular intranets, to increase their global productivity. Here, documents and files are shipped around the world to take advantage of a global, 24-hour workforce. Tele-defined businesses such as consumer service centres, telephone operators, telemarketing and market research, and tele-transacted businesses, such as airline reservations, banking, insurance and administration, have all been quick to explore the possibilities of decentralisation to back-offices.[39] For example, Ireland offers highly skilled, English-language data processing for American and European firms, which send the files at the end of the day and then receive back the updated files when they log on the next morning. In particular, the Irish have been keen to attract back-office work involving skilled processing for financial services, publishing, data processing and software development.[40] One American company employs 600 workers in Shannon, who are connected via a leased AT&T satellite link to its mainframe in Colorado. Similarly, a

New York life insurance company flies in overnight claims from its policy holders for 50 employees in Ireland to process and return the same working day via satellite.[41] Other companies use dedicated phone lines. For example, Mitsubishi offices in Tokyo, London and New York are connected by dedicated leased ISDN connections, and ICI has a similar network spanning 15 European countries.[42]

Lower-skilled clerical and data-entry work, involving the processing and digitising of vast amounts of documentation, is being farmed out to offshore, back-offices in places such as Southeast Asia, the Indian subcontinent and the Caribbean. For example, British Airways bookings are processed in India, and American Airlines in Barbados. The benefits to transnational companies can be significant. For example, Graham and Marvin report that wages are typically 20% of those in the West, staff turnover levels are extremely low, at 1–2%, thus reducing training costs (turnover 35% in North America), and military-type discipline ensures very high levels of accuracy. While there may be significant benefits to corporations, political agencies such as the European Union warn of the potential dangers of farming out such information economy jobs, namely losing employment from home countries and creating an economy dependent on outside interests.[43] In a time when delivery times cannot be used as a competitive argument, they are worried that Europe, which will become increasingly dependent on information industries, will fall behind in the global economy unless it acts now to secure its future.

Similarly to back-offices, the world financial corporations are now using offshore banking operations to maximise profits by exploiting the favourable tax laws in certain areas of the world. As a response, these areas are actively creating new local economies to take advantage of new trade. However, because of the mobility of capital and its increasing separation from employment, offshore banking actually yields very little to the nations in which it occurs (although attendant services industries may). For example, the Cayman Islands, the world's fifth largest banking centre in terms of gross assets, houses 538 foreign banks which employ only 1000 people.[44]

Teleworking, Telecottages and Teleports

In addition to back-offices, the potential decentralisation associated with telecommunication and cyberspatial technologies has led many to explore the possibilities of widespread teleworking. Teleworking refers to the home use of telecommunication services, allowing employees the ability to conduct their everyday working practices from their home, rather than having to commute to a place of work. As such, a teleworker spends a disproportionate amount of time working away from the location of the employer. Teleworking has been a consistent feature of many futurists' predictions over the past twenty years and featured prominently in Toffler's oft-quoted *Third Wave*. The ideas of teleworking can initially be traced back to the early 1970s and the energy crisis, with commentators such as Nilles and Harkness calculating how many barrels of oil could be saved by commuters working from home.[45] The concept also found support from more liberal, reversionist groups preaching a back-to-basics ethic, and decentralised small workplaces linked by telecommunications. Within both visions it is assumed that the worker has the freedom to choose where and whether to work, and also has the necessary skills to be able to work at home. By the 1980s telework was being promoted as a way to allow women into the workforce while still being able to run the family home (a concept that, not unsurprisingly, annoyed many feminists, who already saw women as tied to the home).

Although becoming more popular, so far teleworking has largely not fulfilled the forecasters' predictions (one writer laments that there seem to be more people writing about telework than there are teleworkers![46]), leading Huws to suspect that it 'has acquired a symbolic importance quite out of proportion to its actual prevalence'.[47] To her, the seduction of telecommuting is powerful. It promises the ability to work at a distance from the employer in the comfort of the home, juxtaposing the skyscraper against the cottage, crowded office against home tranquillity, clogged up roads and bustling commuter train against clean and quick telecommunications, expensive travel and time against no travel and saved time. Although figures are extremely difficult to predict accurately, estimates put the current number of teleworkers in the European Union at between 1.25 million (0.8% of the labour force) and 4.6 million (2.8% of the labour force).[48] Future predictions deviate more widely. For example, the US Department of Transport estimates that between 5.2% and 10.4% of the US labour force will be teleworking by the year 2002.[49]

In the main, telework has been forwarded as a positive outcome of the new 'information society', allowing great flexibility to both the worker and the company. For example, a Telecom Australia study of 31 teleworkers found that this group were generally more productive (18%), were happier and healthier, felt more self-reliant and in control of their own lives, but used the phone more to counter missing social interaction.[50] However, several commentators have suggested that any positive effects are counterbalanced by the negative effects of isolation, insecurity, the blurring of the site of leisure with the site of work, the breakdown of worker cohesion and the threat to trade unions. Surveyors of those homeworking during the early 1980s revealed that many teleworkers were underpaid and lacked the benefits of working on site. It is suggested that this polarisation of happier, healthier employees and underpaid, isolated employees largely mirrors the social divisions between telework employees. Teleworkers can be divided into two groups of workers. First, there are the well-educated professionals, with often satisfying and demanding jobs that frequently require entrepreneurial and specialised skills. Second, there are less well-educated workers performing generally less rewarding roles, in the form of low-level, menial tasks like typing or data entry.[51] Weijers *et al.* summarise the costs and benefits as outlined by both employers and employees in a qualitative study in Table 6.3.

Looking at Table 6.3, there clearly needs to be a balance found between the costs and benefits to both employee and employer if telework is going to become a success. Evidence from a Xerox study suggests that there are six features of work organisation necessary to the successful implementation of telework. These are that work organisation should be adaptive rather than rigid; it must have consistently lower overhead

Table 6.3   Costs and Benefits of Teleworking

Costs and benefits for the employer

	Costs	Benefits
1. Mentioned most	Extra equipment Lack of company involvement	Flexibility Productivity More service Less turnover
2. Mentioned often	Training guidance of personnel Adaptation of the organization	Organisation can be contacted Easier/non-office hours Less sick leave
3. Mentioned sometimes	Loss of informal communication	More motivated personnel

Costs and benefits for the employee

	Costs	Benefits
1. Mentioned most	Isolation Insecurity about work and income Furnishing workplace	Flexibility Autonomy Combination with family
2. Mentioned often	Deterioration of labour conditions Less career opportunities	Productivity More possibility to get or keep job
3. Mentioned sometimes	Mixing work and family responsibilities	Less travelling time and costs

---

Source: Weijers *et al.* (1992)

costs; it must enhance individual contributions; it must enhance creativity; it must involve people; and it must motivate the production of quality work.[52] If any of these qualities are missing then telework becomes less viable. Similarly, Weijers *et al.* suggest that benefits accrue to both employee and employer, at the macro and micro scales, so long as the adoption is voluntary rather than forced.[53] To balance the pluses and negatives, a flexible pattern of work could be adopted whereby employees split their time between the office and home. This seems to be the pattern emerging. To explore the possibilities of telework further, the European Union has recently set up pilot teleworking centres in 20 cities, involving at least 20 000 workers. They estimate that by the year 2000, 10 million telework jobs will have been created.[54] The estimates of the total number of jobs that could be carried out via telework are far higher. For example, Weijers *et al.* suggest that a telework post is characterised by part of the work consisting of information processing, part of the work measurable by output, part of the work not dependent on face to face or physical contact, and that the job consists of at least 20% of working time at home. Using these criteria, they suggest that between 1.2 and 1.8 million jobs in the Netherlands alone could be carried out through telework – that is, 37% of all jobs. Handy and Mokhtarian warn, however, that teleworking will not significantly increase without government intervention and awareness initiatives.[55] Government needs to provide examples of successful schemes, support funding and provide education opportunities.

A related idea to telework is the telecottage. These have been promoted as community ventures to link (often isolated) communities into the 'information superhighway', and to provide a training base for IT skills and a place from which to telework. Here, the cost of equipment can be shared, along with expertise and advice. Such a scheme provides a common base, separated from home but nearer than the company office. Telecottage projects are growing in popularity, especially in rural, unemployment blackspots, where they are seen as a potential way to boost the local economy. For example, in the UK, telecottage numbers have risen from 5 in 1989 to 140 in 1995, with nearly all of these situated in rural areas.[56] A related concept, the electronic village hall (EVH), providing community-based information and communication technologies to remote rural locations and inner-city community groups, have also been developed.[57] EVHs were originally developed in Scandinavia and were seen as a potential way to overcome problems of rural isolation. In inner-city areas, such as Manchester, UK, EVHs are seen as a way to develop and strengthen community links. In both cases, EVHs were seen as a way to promote cyberdemocracy at the same time as trying to help modernise the local economy by providing a low-cost and low-risk means of learning about and applying telematic technologies.

A more sophisticated, urban equivalent to the telecottage, and one aimed more towards small to medium-sized companies, is the teleport. The teleport is essentially a high-tech office park offering advanced telecommunications links via satellite and fibre optic connections.[58] By centralising the facilities, teleports provide significant economies of scale to small users who cannot afford private intranet connections by sharing the relatively high fixed costs of technology. Such teleports are seen as the new 'harbour depots' of the information age, performing the same role as harbours in the age of shipping. As such, they provide their users and the host area with a competitive, economic advantage over other places. As a result, teleport projects are appearing in many countries, including some developing nations (e.g. Jamaica, Nigeria) seeking to secure themselves a niche in the global information service economy,[59] for example, to capitalise upon backwater services.

COMPETITIVE ADVANTAGE

One of the main reasons for companies adopting information and communication technologies is to try to gain a competitive advantage.[60] Companies can achieve this through seven different means, by using these technologies:

1. to try to increase productivity, reliability and to reduce costs through employment and organisational restructuring and streamlining operations.
2. to process customer orders and to make a company more responsive to customer needs through rapid communication of needed information, on-line stock guides and after-sales advice and support.[61] There is a growing on-line commercial

market and many companies are now seeking ways to sell their wares direct to the customer via the Internet using encryption keys to protect credit transfers.

3 using the medium as a new space for advertising and marketing, and to create a new public image through the use of value-added services (for example, Fed Ex now allows customers to trace their packages through their journey via the Web[62] and Guinness has created what Barratt calls a 'smartvert' – a screensaver based upon its most successful advert, which can be downloaded over the web, creating a 'legitimacy of presence' on the user's PC).

4 to foster new collaborations, strengthen existing strategic partnerships and increase the efficiency of business relations and communications between partners.[63]

5 as a means of developing competitive intelligence, that is, legally studying a competitor's products, organisations, performance, prices and market strategies, and also studying the market in general and keeping aware of advances, movements and gossip within an industrial sector, and scanning for other useful information such as useful free software, in order to determine ways to outperform competitors.[64]

6 to monitor customer reaction to products and to assess the risks associated with new product ideas.

7 many companies feel they will benefit indirectly through a better-motivated, more flexible and better-informed workforce.[65]

These factors have been summed, for use of the Internet, by Cronin *et al.* in Table 6.4. These benefits can apply across the whole company, improving the corporate value chain, from external suppliers to internal workings to external customer relations (Figure 6.2).

Table 6.4 Key Competitive Advantages to Using the Internet

Indirect advertising	Greater corporate exposure
Informal know-how trading	Accelerated corporate communications
Client prospecting	
Competitor tracking/eavesdropping	Economies of scope
Rapid feedback from customers	Current awareness
Improved responsiveness to customers	Access to distributed expertise
	Passive benchmarking
Access to government data sets	Image enhancement

Source: Cronin *et al.* (1994)

However, the adoption of cyberspatial technologies is not always because of the progressive nature of a company. The overwhelming reason for adoption by companies in the Dabinett and Graham[66] study was 'we had to' in order to fulfil market conditions (e.g. competitiveness, cost, quality, productivity) and shifting cultural expectations

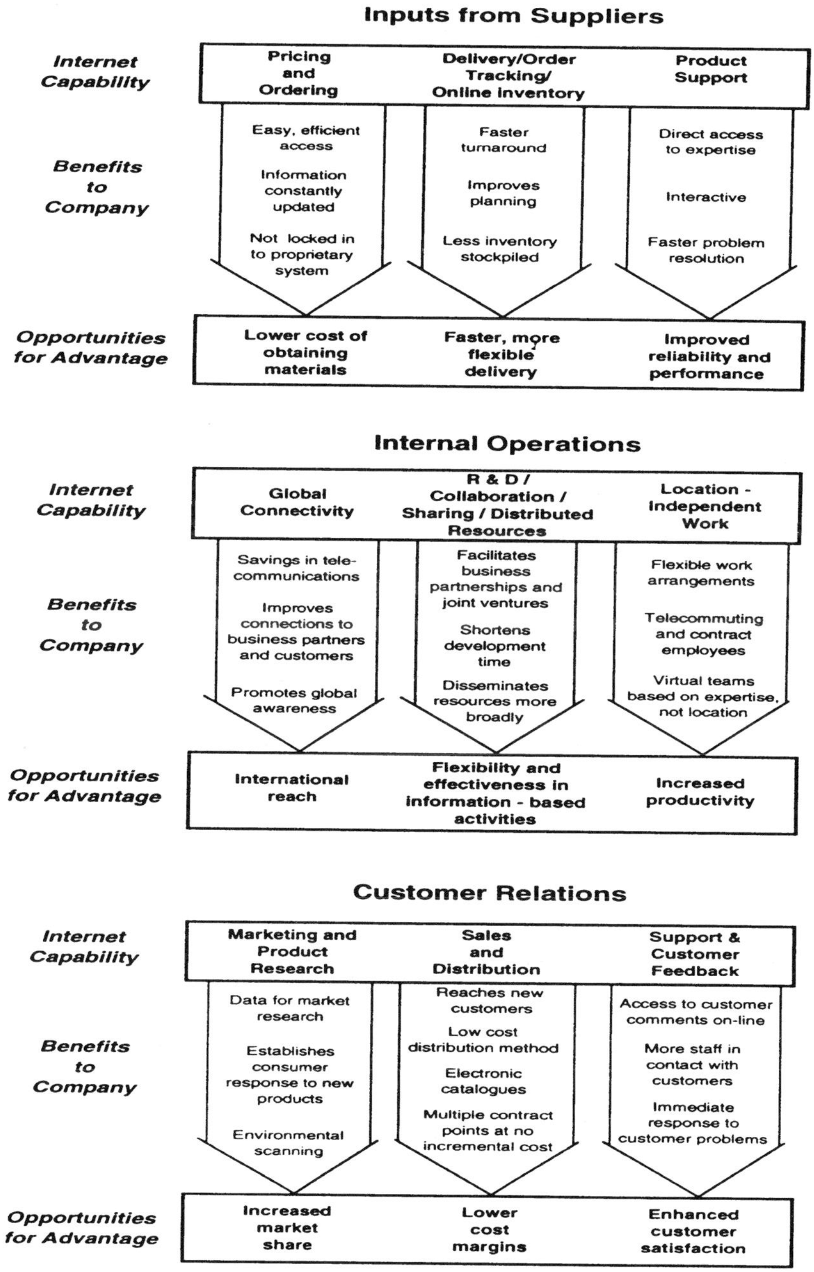

Inputs from Suppliers

Internet Capability	Pricing and Ordering	Delivery/Order Tracking/ Online inventory	Product Support
Benefits to Company	Easy, efficient access / Information constantly updated / Not locked in to proprietary system	Faster turnaround / Improves planning / Less inventory stockpiled	Direct access to expertise / Interactive / Faster problem resolution
Opportunities for Advantage	Lower cost of obtaining materials	Faster, more flexible delivery	Improved reliability and performance

Internal Operations

Internet Capability	Global Connectivity	R & D / Collaboration / Sharing / Distributed Resources	Location - Independent Work
Benefits to Company	Savings in tele-communications / Improves connections to business partners and customers / Promotes global awareness	Facilitates business partnerships and joint ventures / Shortens development time / Disseminates resources more broadly	Flexible work arrangements / Telecommuting and contract employees / Virtual teams based on expertise, not location
Opportunities for Advantage	International reach	Flexibility and effectiveness in information - based activities	Increased productivity

Customer Relations

Internet Capability	Marketing and Product Research	Sales and Distribution	Support & Customer Feedback
Benefits to Company	Data for market research / Establishes consumer response to new products / Environmental scanning	Reaches new customers / Low cost distribution method / Electronic catalogues / Multiple contract points at no incremental cost	Access to customer comments on-line / More staff in contact with customers / Immediate response to customer problems
Opportunities for Advantage	Increased market share	Lower cost margins	Enhanced customer satisfaction

Figure 6.2   Internet Value Chain. Source: Cronin (1994)

(e.g. technology excellence). Many companies, it seems, are still suspicious of computer technology, seeing Internet access as a threat to security, and the use of e-mail and other Internet services as a drain on productivity by providing a distraction that is not easily monitored.[67] In particular, smaller and medium-sized businesses are prone to doubting the relevance of cyberspatial technologies to them. Contrary to popular opinion, it seems that in many cases the move towards information and communication technologies has been reluctant and forced.

THE CHANGING ECONOMIC AND URBAN LANDSCAPE

ORGANISATIONAL AND EMPLOYMENT RESTRUCTURING

These trends, combined together, have led to significant effects upon organisational and employment structures. Clearly, the role of information handling and exchange has grown significantly. For example, Johnston estimates that 50% of all jobs in Europe are in information-based services and 80% of all new jobs are in this sector.[68] However, the relationship between information/communication technologies and employment is complex, with arguments concerning quantity (automation reducing the number of jobs) and quality (automation leading to the deskilling of workers/automation providing greater autonomy in decision making and the gaining of more generic skills) of jobs. Castells[69] further notes that within different countries occupational restructuring differs substantially. While countries such as the US, the UK and Italy have undergone a rapid process of de-industrialisation since the 1970s; in contrast, Japan and Germany have managed to retain much of their manufacturing base. Canada and France occupy a middle ground. As such, there is a complex interplay between global processes and national initiatives, which is leading to a variety of outcomes. He concludes that within Western nations there is a general shift away from manufacturing but this is manifesting itself in two different forms. In the first, there is a rapid phasing out of manufacturing coupled by rapid expansion in service industries. In the second, there is a general maintenance of manufacturing with new growth largely confined to the service sector. He thus proposes two informational models. The first, is the Service Economy Model, represented by the US and UK. The second is the Industrial Production Model, represented by Japan and Germany.

It is clear that information technologies are, regardless of the model, leading to corporate streamlining and changes within the occupational structure. This is because cyberspatial technologies help to provide a new range of opportunities to companies. Castells[70] reports that companies can:

1 downsize the firm, keeping the indispensable highly skilled labour force in Western, developed nations and importing inputs from low cost areas; or,

2 subcontract part of the work to their transnational establishments and to the auxiliary networks whose production can be internalised in the network enterprise system; or,

3 use temporary labour, part-time workers, or informal firms as suppliers in the home country; or,

4 automate or relocate tasks and functions for which the standard labour market prices are considered too high vis-à-vis alternative formulae; or,

5 obtain from their labour force, including the core labour force, acquiescence to more stringent conditions of work and pay as a condition for the continuation of their jobs, thus reversing social contracts established under circumstances more favourable for labour.

All of these strategies have been utilised to restructure the workforce. However, the extent of changes across countries is variable. Within countries such as the US and the UK there have been large-scale redundancies within certain industries. Whereas automation in the factories displaced shop-floor workers, information technology has led to the wide-scale displacement of skilled clerical workers and middle-level managers. Between 1980 and 1993, the 500 largest transnational corporations in the US shed some 4.4 million jobs,[71] many of which were professional and technical posts. In only a few cases has labour restructuring within these companies been offset by job creation through higher demand for an improved, cheaper service/product. Contrary to many people's fears, however, communication and information technologies are having a negligible effect on aggregate levels of unemployment.[72] Rather, they are fostering productivity and economic growth, and expanding employment outside of the high-tech, information industries. Unfortunately, as a result, although there is some growth in highly skilled professional, engineering and technical employment, the overwhelming growth is in low-skilled, low-paid, part-time, casual and menial employment. For example, Kumar reports that 13 million jobs were created in the USA between 1973 and 1980, 70% of which were low-level posts in the service and retail sectors, predominantly part-time or temporary and occupied by women.[73] Consequently, these technologies are helping to foster an increasingly skewed and polarised occupational structure that is becoming common across Western nations. Castells[74] suggests that the new model of employment structure is a core labour force formed by the information workers supported by a more flexible, disposable labour force that can be hired and fired depending upon market demand and costs.

Within the remaining transnational workforce, it is predicted that this wholesale removal of one level of the corporate structure will be accompanied by one of two scenarios. In the first instance, Robins and Webster foresee a Taylorist process of automation, leading to white-collar *de-skilling*.[75] Here, professionals and highly skilled technicians such as architects, bank managers, print typesetters are having their work 'simplified' and made 'easier' as computer programs do all the mental calculations and even decide and implement the best course of action. This in turn will lead to a company with a skewed, hour-glass shaped workforce with a few executives at the top, no middle management and a wide base of clerks and operatives at the bottom.[76]

In contrast to this position, some suggest that with the growing amount of internal and external information to be processed, traditional hierarchical structures will not be able to cope. As a result, it is increasingly expected that staff across the company will become *more skilled*, with powers to synthesise, act upon new information and make low-level decisions, rather than all material being channelled up the management-hierarchical structure.[77] This, it is argued, will lead to power being more evenly distributed across the workforce, as employees become more mobile and companies take on 'adhocracy' rather than hierarchical structures in an effort to speed up 'information metabolism'.[78] Naisbett originally predicted such a vertical and horizontal integration and flattening of a corporation's structure:

> The computer will smash the pyramid: we created the hierarchical, pyramidal, managerial system because we needed it to keep track of people and things people did; with the computer to keep track, we can restructure our institutions horizontally.[79]

However, such a situation is also likely to lead to a polarisation of office work, with relatively unskilled, low-educated data entry clerks at one end (being replaced by automation), and the remaining workforce diversifying in skills and responsibilities (i.e. a football-shaped workforce). For example, bank clerks are largely being replaced by ATMs and telebanking and those remaining are being retrained to selling services, thus upgrading the skills of a smaller number of employees.[80] This employment restructuring has also led to massive infrastructure changes (see next section). In particular, with the shift to automation and telebanking, financial institutions have drastically reduced the number of high street shops, leading to massive job losses. For example, First Direct the telebanking subsidiary of the UK's Midlands Bank, has directly led to 750 high street bank closures and job losses totalling 15 000.[81]

Banking, finance and insurance industries provide good examples of how information technologies are instrumental in altering employment structures. Many of the tasks that use to be carried out by hand have now been computerised. The role of employees has largely changed from implementing a task to monitoring a computer as it performs the task. The role of data entry clerks is also changing as customers are increasingly encouraged to input their own information into the system (e.g. ATMs and automatic telephone systems). No doubt this process of change will increase as the shift towards self-digitisation of forms for postage across the Internet continues, feeding details directly into corporate systems. Automation is also starting to penetrate decision making. Nowhere is this more noticeable than in the stock market, where rather than to save labour, computers are employed to save time, where seconds might mean millions of dollars lost or gained. For some transactions, however, the role of face-to-face contact has not greatly diminished due to the trust relationships developed.[82]

To Castells, then, information technologies and telecommunications are altering the dynamics of office work, allowing greater interconnectivity and complexity of activities whilst being extremely flexible. As such, markets, businesses and organisations that were once separate can merge and the bureaucratic inefficiencies that once limited corporations can be overcome. This, he argues, is producing four new trends in corporate structure: the growing dominance of the large transnational corporation; the decentralisation of management; the subcontracting of operations to smaller companies; and advanced networking linking the elements together. The result is a complex,

hierarchical, diversified organisation, allowing companies to react faster to new situations and to try to gain a competitive advantage over their rivals, improving productivity
by considerably reducing working time per unit of output.[83]

URBAN–REGIONAL RESTRUCTURING

> Modern . . . cities face a 'communications landscape' which is restructuring as rapidly
> as at any time in urban history. Radical technological convergence between pre-
> viously separate areas of telecommunications, broadcasting and computing – to create
> 'telematic' networks and services – is being paralleled by new methods of regulation
> and new types of regulation and new types of national policy regimes. At the same
> time, the urban economic fabric is being re-woven, becoming ever-more dependent
> on telecommunications-rich sectors and activities. This complex and multifaceted
> process of change has profound implications for . . . cities, presenting both threats and
> opportunities to cities and urban policy makers.[84]

There is little doubt among analysts that processes of globalisation, and employment
and organisational restructuring, in part caused by information and communication
technologies, are instrumental in the current restructuring of urban–regional fabric.
Cities were designed as places whose function was to overcome time with space, making communications easier. However, the growth of telecommunications to a certain
extent nullifies this function by making communications easier through the overcoming
of space with time.[85] As such, there is a juxtaposition between urban places and their
electronic counterparts (Table 6.5), which has led several commentators to speculate
that these new, electronic spaces and flows will displace or substitute physical travel
and physical urban functions, and lead to the dematerialisation of the city.

However, as we have seen, telework has yet to replace physical travel. Similarly,
although communication and information technologies are undoubtedly leading to the
physical restructuring of the city, there is little sign that the city is fast dematerialising.
This is because space and time, two traditional constraints to accumulation and

Table 6.5   Urban Places, Electronic Urban Spaces

Urban places (buildings, streets, roads and physical spaces of cities)	Urban electronic spaces (constructed 'inside' telematic networks using computer software)
Territory	Network
Fixity	Motion/Flux
Embedded	Disembedded
Material	Immaterial
Visible	Invisible
Tangible	Intangible
Actual	Virtual/abstract
Euclidean/social space	Logical space

Source: Graham and Marvin (1996)

commodification, have not been fully removed. As such, space–time compression has not led to mass decentralisation. For example, most cities are still expanding, with large building and transport schemes, worsening chronic congestion, gentrification and expanding suburbs. In addition, information flows are not going to be able to provide a substitute for the distribution and collection of material goods and supplies, and the fundamental needs for other infrastructure such as sewerage, oil and gas. There is, however, preliminary evidence to suggest that energy consumption is dropping with the growth in the service sector and that infrastructural development is dropping from the levels at the height of the manufacturing era.[86]

The lure of the benefits from dematerialisation is, however, strong with commentators suggesting that the shift to an information economy could lead to immense savings in terms of time, infrastructure costs and energy consumption, and ultimately to the dissolution of the city. For example, a recent report found that if 10–20% of transportation in the USA could be transferred to telecommuting, teleworking, teleshopping, teleconferencing and electronic document exchange, the daily drive for 6 million commuters, 3 billion shopping trips, 13 million business trips and 600 million truck and airline delivery miles per year could be eliminated.[87] The devastating effects this will have upon local retail trade, transport industries and the people who rely on and work for them is little considered. Moreover, the fact that throughout history physical transportation has always mirrored the growth in communications has been overlooked. It seems that, just like building more roads, reducing travel times just leads to increased use but for different purposes.[88] Further, telematic and other urban infrastructures are becoming mutually interdependent. As a result, city dissolution and dematerialisation is for the foreseeable future likely to be negligible because, as we will see, information and communication technologies are actually reinforcing city life and urban hierarchies through restructuring:

> Telecommunications are not able to simply compress space and time constraints evenly in every location. Geography is still important, not least because telecommunications are unevenly developed and physical transportation is still extremely important for the distribution of people, goods and services. This means that there is still friction in spatial and temporal terms which places important limits on the levels of decentralisation and dispersal away from cities.[89]

At one level organisational restructuring is affecting patterns of investment and development by companies between metropolitan areas. Here, it is argued that telematics are, on the one hand, leading to *centralisation* within large urban areas with affordable, well-developed computer and telecommunications infrastructure. On the other hand, it is contended that telematics are leading to *decentralisation*, as instantaneous, multimedia communications mean that companies can locate in cheaper areas with a suitably skilled workforce, or even transfer routine clerical work electronically to overseas back-offices to create a global, 24-hour office. At another level, employment restructuring, in part caused by information technologies, is leading to *polarisation* of districts within metropolitan areas with the emergence of the 'information haves' and 'information deprived'.

What we are effectively witnessing is the playing out of corporate trade-offs between urban fixity and electronic mobility. It is apparent that rather than the processes which underlie city development being destroyed, electronic spaces are just altering patterns of urban development, and a city's relationship with its surrounding region and other cities.[90]

As such, organisational restructuring suggests that far from the utopian visions of completely footloose industries, electronic cottages and the death of the city, communication technologies are, at one level, actually reinforcing, and in some cases increasing, the role of major business centres.[91] In fact, the world has only become a 'smaller' place for those places that have attracted a disproportionate share of global information and communication services.[92] As such, geography is still of importance and, as we will see, becoming increasingly so. For example, Alles *et al.*[93] report that urban systems are increasingly being dominated by cities that have greater telecommunication infrastructure. Rather than there being a lessening of the pronounced differences between higher order and lower order cities, with a filtering down of economic and social benefits, the differences between 'core' and 'peripheral' cities are becoming more pronounced.[94] This centralisation occurs because if corporations are to take advantage of the global reach of communication technologies they must locate their command and control centres in areas with a suitable infrastructure, at affordable costs. As such, a recursive relationship has developed between the communications industry and the information industries: the communications industry is attracted to the information industries as a source of business, leading to greater density and range of services; as a result, the information industries are, in turn, attracted by the availability of cheap, efficient communication technologies. This process of centralisation is compounded further by:

> [information and communication industries'] nodal positions on global transport (especially airline) networks, their concentrations of a wide range of services, their social and cultural milieux for global business, their locational prestige, their size as centres of property investment, the flexibility that derives from their highly skilled and large labour markets, and the versatility that comes from many possible suppliers and clients within these cities.[95]

Existing structures have been further reinforced by the process of market deregulation, allowing telecommunication companies to create their own strategies of development. Naturally, many chose to target those areas with the highest number of potential customers (e.g. large cities) in order to increase profitability. For example, when the UK telecommunications markets were deregulated, Mercury, the new, second operator, concentrated its efforts on gaining business in London, from where 90% of its initial profits came, and other major UK cities.[96] In addition, the main backbone connections link these major metropolitan areas as the dominant nodes within an emerging hierarchy. Thus, these areas gain competitive advantage through superior international linkages. This hierarchy is perpetuated in the city itself as telecommunication providers favour larger, more lucrative enterprises. As such, deregulation has had significant impacts upon the organisation and the spatial structure of the telecommunication industry,[97] changing the face of the 'communication landscape' (see Table 6.6). Moreover, this centralisation is reinforced because many companies are reluctant to give up the close proximity that fosters social and business connections, supplying tacit information considered vital in some industries, notably the finance sector.

Table 6.6   The Changing 'Communication Landscape'

	Before *(communications monopoly)*	**Now** *(communications market-place)*
Regulation	Single national monopoly	Liberalised competition
Organisations delivering communication services	National monopoly provider (e.g. ATT, BT, NTT)	Wide variety: privatised monopoly, new private entrants, other utilities
Technologies involved	Public switched telephone network (PSTN); mainly copper cables	Wide variety: updated PSTN, ISDN, interlinked and competing with systems and overlays such as radio, microwave, satellite and local cable systems
Services involved	Telephone, telex, some data	Telephone, telex and vast range of data, image and video services
Geographical characteristics	Desired universal diffusion of phone; spatial equalisation	'Cherry picking' of lucrative customers on a global basis in big business centres; spatial polarisation
Urban policy relevance	Negligible; national regulation ensured relatively equal access	Substantial and growing: new importance of access to network plus growing unevenness of 'telegeography'; New policy opportunities

Source: Modified from Graham (1993)

These developments have given rise to some cities taking a proactive role to 'wire' themselves to try to gain a competitive advantage in the global market-place. This is leading to the formation of 'information cities' based around a high tech infrastructure of computer-based networks.[98] For example, Toyko has become a telecommunications, nodal centre for the Pacific Rim, with government initiatives deliberately encouraging the development and integration of information technologies and telecommunications into the urban fabric to gain telematic supremacy.[99] Similarly in Osaka, the metropolitan government has combined with telecommunication operators and information service providers from the private sector to produce and implement an integrated development plan for an information city of 'smart buildings' linked to each other, and the rest of the world, via high speed, satellite and fibre-optic connections.[100] In the US,

New York, Boston, Atlanta and Los Angeles have taken the lead. In Europe, the UK, with its early deregulation of the market-place, has led the way. London quickly became the European capital for finance, broadcasting, publishing, advertising and other information-rich service industries. As a result, London has developed into a major telematic centre, representing some 80% of the UK data communications market.[101] To try to keep its dominant edge, the redevelopment of the London Docklands saw the formation of a teleport linking a range of telecommunication technologies. Similar telematic developments are occurring in Manchester, Hamburg, Cologne, Barcelona, Amsterdam and Rotterdam. Elsewhere, Singapore, in particular, has taken a proactive approach, led by the government's National Computer Board and Telecommunications Authority, in an effort to create an 'intelligent island'. As a result, Singapore has an incredibly sophisticated and dense telecommunication infrastructure, incorporating leased circuits, fibre-optic networks, household teleboxes and ubiquitous remote computer access as it tries to move from unskilled, low-wage manufacturing to value-added business services and financial markets.[102] Gibbs and Leach[103] suggest that failure by individuals, firms and areas to take such a proactive approach will have important negative effects, ultimately leading to economic marginalisation, especially as local economies are increasingly being tied into global markets and strategies. They suggest that local government agencies should increasingly try to encourage adoption of telematic technologies and take a proactive stance as reliance on market forces is likely to lead to further economic polarisation between core and peripheral regions.

In contrast to this process of centralisation, many office activities, business services and production centres are decentralising. This is because locating in the centre of major cities carries considerable penalties in terms of high rent costs, high labour costs, recruitment problems, congestion, poor environmental quality and overcrowding.[104] Decentralisation takes one of two forms. Firstly, many companies are decentralising within and across regions to smaller cities and non-metropolitan areas to capitalise on lower workforce and operating costs. Secondly, decentralisation is occurring across the city to the suburbs, to take advantage of lower worker turnover, worker accessibility and a skilled, cheaper, suburban labour pool, without overly compromising customer accessibility.[105]

While this process of decentralisation is occurring across well-connected large cities from the centre to the suburbs, Alles *et al.* suggest that many small and medium-sized cities are not benefiting, and are in fact becoming increasingly dominated by large cities who are increasing their competitive advantage. Contrary to this view, Omaha, Nebraska, claims to have created 100 000 tele-related jobs through back-office relocation.[106] Alles *et al.*, however, assert that, in the main, smaller cities and non-metropolitan areas are limiting because of their underdeveloped communications infrastructure. This is compounded, in the US at least, by the reduced availability of air-connections for quick personal decision-making visits.[107] Omaha, is an exception rather than the rule, being located on the crossroads of several, major fibre-optic connections. What is more, this process of decentralisation of some company sectors is actually reinforcing the need for the centralisation of control and coordination in the form of global command centres.[108] That is, the greater the decentralisation of some sectors, the greater the centralisation of others. Graham and Marvin illustrate this mechanism well in Figure 6.3, detailing the processes underlying the widening divisions between cities.

Within metropolitan areas, employment restructuring, in part caused by communication and information technologies, is reconfiguring the social and economic fabric of the city. The demise of middle-level employment is reducing the number of traditional middle class jobs and leading to a polarisation of residents across districts. This is leading to (in the US at least), what Castells terms, the 'rise of the dual city' comprising (i) those involved in the emerging information economy, accompanied by those with professional, engineering or technical jobs in other employment sectors, and (ii) those involved in low-level, low-skilled information economy/service positions, employees in attendant industries such as retailing, catering and leisure services, who are generally low-wage, part-time and casual, accompanied by those on welfare, and the informal and criminal economies. These two groupings (high skill/low skill) are becoming more spatially localised and distinct, leading to increased social and spatial divisions. Adding to this spatial polarisation, especially in world cities such as London, New York and Tokyo, is the well-paid nature of many of the white-collar and administrative jobs associated with the information service sector, including financial workers. These wealthy workers have sent real-estate prices soaring, leading to fresh gentrification and further impoverishment for more disadvantaged populations living near by. As a result, urban policy makers are having to weigh up the benefits of restructuring, over increasing social and spatial divisions. Again, the processes of this social and spatial polarisation dilemma are well illustrated by Graham and Marvin in Figure 6.4.

SOFT- OR CYBER-CITIES

> In a world of ubiquitous computation and telecommunication, electronic augmented bodies, postinfobahn architecture, and big-time bit business, the very idea of a city is challenged and must be eventually reconceived. Computer networks become as fundamental to urban life as street systems. Memory and screen space become valuable, sought-after sorts of real estate. Much of the economic, social, political, and cultural action shifts into cyberspace. As a result, familiar urban design issues are up for radical reformulation. . . . we have the opportunity to rethink received ideas of what buildings and cities are, how they can be made, and what they are really for. The challenge is to do this right – to get us the good bits.[109]

This urban–regional restructuring and the globalisation of the world economy is, as detailed, leading towards what some call soft- or cyber-cities and other technopoles. These are cities whose infrastructure is increasingly becoming composed of cyberspatial connections and whose existing infrastructure is increasingly being monitored and controlled by computer networks. Here, a recursive relationship exists between the city and computer as the city becomes increasingly managed and controlled by the computer, at the same time as its infrastructure becomes a vast network of computers. This relationship is strengthened by the introduction of smart and responsive technologies to building design, using microchip-based technologies to allow building features to respond to the occupants' movements and desires.

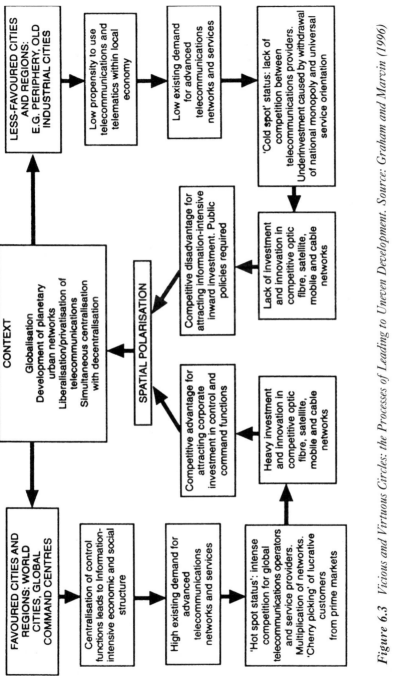

Figure 6.3 *Vicious and Virtuous Circles: the Processes of Leading to Uneven Development. Source: Graham and Marvin (1996)*

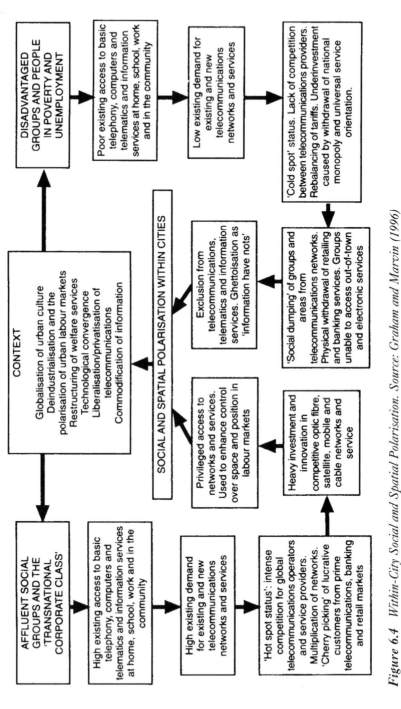

Figure 6.4 Within-City Social and Spatial Polarisation. Source: Graham and Marvin (1996)

For Mitchell, this recursive relationship is going to have a number of effects upon urban life and urban use. Most notably, as mentioned, work and travel behaviour will change; instead of travelling the roads, we'll be surfing the (information) superhighways. Other effects will see the changing role of public buildings. Libraries, museums and galleries will come on-line as the world's information, knowledge and artefacts become bits for on-screen consumption. Hyperlinks will allow all this material to be joined together to form some sort of super, multimedia laboratory. Other information providers – bookshops, newsagents, audio warehouses, video stores – will start to disappear from the urban fabric, replaced by on-line, multimedia bitstores allowing customers to download straight to the VCR, stereo, computer or laser printer. A similar fate awaits places of entertainment such as theatres, cinemas and sports arenas as they are replaced with virtual auditoriums and virtual arenas, finishing the job started by television and continued by video. In fact, this process is set to affect all public settings, as educational establishments are replaced by the on-line school/university, hospitals and healthcare facilities decline in the wake of telemedicine, banks, finance houses and stock markets are replaced by 'invisible' back offices and ATM machines, retail outlets, from department stores to corner shops, are replaced by electronic shopping malls accessed by high-tech virtual reality suits that even let you feel and smell the goods. Eventually the city will become the computer and the computer the city, perfectly meshed and radically altering the contemporary urban fabric and form. Here, the home will take on new meaning, as it slowly becomes not just a place to live and to relax but also the (smart) site of work, entertainment, education etc.

Such soft cities are still the imaginings of some utopian analysts, the urban fabric of the near future. However, a few places in the world are actively exploring the possibilities of reconfiguring their urban fabric, of becoming a soft-city. Such a city is Singapore, which is aggressively seeking to become one of the world's first cyber-cities. Its principal aim is to have all places of work, homes and schools 'wired' by the year 2000. Here, the city is being re-worked and re-thought as new technological infrastructures are set in place under the auspices of the government's IT2000 master plan.[110] The government's hope is to transform the city-state into a networked, intelligent island, using information and communication technology to utilise its intellectual capital and to sustain economic growth. There are five strategic themes which define the intelligent island vision: to become a global business hub; to boost Singapore's economic engine; to enhance individual potential; to link its communities both locally and nationally; and to improve quality and standard of life. Through strong government intervention and strategic partnerships with industry, Singapore hopes to become the world's first fully networked nation, with every citizen and corporation having access to a range of information services. In turn, information and communication technologies will be used to increase economic competitiveness, attract inward investment and achieve an 'intelligent society', encouraging learning and innovation.[111] Kawasaki in Japan has adopted a similar approach and is developing a series of eighteen 'intelligent plazas' consisting of smart buildings full of fibre-optic and cable services in a bid to create an 'on-line' city.[112] These plazas, which each aim to employ 1000 workers, are used to link new themed areas and are sequentially linked through a main fibre-optic grid with connecting subsidiary links to other nodes (Figure 6.5). The themed areas include a 'techno-venture' park where new telematic applications can be developed, a 'techno-community' where older industries using telematics reside, a 'technopia' representing the existing city centre and a 'technoport' representing the existing sea port. A hope is that as well as stimulating growth in telematic industries, the plan will see attendant growth in subsidiary industries such as retail and leisure services.

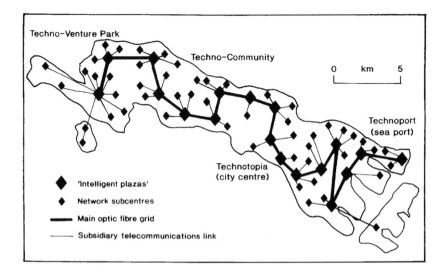

Figure 6.5 *Telematics-Based Urban Plan for Kawasaki. Source: Batty (1991)*

These initiatives go well beyond the city implementations of ad hoc telematic schemes or the development of a teleport that characterise many government initiatives concerning information and communication technologies. Indeed, these attempts to become the first cyber-cities of the future are not being so enthusiastically adopted by governments elsewhere. For example, the Bangemann Report of the European Union and the NII in the US have both signalled that the development of suitable infrastructure should be in the hands of private enterprise, with uptake being market-led. Here, the prime task of government is to safeguard competitive forces. This may mean that the cyber-cities of America and Europe will take on a different shape to those in the Far East, where infrastructural developments in places, such as in Singapore and Japan, are highly coordinated.

Within this changing context of city life, analysts argue we need to reconceptualise the urban planning process, to re-think the city as a site of home, work and play, incorporating at the heart of any new urban plan information and communication technologies. These technologies are going to have profound effects upon the urban fabric and form of Western cities, and their significance as agents of restructuring and stimulants to economies needs to be acknowledged and accounted for. However, as Graham and Marvin warn, these technologies should not be viewed as some sort of short-term, technical fix, creating employment and providing the catalyst for urban regeneration. Unless woven as technological tools into a wider set of social, institutional and political processes of change, telematic technologies will not fulfil much of their promise as agents to bring together urban fragments and add coherence and capacity to urban policy making.

THE POSTMODERN CITY

Some analysts suggest that we are not only witnessing the restructuring of the economic basis of urban landscapes but that urban form is also changing in other significant ways. For example, Zukin[113] contends that how we see and organise the city is changing as the consumption of space is abstracted from the logic of industrial production. This, she suggests, is part of a broad change into a postmodern society, where the city becomes a spectacle for consumption, and developers seek to construct simulated landscapes that the public then consume. Liverpool's Albert Dock and London's Covent Garden are two examples of simulated places, overlain on the original buildings to become pastiches of their former selves. When shopping at these sites you are not only consuming the goods but also the site of sale. Specifically redeveloped as sites of consumption, they are examples of what Baudrillard[114] has described as 'hyperreal' places. These are places that have been redeveloped into 'authenticated' sites; representations of the original, where the fake substitutes itself for the real and in the process becomes more real than the real (e.g. 'olde world' theme pubs). Sorkin[115] suggests that informational technologies (cyberspace, television etc.) are helping to rewrite the city in significant ways by rendering time and space obsolete, thus creating cities that are 'ageographical' because they have no 'sense of place'. These technologies have helped to generate a 'simulated real' and cities that are 'placeless', adopting a global identity. He terms these new global cities as the 'cit[ies] of simulation', which are shrines to global capital and consumption. Soja's analysis of Los Angeles confirms Sorkin's globalising, merging thesis, suggesting that LA is becoming a pastiche of everywhere else so that its unique features become obscured in its sameness. This sameness is the result of decentring accompanied by homogenous, satellite development, gentrification reworking the old and unique into the new and the same, and new buildings adopting architectural pastiches that do not relate to local, historical styles. Castells and Hall[116] thus suggest that if dropped by parachute into new 'soft-cities' such as Cambridge, UK or Massachusetts, Mountain View, California, or Munich, Germany we would not recognise the country, let alone the city. For Jameson[117], this erasure of difference is the logic of late capitalism – a global, homogenous market-place. Cyberspace contributes to this development by helping to collapse space and time, making capital and culture more mobile.

———

While Jameson's theory might be persuasive, it is clear that while cities are changing in both their form and function, they are also seeking to capitalise upon their heritage and their uniqueness. As such, the processes of globalisation do not make the local and historical obsolete but rather there is a rewriting of the city spaces developed during the period of Enlightenment and shaped by the processes of modernism, imperialism and colonialism.[118] There has been a realisation that culture and heritage are desirable commodities in urban areas, attracting consumption, inward investment and tourism.[119] As such, cities are increasingly seen as sites of cultural production and marketed as cultural commodities to be consumed by both residents and visitors. Lash and Urry[120] suggest that this restructuring is part of an emerging 'economy of signs' that is expressed through an intensifying of cultural industries such as arts, tourism and leisure, and which is part of the growing service sector economy. Cultural resources are thus being manipulated and 'sold' to provide capital gain.[121] Cyberspace is one particular medium through which cities are seeking to seduce consumption and through which the city is being reworked. City authorities are increasingly creating an on-line presence aimed at attractively marketing the city. Further, cyberspace is helping to blur the distinction between virtuality and reality, between the hyperreal and the real.

The postmodern city then, like urban–regional restructuring, seems to be developing in two directions at the same time. At one level, the city is becoming less distinct, more global and more homogenous; at another level the city is trying to market itself as more unique, set apart from other places, in order to attract consumption. As such, there is an emerging complex interplay between the local and global, authenticated and simulated. As noted, cyberspace is implicated in this interplay in three main ways. Firstly, cyberspace is seen to be aiding the collapse of space and time, thus allowing the rapid movement of capital and leading to significant urban–regional restructuring. Secondly, cyberspace is providing a new space in which city developers can promote and market their city as different and unique while being effectively linked into the global network of travel (lots to do, easy to get to). Thirdly, cyberspatial technologies are helping to blur virtuality with reality, masking the simulated nature of sites of consumption.

THE FUTURE LANDSCAPE

As we have seen throughout this chapter, information and communication technologies are having profound effects on the organisation and structure of employment, corporations and the cities we live in. Unlike much of the analysis concerning culture and society, the appraisals reviewed, in general, have tended to be more balanced with a stronger empirical base to draw upon. As a result, many of the accounts did not paint overly utopian pictures of the future but rather sought to contextualise and interpret their predictions within the patterns emerging in their own research. While many of these researchers are optimistic for the future, their predictions are more guarded. Developments have been much slower than utopian forecasters first estimated, and rather than benefits being universally spread across space and society, it is clear that information and communication technologies further accentuate existing spatial and social divisions. Clearly, cyberspatial technologies are leading to rapid globalisation but within this global economy there is much activity and restructuring as places seek to gain competitive advantage. As a result, a pattern of corporate centralisation towards major, global cities with strong telematic networks, accompanied by cost-saving, decentralisation of backwater offices to the suburbs, smaller cities and nations with cheaper costs, is occurring. This reorganisation, rather than leading to wide-scale, well-paid, professional employment, has actually led to corporate downsizing and a growth in non-technical, part-time, menial employment. This pattern of regional and employment restructuring is likely to continue for sometime as places battle for position before stabilising into a coherent shape. Globalisation is also being shaped by the policies of nation states and is not an even process; the global economy is asymmetric in nature both across nations and within nations.

As such, the utopian predictions of an egalitarian, integrated information society seem overly optimistic. Roszak is quick to point to the deficiencies of the early utopian predictions from futurists such as John Naisbett and Alfin Toffler. He suggests that their forecasts of very rapid restructuring and universal benefits have not materialised for three main reasons. First, these authors fell into the trap of confusing information with knowledge. For example, Naisbett, describing the move from industrial to information society, describes the new economic order as one in which:

> we now mass-produce information the way we used to mass-produce cars. In the information society, we have systematized the production of knowledge and amplified our brain-power. To use an industrial metaphor, we now mass-produce knowledge and this knowledge is the driving force of our economy.

For Naisbett, information and knowledge are the same. If you possess information, you possess knowledge. However, information only becomes knowledge if it is synthesised, digested and used in such a manner as to produce an original analysis of a given situation. The computer just transfers and processes bits of information. It does not create knowledge. Expert users capable of taking the information and synthesising and interpreting it create knowledge. Roszak suggests that we do not yet possess a large, sophisticated 'information society', educated to sufficient level to fully maximise the economic potential achievable when information is turned into knowledge.

Second, even if we accept that information is becoming more important in business, he suggests that we must remember that it is only a service. Futurologists seem to predict the end of the industrial society and the move to an information society; a move from the mode of capital/labour to the mode of information. Here, knowledge (information) will be the principal product of our economic life. However, information is predominantly used within a business context not as a principal product but as a service to aid the development, manufacture and marketing of a product. Even within the service sector, where information may be the principal product, the system is reliant on (high tech) manufacturing industries, which in turn are reliant on primary industries. Within this postindustrial society information does have an important role, but it is yet to, and unlikely to, surpass capital and labour. Roszak suggests that if information technologies are to provide a long-term, economic return then they must be grafted onto the existing industrial system, using its skills, labour, resources and manufacturing centres. High tech is not going to abruptly supersede the current system and create some all-new 'information economy'. High tech industries, including cyberspatial technologies, are another stage of industrial development; they do not displace everything that has gone before them: 'they overlap, compound, and must be coordinated'.[122] Trying to jump to some 'information economy' without embedding it in what currently exists and ignoring the shifts in the global economy will ultimately lead to disaster. Humans cannot live on information alone.

Thirdly, utopian futurologists rather than questioning how the global economy is restructuring and the consequences of moving manufacturing to developing and newly industrialised countries have mainly focused their attention on the benefits to be gained by Western, professional, affluent middle-class people. Typically, they focus on life styles, new commodities and consumer fashions of an 'information age', and ignore deeper and broader, social/economic consequences of this line of 'progress'. Roszak[123] accuses these writers of practising:

> noncontroversial trendiness that easily catches on among business types and public officials in search of attractively packaged convenience food for thought. . . . [Achieved through] an ungainly hybrid of potted social science, Sunday supplement journalism, and soothsaying. They feature breezy scenarios of things to come pitched at about the intellectual level of advertising copy. Sensational snippets and zany catchphrases fill every page with breathtaking amazements; glittering predictions whiz by on all sides.

In reality, cyberspatial technologies have profound social and economic consequences. As such, in our analysis, we must remember that these technologies have been adopted because they increase corporate profits by increasing productivity while reducing costs. As we have discovered, this has meant corporate streamlining of the workforce, and restructuring operations to take advantage of cheaper back-office operations and advanced telematic hubs. This, in turn, has led to widening social and spatial divisions, not to universal benefits. Any technology that can fulfil this role of producing capital gains will be appropriated by transnationals for this purpose. We should remember that transnationals are run to make profits, not to make an egalitarian society. As such, it is increasingly unlikely that such society is likely to emerge under the present wealth production cycle.

Given this, utopian predictions seem hopelessly out of tune with the patterns emerging, especially as social and spatial divisions are widening, not closing. And this is before the real test of information and communication technologies has begun: whether the general public will opt for a cyberspatial future on a grand scale. If multimedia services such as teleshopping, home entertainment and teleworking do not capture *and* keep the imagination of the majority of the public then the cyberspatial/information revolution will ultimately be confined to corporate industry, rapidly stabilising and losing momentum. The massive investment by telecommunication, computing and entertainment industries is in anticipation of widespread public use. As Makridakis points out, the question of public adoption divides experts.[124] At present, most cyberspatial users are major corporations, university and research workers and a few enlightened individuals. The real questions concern whether society will take to home shopping, where they cannot touch their intended purchases and judge quality and value. Will people take wholesale to home entertainment and shun more social activities such as going to the movies, restaurants, bars and football matches? Experts point to the poor performance of catalogue sales, the new commercialisation of the shopping mall and sport entertainment, the growth of specialist shops, the failure of early videotext systems, the social instinct of human beings and the desire for physical meetings as reasons why growth might not fulfil expectations. In contrast, others point to the growing ritual of watching television, phoning rather than meeting friends, the high number of services completed over the telephone or post such as insurance renewal, paying bills, etc., the growing number of teleworkers[125] and the fact that systems will become more user-friendly, more interactive and more fun as reasons why cyberspatial use will grow unabated for some time. The fundamental question is 'will cyberspatial technologies provide *wanted* services and provide *real* value to customers?. As discussed, these questions will only be answered with time. However, to me at least, the demand for cyberspatial services, although substantial, will not live up to many of the expectations of analysts and companies. I subscribe to the social animal theory that humans like the company of others and, as such, generally like meeting each other, attending and participating in social events. They will not completely forsake personal interaction for the computer screen. There will be many corporate causalities, which have over-zealously predicted the public adoption of cyberspace. Of course, if I am wrong, then these investment companies are set to make a fortune in profits and it will be the more cautious enterprises that suffer. This is not to deny that there is a current explosion of information-related industries, but rather that this explosion may well reach its ceiling in the near future (next 20 years), slowing to a steady rate of development, as the current wave of employment and organisational and urban–regional restructuring stabilises and takes shape. Such a conviction is based upon the notion that the demand for information cannot increase exponentially forever. At some point, we must reach saturation or balance point, where the benefits of information will not exceed the costs of collection, processing and synthesis. Moreover, as a society we cannot exist on a diet of information alone.

As has been argued throughout the book, it is suggested that if we are to gain a deeper understanding of the information economy, and its effects upon corporate organisation and employment structures, and urban–regional development, a postmodern approach linked with aspects of social constructivism and political economy should be adopted. As Graham and Marvin have persuasively argued, such an approach appreciates that the development and implications of technologies are played out in an intricate fashion, with local, social and cultural processes recursively situated within broader political and economic structures and mechanisms working at the national and global scale. This approach explicitly recognises that the relationship between technology and society is not framed purely within political–economic structures and processes, or sociocultural structures and processes, but is rather an interplay of the two. Therefore, organisational and employment restructuring and urban–regional reconfiguration are best understood by carefully analysing the cultural and social processes underlying the decisions of corporate decision makers, urban planners and regional government and assessing the interplay between individuals and institutions, while appreciating historical context and the strong influences of broader scale, political and economic processes and mechanisms. It is suggested that using such a strategy will allow us to gain a better understanding of the processes at play today and to proffer more realistic predictions of the future.

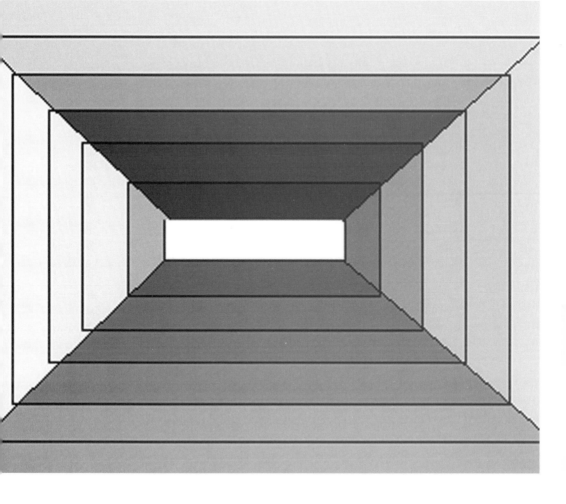

CHAPTER 7

ENTWINING THEMES

CHAPTER 7

ENTWINING THEMES

This book aimed to introduce the central arguments and theories of those who have studied the implications of cyberspatial technologies, and to try to provide a balanced, well-reasoned overview that contextualises cyberspace within the world we live in. In part, the book has been motivated by a deep-seated conviction that we are, in general, failing to adequately conceptualise and understand the impact of cyberspatial technologies upon our society because we are examining the implications of cyberspace, whether they be social, cultural, political or economic, separately.[1] Underlying the analysis and arguments that have been presented is a belief that these separate components of our lives cannot be viewed independently; they are interdependent and complexly entwined. In Chapter 3, I critically reviewed the theoretical perspectives adopted by scholars seeking to understand cyberspatial technologies. I argued that to fully conceptualise and understand the development, and wide-ranging consequences, of cyberspatial technologies, a position combining postmodernism with social constructivism and political economy needs to be adopted. This position has been used throughout the book to underpin the discussion presented. I have consistently argued that using this approach allows us to contextualise our analysis within the world we do inhabit and allows us to move away from the overburden of hype so that we can appreciate fully the complex relationships between technology and society. Such an approach allows us to carefully deconstruct the processes of development and appropriation of cyberspatial technologies and the ways in which the sociocultural and politico-economic intersect at both the local and global scales. In this last chapter, I will try to draw together and interweave the themes of society, culture, politics and economics, in an effort to gain some composite understanding of the impact of cyberspatial technologies and to assess the predictions concerning cyberspatial developments.

REMAKING THE KNOT

To fully understand the implications of cyberspatial technologies we need to remake the knot. That is, we need to tie the cultural, social, political and economic strands back together. As separate entities each strand can be presented to give us a picture of cyberspace. However, it is a selective picture, which fails to demonstrate the complex ways in which these strands interact and shape each other. In this section I seek to demonstrate with three worked examples the complex nature of cyberspace. The examples I have chosen centre upon the three main promises that Critical Art Ensemble identified as underlying cyberspace's appeal (new body, community, democracy).[2] It should become clear that these promises hold appeal only when viewed from one position – as soon as they are seen from other positions their utopian claims lose credibility and the complex nature of their consequences are revealed. My argument is that we need to view cyberspace from many positions and tie together the various vistas to understand its development and appropriation.

The first of the utopian promises is that cyberspace creates a new body. As discussed in Chapter 4, many theorists suggest that cyberspace will further widen the gap between mind and body and allow us to assign ourselves a new body constructed in whatever form we wish and given flesh through the words or graphics we use. In cyberspace we will be accepted on the basis of our words, not on the body or position they are spoken from. While there is a degree of truth in the formulation of a new body and disembodied spaces, this has to be put in context. Virtual spaces are, at present, embodied spaces, they are selective spaces and they are monitored spaces. While there is a certain amount of ability to play with gender roles, the gender assumed by a person is treated in the same way on-line as off-line. As such, the disembodying nature of cyberspace is not leading to qualitatively different spaces for women unless they are prepared to deny their gender. The same is true of disability, sexuality and race. You are only accepted as being equal if you pretend to be someone you are not. The alternative is closed and monitored forums where only like communicate with like. In addition, while cyberspace might provide a protective space for gay people to meet and interact, it does not negate the fact that if these people live in areas of homophobia or where homosexual practice is illegal they will be unable to openly act on their desires. Ironically, the groups for which cyberspace is meant to be most liberating are generally excluded through fiscal constraints and computer literacy. As such, the factors that regulate society off-line are currently regulating space on-line (e.g. class, lifestyle, gender, sexuality). That is, the cultural and economic ideologies that reproduce non-virtual society are not circumvented but rather directly impinge upon life on-line.

It must not be forgotten that cyberspaces were developed for military purposes, that cyberspaces are increasingly commercial spaces and that cyberspatial appropriation and development are heavily influenced by government policies and regulation. Commercial interests have been quick to invest in the business potential of cyberspace. Large transnational companies such as CompuServe and AOL now own and provide access to the Internet. Intranets are now big business, providing transnational companies with the capabilities to more effectively run their global operations. The US government was (and still is) largely responsible for the growth of the Internet, providing monetary support necessary for research and development. Governments around the world still wield a large influence concerning development and regulation. As we saw in Chapter 5, many governments have started to introduce formal legal frameworks to help govern virtual interactions. They also help to guide commercial investment and open up new markets through regional development schemes and government initiatives. For example, in recent years we have seen the deregulation of the telecommunications industry, government investment in telematic initiatives and wide-scale promotion of the information society.

The new body sits uncomfortably with such commercial and government interests. The new body is a body of the public sphere. It can say what it wishes, do what it wants. Cyberspace is increasingly becoming a public sphere with private owners. While there are little oases of seemingly free speech, the spaces provided by commercial service providers and the access provided to employees by companies are highly regulated and monitored. In reality this has always been the case – before the commercial owners, cyberspace was controlled by all-powerful sys-ops. While the ethic of cyberspace was to allow free speech the sys-ops had the power to step in and remove access rights. The new body in this context is an illusion. Speech and interactions in commercially owned spaces are regulated and monitored so that the new body becomes accompanied by what Critical Art Ensemble[3] calls a data body. A data body is also a virtual body but consists of facts and figures about an individual's actions within virtual and non-virtual worlds. For example, the data body of virtual interactions might consist of a log of all e-mail, recordings of chat dialogue and a record of web sites visited. A data body of off-line information might include credit card transactions, health records and government records. As such, while the new body represents a fluidity and freedom in identity construction it is accompanied by the creation of an exclusive space and a loss of privacy. The new body does not represent a utopian ideal when viewed from different positions. The new body is embodied and situated in the cultural and economic ideologies that currently reproduce society off-line. There can be no denying that cyberspace does provide an interesting arena in which to study identity and the body, but we need to carefully deconstruct this new body in the context of wider sociocultural and politico-economic processes in the world that we do live in.

The second utopian promise is that cyberspace will revitalise our sense of community by providing a new medium of interaction that is free of the constraints of place. MUDs, bulletin board discussion groups, mailing lists and IRC are all seen as providing new sites of communication where people can forge new senses of community based upon shared ideas and beliefs. For utopists such as Rheingold, these cyberspaces provide a viable alternative to the social spaces that are disappearing from our cities. Again, while there is a degree of truth in Rheingold's claims – there is evidence of community-like social relations in cyberspace – these claims need to be placed into a wider context. As such, we need to start questioning beyond whether such communities are forming and their nature, to ask whether such communities are desirable, whether they really can replace real-world communities, and how wider politico-economic processes and structures feed into their development. As argued in Chapter 4, there is little evidence that on-line communities are any more than pseudo-communities. They are communities in which there is little social responsibility and poor democracy. They are communities you can leave by just turning off the computer. They are communities that seek to ignore the problems of weakened communities in real space where we do all live.

As already argued, virtual spaces are embodied spaces, they are selective spaces and they are monitored spaces. Rheingold's vision of new public and open free spaces is a misnomer. There are very few unregulated spaces on-line. If virtual spaces are not controlled by a commercial Internet Service Provider (ISP) then they are controlled by a sys-op. Access to these communities is regulated by money and computer literacy. Virtual spaces then are private spaces, often owned by transnational companies seeking to make large profits from on-line interactions and selective communities. Even on free or open spaces, such as many bulletin boards, for those outside the US there are the phone bills to pay. Similarly, while these communities give the illusion that they are disembodied and disengaged from the non-virtual world, as with the new body, they are tied into the same sociocultural and politico-economic ideologies that reproduce and regulate real space. As such many of the concerns that have been expressed in relation to the new body, such as the role of governments and business, also apply to new communities. While virtual communities do provide interesting arenas in which to interact with others, it must be recognised that it is from the site of the real world that we engage in virtual interactions, it is to the real-world we return when the machine is switched off, and it is interactions and decisions in the real world (by governments and businesses) that most often guide cyberspatial development and appropriation. In our studies of on-line communities, then, we need to appreciate the influence of the real world upon the virtual and deconstruct the complex interplay between the two to reveal not only the nature and form of on-line communities but also why they are formed, how they are regulated and reproduced, and what their effect upon real-world communities is.

A third promise of cyberspace has been a new age of democracy. Cyberspatial connections will allow us to become a more democratic society by allowing everybody to voice their opinion and vote on specific issues. Cyberspace will wrench control from our political representatives or masters and place it back into the hands of the people. Cyberspace will thus undermine the pyramid of authority and lead to a flatter, more egalitarian society. Again, there is a grain of truth in this promise – cyberspace does allow people to freely communicate with everybody else who is on-line – but the utopian predictions concerning politics and polity need to be put into the context of wider social and economic processes and structures. Cyberspace is largely owned and controlled by transnational corporations and regulated within current government policies. Both business and governments are not overly keen on transferring power to their employees or electorate. Cyberspace is now run not as a medium of public interest, but as a commercial concern supplying mass entertainment and a global communications network. It is not an egalitarian space and access is restricted. At present, cyberspace is being used to reproduce hegemonic structures and to reinforce sociocultural and politico-economic ideologies which structure society. While cyberspace does lead to highly permeable borders, susceptible to information transfer, sovereignty is still highly guarded in 'real' space, across which tangible trade is highly regulated. Nation states will continue to exist as necessary organisational structures, fuelled by deeply entrenched historical prerogatives. Where experiments in cyberdemocracy have occurred, notably free-nets, the Internet has merely been used to extend the current structure by giving the electorate the opportunity for greater dialogue with their elected officials. In other forums such as *City Talks* the discussions soon became dominated by the same voices that dominate traditional forms of political dialogue. There seems to be an assumption that everybody wants to vote on every issue, has the political conviction to understand all the arguments, and will vote for the common good. The reality, of course, is that not everyone wants to vote, not everyone understands all issues, people will vote for their own gain and political mobilisation on-line will be weak. Government is complex and requires an understanding of complex issues. That is why we elect officials to represent our interests on a full-time basis.

This is not to deny that cyberspace does have significant beneficial impacts upon the democratic process. PENs have been used effectively to lobby local government on a number of issues, most notably by those who are most disenfranchised (e.g. the homeless in Santa Monica). The Internet does provide a forum in which to discuss significant issues and to mobilise support. The Internet is allowing people greater access to government information and other databases in the public domain. However, this is not going to lead to a radical transformation of our democratic structures and to the dissolution of place-based political organisation. The political implications of cyberspace need to be contextualised into wider economic concerns relating to ownership, control and regulation and into social concerns relating to voter behaviour and political mobilisation. In our studies of democracy on-line, then, we need to deconstruct the recursive relationship between on-line and off-line political spaces.

THE FUTURE OF THE CYBERSPACE

> In many ways it is futile to think about the future. There are far too many variables involved and it is almost impossible to make accurate predictions.[4]

The future of cyberspace is ensured for four reasons. First, cyberspace does offer a new medium of interaction, changing the nature of mass-media communications; it does have profound affects upon space–time relations; and it does further blur the distinctions between categories such as reality and virtuality, nature and technology. These changes are altering the way we live our lives, often in subtle and complex ways. Second, a critical mass has been reached and exceeded: millions of people interact with cyberspatial technologies everyday, either related to work, a form of entertainment or as resource. Third, many millions of different currencies are being spent on Internet and VR research, development and implementation by a variety of agencies. Government, industry, the military and space agencies are all investing heavily in cyberspatial technologies, with governments wanting to secure a world platform and industries wanting to make and secure a world market. In addition, there seems to be an entrepreneurial undercurrent, with many new companies based on home-brew ideas. Fourth, we are witnessing, at present, a digital convergence of many industries towards cyberspace. Information such as voice, sounds, text, graphics, data and video are all being digitised and can all be transmitted through cyberspatial technologies. Mitchell[5] can imagine a future where electronic interaction will become multimodal, where the digital convergence will be complete. We will be able to virtually meet, face-to-face in cyberspace, using sophisticated virtual reality technologies hooked up to the Internet. Telepresence will be a reality. As such, the Internet is going to grow explosively in size and use over the next few years.

The shape of the cyberspatial future is, however, more difficult to predict. Rapid technological developments mean that the nature of cyberspace is constantly changing. In addition, while virtual reality developments remain largely in private hands, there is a largely silent power struggle taking place for the control and regulation of the Internet. At present, corporate conservatives who want the Internet developed and regulated by transnationals and a few select start-up companies seem most likely to direct future developments. This is particularly the case in the US, where the Clinton administration is promoting a strategy where for-profit firms will develop the Internet. This is going to lead to the Internet becoming increasingly controlled and regulated by large transnational companies providing value-added services. As such, the largely unregulated nature of many cyberspaces will be increasingly squeezed out and marginalised. This means that while large forums such as Usenet will continue to flourish, new users will be largely directed into the closeted spaces of ISPs such as AOL and Prodigy. Barratt[6] reports that the Internet will only be stifled if there is insufficient infrastructure investment, excessive and stifling legislation or legal challenge and prohibition. At present, these three possible stifling agents are unlikely to occur. Investment is high, governments are working to keep the amount of legislation and regulation to a minimum and legal challenges have, so far, been few and far between. Cyberspace is largely going to be regulated through market-led rules and customary laws with the minimum of formalised laws. Where formalised laws have been introduced they generally seek to build upon laws that underpin real-world interactions and protect individual and business concerns. In those cases where the law has been extended beyond those in the non-virtual world, such as the CDA, challenges by lobby groups seek to redress the balance. For example, the CDA was ruled unconstitutional in recent test cases and was finally repealed in June 1997.

Clearly there are many imponderables concerning the future of cyberspace, and the picture painted is just one possible future. Within this discussion it might seem that cyberspatial technologies have been reappropriated by commercial interests to the detriment of individual users. However, these commercial interests are competing to provide a service for individuals users. It was inevitable that transnational companies would have to adopt the Internet to provide the level of investment needed to rapidly expand access and services. ISPs, while raising a number of questions concerning freedom of speech and privacy, are regulated, then, through market forces. As such, it is my thesis that cyberspatial technologies will be appropriated for the good. There are negative aspects to all technologies. In the case of cyberspatial technologies the potential benefits will outweigh the negative aspects and most of us will be willing to trade gains in terms of entertainment and service provision for losses in terms of confidentiality. Computing and cyberspatial technologies, although designed for profit or defence, are generally designed to make our lives easier, safer or more enjoyable. They do have downsides, such as making the world's financial markets more unstable, but in general, they are positive inventions of the latter part of the twentieth century.

LAST WORDS

The broad scope of issues covered within this book illustrate the depth and breadth of the potential implications of cyberspatial technologies. Cyberspace is one of the most significant technological developments of the late twentieth century. Cyberspatial technologies are clearly transformative technologies, which are changing the way we live our lives regardless of whether we undertake on-line interaction. Cyberspace does have significant implications for entertainment and commercial enterprise, changing our patterns of leisure availability, leisure time and our leisure choice and leading to radical restructuring of employment structures and urban–regional infrastructure. Cyberspace is increasing the processes of globalisation, decentring and fragmentation. Cyberspace is also raising a number of ethical issues by providing the basis for an increase in surveillance and creating a new space of deviancy. The claims concerning the more social and cultural aspects of cyberspace are less clear. The role of cyberspace in identity formation, community relations and political reform, as argued earlier, is at present generally unknown. While some commentators predict that cyberspace will have significant impacts upon identity, community and democracy, I am not so sure. Cyberspaces do offer new forms of communication and are new spaces of interaction but they are embodied spaces that are essentially extensions of real-world spaces, governed by the same cultural ideologies. Cyberspaces supplement rather than replace real-world activities.

It is clear that the study of cyberspace is an important venture and will become increasingly so. This book has aimed to highlight the sorts of questions that researchers should be engaging and has attempted to provide a theoretical framework in which to contextualise these studies. It is important that we realise that cyberspace, while having a different form to real space, is just an extension of the real world – we access cyberspace from the real world and many of our actions in cyberspace have real-world implications. Cyberspace exists in a symbiotic relationship with real space and it is this relationship that we must seek to understand. The implications of cyberspatial technologies are many and the social, cultural, political and economic effects are interdependent and should be studied as such. An approach that combines postmodernist ideas with social constructivism and political economy allows us to carefully deconstruct the implications of cyberspatial technologies within the context of the world we do live in and understand the symbiotic relationship between the virtual and non-virtual worlds.

NOTES

PREFACE

1. Lemke (1994) Cultural dynamics and virtual culture. *The Arachnet Electronic Journal of Virtual Culture* 2(1).
2. Critical Art Ensemble (1995) Utopian promises - Net realities.
3. BBC (1996) *The technophobes guide to computing.* Broadcast BBC 2, Tuesday 30 April. Estimates, however, vary from 4 to 96 million. These estimates are calculated by deciding how many people are likely to be connecting with each Internet host. There are estimated to be between 4 and 9.6 million hosts worldwide (see Figure 2.6 and http://nic.merit.edu/nsfnet/statistics/history.hosts), each thought to be supporting between 1 and 10 users.
4. Some analysts estimate a growth of 20% per month (Barr and Batty 1994) and that 50% of all homes in the USA will have a modem by the year 2000 (Alter 1995). Barrett (1996) reports that 150 000 people are going on-line every month and projections of users stand at 100 million by 1998 and 200 million by 2002.
5. Barratt (1996) reports that the UK Internet market is worth £35 million in 1996 with a current growth rate of 200% and expected market of £1 billion by 2001. Given that the UK market represents only 6% of the world market it is clear that many now envisage that cyberspace is set to become a major new business arena. However, the profits have been made by relatively few on-line service providers. Many start-up companies are ailing as a process of 'natural selection' ensues. In addition to on-line services Barratt suggests that value-added services would be over £65 million in the UK in 1996. These value-added services include consultancy concerning corporate home pages, Internet security against hackers, insurance etc.
6. Miller (1996) *Civilising Cyberspace: Power, Policy and the Information Superhighway.* New York: ACM Press.
7. Lyon (1988) *The Information Society: Issues and Illusions.* Oxford: Polity Press.
8. A recent survey by IDS Direct Marketing estimates that only 332 of Northern Ireland's 60 000 businesses are on-line (0.56%). *Sunday Business Post*, 4 May 1997, p. 3.

CHAPTER 1

1. Gibson (1984) *Neuromancer*, p. 67.
2. Shields (1996) Introduction: virtual spaces, real histories and living bodies. In Shields, R. (ed.) *Cultures of Internet*, pp. 1–10, 6.
3. The word cyberspace has been used in a number of ways. As well as referring to computer-mediated communication, it has also been used to discuss future developments and smart technologies which imbue objects with the ability to react to human presence. Benedikt (1991) (Introduction. In Benedikt (ed.) *Cyberspace: First Steps*, pp. 1–25, 1–3) produces a number of definitions of cyberspace which cover a broad spectrum of real and possible human–computer scenarios:

   > Cyberspace: A new universe, a parallel universe created and sustained by the world's computers and communication lines. A world in which the global traffic of knowledge,

secrets, measurements, indicators, entertainments, and alter-human agency takes on form . . .

Cyberspace: Accessed through any computer linked into the system; a place, one place, limitless . . .

Cyberspace: . . . a virtual world. Everywhere and nowhere, a place where nothing is forgotten and yet everything changes.

Cyberspace: A common mental geography, built, in turn, by consensus and revolution, canon and experiment; a territory swarming with data and lies, with mind stuff and memories of nature . . . in a silent, invisible concert of enquiry, deal making, dream sharing, and simple beholding.

Cyberspace: Its corridors form wherever electricity runs with intelligence. Its chambers bloom wherever data gathers and is stored. . . . Billowing, glittering, humming, coursing, a Borgesian library, a city; intimate, immense, firm, liquid, recognizable and unrecognizable at once.

Cyberspace: . . . From vast databases that constitute the culture's deposited wealth, every document is available, every recording is playable, and every picture is viewable.

Cyberspace: . . . everything informational and important to the life of individuals – and organizations – will be found for sale, or for the taking, in cyberspace.

Cyberspace: The realm of pure information . . . the soft hail of electrons.

4. Stone (1991) Will the real body please stand up?: Boundary stories about virtual cultures. In Benedikt (ed.) *op cit.*, pp. 81–118.
5. Plant (1996) On the matrix: cyberfeminist simulations. In Shields (ed.) *op cit.*, pp. 170–184. The word anarchic is not being used to imply some ungovernable space with free-form violence and rabid individualism but rather to suggest that virtual society is not governed by a central authority.
6. Shields, *op cit.*, p. 1.
7. A worldwide list and details of cybercafes can be found at http://www.cyberiacafe.net/cyberia/guide/ccafe.htm.
8. Correll (1995) The ethnography of an electronic bar: The lesbian cafe. *Journal of Contemporary Ethnography* 24: 270–298.
9. Stone (1995) Sex and death among the disembodied. In Star (ed.) *The Cultures of Computing*, pp. 243–274.
10. Poster (1995a) *The Second Media Age.*
11. Langdale (1989) The geography of international business telecommunications. *Annals of the Association of American Geographers* 79: 501–522.
12. Mitchell (1995) *City of Bits: Space, Place and the Infobahn.*
13. Benedikt, *op cit.*
14. Sherman and Judkins (1992) *Glimpses of Heaven, Visions of Hell.*
15. Coyle (1993) The genesis of virtual reality. In Hayward and Wollen (Eds) *Future Visions: New Technologies of the Screen.*
16. Stone (1991) *op cit.*
17. Lajoie (1996) Psychoanalysis and cyberspace. In Shields (ed.) *op cit.*, pp. 153–169, 155.
18. Heim (1991) The erotic ontology of cyberspace. In Benedikt (ed.) *op cit.*, pp. 59–80, 68.
19. *Ibid.*, p. 70.
20. Robins (1995) Cyberspace and the world we live in. In Featherstone and Burrows (eds) *Cyberspace, Cyberbodies and Cyberpunk*, pp. 135–156.
21. Gibson, *op cit.*
22. Rheingold (1991) *Virtual Reality.*

23. Miller (1996) *Civilising Cyberspace.*
24. Haraway (1991) A cyborg manifesto: science, technology, and socialist-feminism in the late twentieth century. In *Simians, Cyborgs and Women.*
25. Poster, *op cit.*
26. Graham and Marvin (1996) *Telecommunications and the City: Electronic Spaces, Urban Places.*
27. Mitchell, *op cit.*
28. Elkin-Koren (1996) Public/private and copyright reform in cyberspace. *Journal of Computer-Mediated Communication* 2(2).
29. Morris and Ogan (1994) The internet as mass medium. *Journal of Computer-Mediated Communication* 1(4).
30. Palme (1993) Legal and ethical aspects of computer-mediated communication. *The Arachnet Electronic Journal on Virtual Culture* 1(4).
31. Castells (1996) *The Rise of the Network Society.*
32. Marvin (1994) Spoof, spam, lurk and lag: the aesthetics of text-based virtual realities. *Journal of Computer-Mediated Communication.*
33. *Ibid.*
34. *Ibid.*
35. Lee (1996) Addressing anonymous messages in cyberspace. *Journal of Computer-Mediated Communication* 2(1).
36. Danet, Ruedenberg-Wright and Rosenbaum-Tamari (1996) 'Hmmm . . . where's that smoke coming from?' Writing, play and performance on Internet Relay Chat. *Journal of Computer-Mediated Communication* 2(4).
37. Soja (1989) *Postmodern Geographies.*
38. Harvey (1989) *The Condition of Postmodernity.*
39. Benedikt (1991) Introduction. In Benedikt (ed.) *op cit.*, pp. 1–25, 10
40. *Ibid.*
41. Robins and Hepworth (1988) Electronic spaces: new technologies and the future of cities. *Futures* 20: 155–176.
42. Castells, *op cit.*
43. Gillespie and Williams (1988) Telecommunications and the reconstruction of regional comparative advantage. *Environment and Planning A* 20: 1311–1321.
44. Hauben (1995) Preface. In *The Net and Netizens.*
45. Critical Art Ensemble (1995) Utopian promises – Net realities.
46. Griswold (1994) *Cultures and Societies in a Changing World.*
47. Castells, *op cit.*
48. Morley and Robins (1995) *Spaces of Identity.*
49. Castells, *op cit.*
50. Tomas (1991) Old rituals for new space: Rites de passage and William Gibson's cultural model of cyberspace. In Benedikt (ed.) *op cit.*, pp. 31–48.
51. Morley and Robins *op cit.*, p. 116.
52. Batty (1996) Virtual geography (unpublished manuscript).
53. Hillier and Hanson (1984) *The Social Logic of Space*; Harvey, *op cit.*; Gregory (1994) *Geographical Imaginations.*
54. Stone (1991) *op cit.*
55. McCaffery (1991) An interview with William Gibson. In McCaffery (ed.) *Storming the Reality Studio*, pp. 263–285.
56. Mitchell, *op cit.*
57. Benedikt, *op cit.*
58. McCaffery, *op cit.*, Introduction.
59. See Poster (ed.) (1988) *Jean Baudrillard: Selected Writings.*
60. Kumar (1995) *From Postindustrial to Postmodern Society*, p. 124.

61. Wilson (1994) Cyberwar, God and television: Interview with Paul Virilio.
62. Castells, *op cit.*
63. *Ibid.* p. 375.
64. Slouka (1996) *War of the Worlds: The Assault on Reality.*
65. Lajoie, *op cit.*
66. Slouka, *op cit.*
67. Lanier and Biocca (1992) An insider's view of the future of virtual reality. *Journal of Communication* 42.
68. Haraway, *op cit.*
69. Plant (1993) Beyond the screens. *Variant* 14: 12–17.
70. Featherstone and Burrows (1995) Cultures of technological embodiment: an introduction. In Featherstone and Burrows (eds) *op cit.*, pp. 1–20.
71. Balsamo (1995) Forms of technological embodiment. In Featherstone and Burrows (eds) *op cit.*, pp. 215–238.
72. Escobar (1994) Welcome to Cyberia. *Current Anthropology* 35: 211–231.
73. *Ibid.* p. 217.
74. Stone, *op cit.*
75. Slouka, *op cit.*, pp. 131, 81.
76. Stallabrass (1995) Empowering technology: the exploration of cyberspace. *New Left Review* 78: 3–32.
77. Castells (1988) *The Informational City.*
78. Slouka, *op cit.*
79. Tomas, *op cit.*
80. Laurel (1991) *Computers as Theatre*, pp. 197–198.
81. Stallabrass, *op cit.*
82. Heim, *op cit.*, p. 59.
83. Heim (1995) The design of virtual reality. In Featherstone and Burrows (eds) *op cit.*, pp. 65–78.
84. Tomas, *op cit.*
85. Novak (1991), Liquid architectures in cyberspace. In Benedikt (ed.) *op cit.*, pp. 225–254.
86. Sherman and Judkins, *op cit.*, p. 17.
87. *Ibid.*, p. 126.
88. *Ibid.*, p. 134.
89. Stenger (1991) Mind is a leaking rainbow. In Benedikt (ed.) *op cit.*, pp. 49–58.
90. Mitchell, *op cit.*, pp. 109–111.
91. Benedikt, *op cit.*
92. Morse (1994) What do cyborgs eat? *Discourse* 16: 86–123.
93. Penny (1994) Virtual reality as the completion of the Enlightenment project. In Bender and Druckery (eds) *Culture on the Brink*, pp. 231–248, 237.
94. Tomas, *op cit.*
95. Mnookin (1996) Virtual(ly) law: The emergence of law in LambdaMOO. *Journal of Computer-Mediated Communication* 2(1).
96. Robins, *op cit.*
97. Sardar (1995) alt.civilisations.faq: cyberspace as the darker side of the West. *Futures* 27: 777–794; Stallabrass, *op cit.*; Slouka, *op cit.*
98. Robins, *op cit.* p. 136.
99. *Ibid.* p. 137.
100. *Ibid.* p. 153.
101. Novak, *op cit.* p. 225.
102. Roszak (1994) *The Cult of Information.*
103. Rheingold, *op cit.*
104. Dery (1996) *Escape Velocity.*

105. Roszak, *op cit.*, p. xlvi.
106. Robins, *op cit.*
107. Critical Art Ensemble, *op cit.*
108. Rheingold, *op cit.*
109. Woolley (1992) *Virtual Worlds*, p. 35.
110. Lajoie, *op cit.*, p. 168.

CHAPTER 2

1. Hillman (1991) *Revolution or Evolution?*, p. 1.
2. Graham and Marvin (1996) *Telecommunications and the City: Electronic Spaces, Urban Places*, p. 3.
3. Woolley (1992) *Virtual Worlds: A Journey in Hype and Hyperreality*.
4. Rheingold (1994) *The Virtual Community*.
5. *Ibid.*
6. O'Neill (1995) The role of ARPA in the development of the ARPANET, 1961–1972. *IEEE Annals of the History of Computing* 17(4): 76–81.
7. Salus (1995) *Casting the Net*.
8. O'Neill, *op cit.*
9. Hart, Reed and Bar (1992) The building of the Internet: implications for the future of broadband networks. *Telecommunications Policy* 16: 666–689.
10. O'Neill, *op cit.*
11. Salus, *op cit.*
12. *Ibid.*
13. O'Neill, *op cit.*
14. O'Neill, *op cit*; Salus, *op cit.*
15. O'Neill, *op cit.*
16. *Ibid.*
17. Salus, *op cit.*
18. Hart *et al.*, *op cit.*
19. Salus, *op cit.*
20. Hart *et al.*, *op cit*; O'Neill, *op cit.*
21. Salus, *op cit.*
22. Hart *et al.*, *op cit.*
23. O'Neill, *op cit.*
24. Salus, *op cit.*
25. Hart *et al.*, *op cit.*
26. Hardy (1993) The history of the net.
27. Cerf (1995) Foreword. In Salus *op cit.*
28. Salus, *op cit.*
29. Hart *et al.*, *op cit.*
30. Salus, *op cit.*
31. Zakon (1996) Hobbes' internet timeline.
32. Lemos (1996) The labyrinth of Minitel. In Shields (ed.) *Cultures of Internet: Virtual Spaces, Real Histories and Living Bodies*, pp. 33–48.
33. Rheingold, *op cit.*
34. *Ibid.*
35. Stone (1991) Will the real body please stand up? In Benedikt (ed.) *Cyberspace: First Steps*, pp. 81–118.
36. Rheingold, *op cit.*

37. Cerf, *op cit.*
38. Salus, *op cit.*
39. Rheingold, *op cit.*
40. Salus, *op cit.*
41. Rheingold, op cit; Salus, *op cit.*
42. Rheingold, *op cit.*
43. *Ibidt.*
44. Hardy, *op cit.*
45. Mitchell (1995) *City of Bits: Space, Place and the Infobahn.*
46. Bruckman (1993) Gender swapping on the Internet.
47. Hart *et al.*, *op cit.*
48. Salus, *op cit.*
49. Zakon, *op cit.*
50. Salus, *op cit.*
51. O'Neill, *op cit.*
52. Hart *et al.*, *op cit.*
53. *Ibid.*
54. Zakon, *op cit.*
55. Rheingold, *op cit.*
56. Schuler (1995) Public space in cyberspace. *Internet World*, December: 89–95.
57. *Ibid.*
58. Rheingold, *op cit.*
59. Salus, *op cit.*
60. Rheingold, *op cit.*
61. Hollifield and McCain (1995) A national network in the global village. *Social Science Computer Review* 13: 183–206.
62. *Ibid.*
63. Zakon, *op cit.*
64. Stix (1993) Domesticating cyberspace. *Scientific American* 269(2): 85–92.
65. European Union (1996) *The Information Society.*
66. *Ibid.*
67. Miller (1996) *Civilising Cyberspace.*
68. Stix, *op cit.*
69. Morley and Robins (1995) *Spaces of Identity.*
70. Miller *op cit.*
71. Stix, *op cit.*
72. McChesney (1995) The Internet and US communication policy-making in historical and critical perspective. *Journal of Computer-Mediated Communication* 1(4).
73. Sherman and Judkins (1992) *Glimpses of Heaven, Visions of Hell.*
74. Rheingold, *op cit.*; Salus, *op cit.*
75. Rheingold (1991) *Virtual Reality.*
76. Rheingold (1991) *op cit.*
77. Coyle (1993) The genesis of virtual reality. In Hayward and Wollen (eds) *Future Visions: New Technologies of the Screen*, pp. 148–165.
78. Machover and Tice (1994) Virtual reality. *IEEE Computer Graphics and Applications*, January: 15–16.
79. Rheingold (1991) *op cit.*
80. *Ibid.*
81. *Ibid.*
82. Ellis (1994) What are virtual environments? *IEEE Computer Graphics and Applications*, January: 17–22.

83. *Ibid.*
84. Rheingold (1991) *op cit.*.
85. Ellis, *op cit.*
86. Rheingold (1991) *op cit.*.
87. Ellis (1991) Nature and origins of virtual environments. *Computing Systems in Engineering* 2(4): 321–347.
88. Boman (1995) International survey: virtual environment research. *Computer* June: 57–65.
89. Sherman and Judkins, *op cit.*
90. Encarnacao, Gobel and Rosenblum (1994) European activities in virtual reality. *IEEE Computer Graphics and Applications* January: 66–74.
91. Rheingold, *op cit.*
92. Encarnacao, *et al.*, *op cit.*
93. *Ibid.*
94. *Ibid.*
95. Bowonder, Miyake and Linstone (1994) The Japanese institutional mechanisms for industrial growth: a systems perspective – part 1. *Technological Forecasting and Social Change* 47: 229–254.
96. Kahaner (1994) Japanese activities in virtual reality. *IEEE Computer Graphics and Applications* January: 75–78.
97. Rheingold (1991) *op cit.*
98. Golledge, Loomis, Klatzky, Flury and Yang (1991) Designing a personal guidance system to aid navigation without sight: progress on the GIS component. *International Journal of Geographical Information Systems* 5: 373–395.
99. Pratt, Zyda and Kelleher (1995) Virtual reality: In the mind of the beholder. *Computer* 17–19.
100. Polis, Gifford and McKeown (1995) Automating the construction of large scale virtual worlds. *Computer* July: 57–65.
101. Ribarsky, Bolter, Op den Bosch and van Teylingen (1994) Visualization and analysis using virtual reality. *IEEE Computer Graphics and Applications*, January: 10–12.
102. Ellis (1994) *op cit.*
103. Machover and Tice, *op cit.*
104. Boman, *op cit.*
105. Sherman and Judkins, *op cit.*

CHAPTER 3

1. Graham and Marvin (1996) *Telecommunications and the City: Electronic Spaces, Urban Places.*
2. *Ibid.*, p. 85.
3. Aronowitz (1994) Technology and the future of work. In Bender and Druckery (eds) *Culture on the Brink*, pp. 15–29.
4. Roszak (1994) *The Cult of Information.*
5. *Ibid.*
6. Kroker and Weinstein (1994) *Data Trash: The Theory of the Virtual Class.*
7. Gray and Driscoll (1992) What's real about virtual reality? Anthropology of, and in, cyberspace. *Visual Anthropology Review* 8: 39–49.
8. Winner (1986) *The Whale and the Reactor.*
9. Robins (1995) Cyberspace and the world we live in. In Featherstone and Burrows (eds) *Cyberspace, Cyberbodies and Cyberpunk*, pp. 135–156.
10. Edge (1995) The social shaping of technology. In Heap, Thomas, Einon, Mason and MacKay (eds) *Information Technology and Society.*
11. Morley and Robins (1995) *Spaces of Identity.*

12. Mackenzie and Wajcman (1985) *The Social Shaping of Technology*.
13. Woods (1995) A question of space. In Aronowitz and Menser (eds) *Technoculture*. New York: Routledge.
14. Mackenzie and Wajcman, *op cit.*, p. 2.
15. Graham and Marvin, *op cit.*
16. Poster (1995a) *The Second Media Age*.
17. Penley and Ross (1991) *Technoculture*.
18. Haraway (1991) A cyborg manifesto: science, technology, and socialist-feminism in the late twentieth century. In *Simians, Cyborgs and Women*.
19. Bijker and Law (1992) *Shaping Technology, Building Society*.
20. White (1978) *Medieval Technology and Social Change*, cited in Mackenzie and Wajcman, *op cit.*, p. 6.
21. Penley and Ross, *op cit.*
22. Escobar (1994) Welcome to Cyberia: notes on the anthropology of cyberculture. *Current Anthropology* 35: 211–231.
23. Lemos (1996) The labyrinth of Minitel. In Shields (ed.) *Cultures of Internet: Virtual Spaces, Real Histories and Living Bodies*, pp. 33–48.
24. Escobar, *op cit.*
25. Hess (1995) *Science and Technology in a Multicultural World*.
26. Lyon (1988) *The Information Society*.
27. Chapman (1994) Making sense out of nonsense: rescuing reality from virtual reality. In Bender and Druckery (eds) *op cit.*, pp. 149–155.
28. Graham and Marvin, *op cit.*
29. *Ibid.*, p. 105.
30. Escobar, *op cit.*
31. Winner (1993) Upon opening the black box and finding it empty. *Science, Technology, and Human Values* 18: 362–378.
32. Graham and Marvin, *op cit.*
33. *Ibid.*
34. Penley and Ross, *op cit.*
35. Aronowitz, *op cit.*, p. 16.
36. Waters (1995) *Globalisation*.
37. Kumar (1995) *From Postindustrial to Postmodern Society*.
38. Walker (1985) Is there a service economy? *Science and Society* 49: 42–83.
39. Poster, *op cit.*, p. 78.
40. Haraway, *op cit.*
41. Dery (1996) *Escape Velocity: Cyberculture at the End of the Century*, p. 3.
42. Kroker and Weinstein, *op cit.*
43. Interrogate the Internet (1996) Contradictions in cyberspace: collective response. In Shields (ed.) *op cit.*, pp. 125–132.
44. Tomas (1991) Old rituals for new space: rites de passage and William Gibson's cultural model of cyberspace. In Benedikt (ed.) *Cyberspace: First Steps*, pp. 31–48.
45. Slouka (1996) *War of the Worlds: The Assault on Reality*.
46. Poster, *op cit.*
47. Graham and Marvin, *op cit.*
48. *Ibid.*, p. 113.
49. Dear (1988) The postmodern challenge: reconstructing human geography. *Transactions of the Institute of British Geographers* 13, 262–274.
50. Cloke, Philo and Sadler (1991) *Approaching Human Geography: An Introduction to Contemporary Theoretical Debates*.
51. Druckery (1994) Introduction. In Bender and Druckery (eds) *op cit.*, pp. 1–12, 1.

52. Cloke *et al.*, *op cit.*
53. Lyon (1994) *Postmodernity*, p. 11.
54. *Ibid.*, p. 11.
55. Rosenau (1992) *Postmodernism and the Social Sciences.*
56. Brian McHale, cited in Woolley (1992) *Virtual Worlds: A Journey in Hype and Hyperreality.*
57. Crook, Pakulski and Waters (1992) *Postmodernization: Change in Advanced Society.*
58. Rosenau, *op cit.*
59. *Ibid.*
60. *Ibid.*, p. 3.
61. Poster, *op cit.*
62. Poster, *op cit.*; Poster (1995b) Postmodern virtualities. In Featherstone and Burrows (eds) *op cit.*, pp. 79–96.
63. Kumar, *op cit.*
64. Winner (1994) Three paradoxes of the information age. In Bender and Druckery (eds) *op cit.*, pp. 191–197.
65. Rosenau, *op cit.*
66. Griswold (1994) *Cultures and Societies in a Changing World.*
67. Lyon, *op cit.*
68. Kumar, *op cit.*
69. *Ibid.*, p. 112.
70. Jencks (1989) *What is Post-Modernism?*
71. McCaffery (1991) Introduction: in the desert of the real. In McCaffery (ed.) *Storming the Reality Studio*, pp. 1–16.
72. Schroeder (1994) Cyberculture, cyborg post-modernism and the sociology of virtual reality technologies. *Futures* 26: 519–528.
73. Druckery, *op cit.*
74. *Ibid.*, p. 2.
75. Poster, *The Second Media Age.*
76. Thu Nguyen and Alexander (1996) The coming of cyberspacetime and the end of polity. In Shields (ed.) *op cit.*, pp. 99–124.
77. Emberley (1988) Technology, values and nihilism. *Science, Technology and Politics* 3: 41–58.
78. Morley and Robins, *op cit.*, p. 74.
79. Roseneau, *op cit.*
80. Poster, *The Second Media Age.*
81. *Ibid.*
82. Peet and Thrift (1989) Political economy and human geography. In Peet and Thrift (eds) *New Models in Geography*, Vol. 1, pp. 1–27.
83. Brown (1995) Postmodernism, the wheel of retailing and the will to power. *International Review of Retail, Distribution and Consumer Research* 5, 387–414.
84. Cloke *et al.*, *op cit.*, p. 192.
85. Morley and Robins, *op cit.*
86. *Ibid.*, p. 218.
87. *Ibid.*, p. 219.
88. Bromberg (1996) Are MUDs communities? Identity, belonging and consciousness in virtual worlds. In Shields (ed.) *op cit.*, pp. 143–152.
89. Interrogate the Internet, *op cit.*, p. 125.
90. Berman (1992) Why modernism still matters. In Lash and Friedman (eds) *Modernity and Identity.*
91. Kumar, *op cit.*, p. 3.
92. *Ibid.*, p. 32.
93. Berman, *op cit.*

94. *Ibid.*
95. Rosenau, *op cit.*
96. Kramarae (1995) A backstage critique of virtual reality. In Jones (ed.) *Cybersociety: Computer Mediated Communication and Community*, pp. 36–56.
97. Interrogate the Internet, *op cit.*
98. Shade (1994) Gender issues and computer networking. *Electronic Journal on Virtual Culture* 2(3).
99. Brants, Huizenga and van Meerten (1996) The new canals of Amsterdam: an exercise in local democracy. *Media, Culture and Society* 18: 233–247.
100. Kramarae, *op cit.*, p. 41.
101. *Ibid.*
102. Coyle (1996) How hard can it be? In Cherney and Reise (eds) *Wired Women: Gender and New Realities in Cyberspace*, pp. 42–55.
103. Borsook (1996) The memoirs of a Token: An aging Berkeley feminist examines Wired. In Cherney and Reise (eds) *op cit.*
104. Kramarae, *op cit.*, p. 43.
105. Herring (1993) Gender and democracy in computer-mediated communication. *Electronic Journal of Communication* 3(2): 1–17.
106. We (1994) Cross-gender communication in cyberspace. *The Arachnet Electronic Journal of Virtual Culture* 2(3).
107. Lakoff (1975) *Language and Women's Place.*
108. Witmer and Katzman (1996) On-line smiles: does gender make a difference in the use of graphical accents? *Journal of Computer-Mediated Comunication* 2(4).
109. Bellman, Tindimubona and Arias (1993) Technology transfer in global networking: capacity building in Africa and Latin America. In Harasim (ed.) *Global Networks: Computers and International Communication*, pp. 237–254.
110. We, *op cit.*
111. Haraway, *op cit.*; Plant (1996) On the matrix: cyberfeminist simulations. In Shields (ed.) *op cit.*, pp. 70–184; Light (1995) The digital landscape: a new space for women? *Gender, Place and Culture* 2(2): 133–146.
112. Hall (1996) Cyberfeminism. In Herring (ed.) *Computer Mediated Communication.*
113. Light, *op cit.*, p. 134–135.
114. *Ibid.*
115. Hall, *op cit.*
116. Clerc (1996) Estrogen brigades and 'big tits' threads: media fandom online and off. In Cherney and Reise (eds) *op cit.*, pp. 73–97.
117. Sutton (1996) Cocktails and thumbtacks in the Old West: what would Emily Post say? In Cherney and Reise (eds) *op cit.*, pp. 169–187.
118. Brail (1996) The price of admission: harassment and free speech in the wild, wild west. In Cherney and Reise (eds) *op cit.*, pp. 141–157.
119. *Ibid.*
120. Hall, *op cit.*
121. Graham and Marvin, *op cit.*
122. *Ibid.*
123. *Ibid.*
124. Druckery, *op cit.*

CHAPTER 4

1. Postman (1992) *Technopoly: The Surrender of Culture to Technology*, p. 20.

2. Squire (1996) Re-territorializing knowledge(s): electronic spaces and virtual geographies. *Area* 28: 101–103.
3. Griswold (1994) *Cultures and Societies in a Changing World.*
4. Druckery (1994) Introduction. In Bender and Druckery (eds) *Culture on the Brink*, pp. 1–12.
5. Guattari (1992) Regimes, pathways, subjects. In Crary and Kwinter (eds.) *Zone 6: Incorporations*, p. 18.
6. Poster (1995) *The Second Media Age.*
7. Poster (1995) Postmodern virtualities. In Featherstone and Burrows (eds) *Cyberspace, Cyberbodies and Cyberpunk*, pp. 79–96.
8. Thu Nguyen and Alexander (1996) The coming of cyberspacetime and the end of polity. In Shields (ed.) *Cultures of Internet: Virtual Spaces, Real Histories and Living Bodies*, pp. 99-124.
9. *Ibid.*
10. Tomas (1991) Old rituals for new space: rites de passage and William Gibson's cultural model of cyberspace. In Benedikt (ed.) *Cyberspace: First Steps*, pp. 31–48.
11. Schroeder (1994) Cyberculture, cyborg post-modernism and the sociology of virtual reality technologies. *Futures* 26: 519–528.
12. Escobar (1994) Welcome to Cyberia: notes on the anthropology of cyberculture. *Current Anthropology* 35: 211–231.
13. Jones (1995) Introduction: from where to who knows. In Jones (ed.) *Cybersociety: Computer Mediated Communication and Community*, pp. 1–9.
14. Rheingold (1994) *The Virtual Community: Surfing the Internet*, p. 3.
15. Baym (1995) From practice to culture on Usenet. In Star (ed.) *The Cultures of Computing*, pp. 29–52.
16. *Ibid.*
17. Correll (1995) The ethnography of an electronic bar: the lesbian cafe. *Journal of Contemporary Ethnography* 24: 270–298.
18. *Ibid.*, p. 281.
19. Bruckman and Resnick (1995) The MediaMOO project: constructionism and professional community. *Convergence* 1(1); Mnookin (1996) Virtual(ly) law: the emergence of law in LambdaMOO. *Journal of Computer-Mediated Communication* 2(1); Reid (1995) Virtual worlds: culture and imagination. In Jones (ed.) *op cit.*, pp. 164–183; Turkle (1996) *Life on the Screen: Identity in the Age of the Internet.*
20. Telnet jhm.ccs.neu.edu then type connect guest
21. Turkle *op cit.*
22. Bruckman and Resnick *op cit.*
23. Mnookin, *op cit.*
24. This process of democratisation and social accounting began after the infamous 'rape in cyberspace' where one 'player' used sophisticated programming to take over another person's character and forced them to perform sexual acts for his character. For full details see Dibbell (1994) A rape in cyberspace. *The Village Voice* 21 December: 36–42.
25. Mnookin, *op cit.*
26. Castells (1996) *The Rise of the Network Society.*
27. Martin, Gutman and Hutton (eds) (1988) *Technologies of the Self: A Seminar with Michel Foucault.*
28. Aycock (1995) 'Technologies of the Self': Foucault and internet discourse. *Journal of Computer-Mediated Communication* 1(2).
29. Poster, *The Second Media Age.*
30. Robins (1995) Cyberspace and the world we live in. In Featherstone and Burrows (eds) *op cit.*, pp. 135–156, 138.
31. Hayles (1993) Virtual bodies and flickering signifiers. *October* 66: 69–91, 72.
32. Morse (1994) What do cyborgs eat? In Bender and Druckery (eds) *op cit.*, pp. 157–189, 157.

33. Lupton (1995) The embodied computer/user. In Featherstone and Burrows (eds) *op cit.*, pp. 97–112.

34. Kroker and Weinstein (1994) *Data Trash: The Theory of the Virtual Class.*

35. Lupton, *op cit.*, p. 100.

36. Dery (1996) *Escape Velocity: Cyberculture at the End of the Century.*

37. Wilson (1994) Cyberwar, God and television: Interview with Paul Virilio.

38. Morse, *op cit.*

39. Turkle, *op cit.*

40. Rheingold, *op cit.*, p. 61.

41. Stone (1991) Will the real body please stand up? In Benedikt (ed.) *op cit.*, pp. 81–118.

42. Kane (1994) *Hitchhiker's Guide to the Electronic Highway*, p. 204.

43. Mitchell (1995) *City of Bits: Space, Place and the Infobahn*, p. 12.

44. Heim (1991) The erotic ontology of cyberspace. In Benedikt (ed.) *op cit.*, pp. 59–80.

45. Baym, *op cit.*

46. Correll, *op cit.*

47. Aycock and Buchignani (1995) The e-mail murders: reflections on 'dead' letters. In Jones (ed.) *op cit.*, pp. 184–227.

48. Lanier (1989) Virtual environments and interactivity: windows to the future (panel session). *Computer Graphics* 23(5): 8.

49. Thu Nguyen and Alexander, *op cit.*

50. Leary (1994) How I became an amphibian. In *Chaos and Cyberculture*, p. 5.

51. Lemos (1996) The labyrinth of Minitel. In Shields (ed.) *op cit.*, pp. 33–48.

52. Turkle, *op cit.*

53. Pile and Thrift (1995) *Mapping the Subject: Geographies of Cultural Transformation.*

54. Stone, *op cit.*

55. Slouka (1996) *War of the Worlds: The Assault on Reality.*

56. Bechar-Israeli (1995) From <Bonehead> to <cLoNehEAd>: nicknames, play and identity on Internet Relay Chat. *Journal of Computer-Mediated Communication* 1(2).

57. Robins, *op cit.*

58. *Ibid.*, p. 139.

59. Foucault (1978) *The History of Sexuality*, Vol. 1; Foucault (1979) *Discipline and Punish, the Birth of a Prison.*

60. Haraway (1991) A cyborg manifesto: science, technology, and socialist-feminism in the late twentieth century. In *Simians, Cyborgs and Women*, p. 222.

61. Thu Nguyen and Alexander, *op cit.*

62. Sobchack (1995) Beating the meat/surviving the text, or how to get out of this century alive. In Featherstone and Burrows (eds) *op cit.*, pp. 205–214.

63. Woodward (1994) From virtual cyborgs to biological time bombs: technocriticism and the material body. In Bender and Druckery (eds) Culture *op cit.*, p. 51.

64. Stone, *op cit.*, p. 113.

65. Argyle and Shields (1996) Is there a body in the net? In Shields (ed.) *op cit.*, pp. 58–69, 58.

66. Kawakami (1993), cited in Aoki (1994) Virtual communities in Japan.

67. Haraway, *op cit.*, p. 151.

68. Featherstone and Burrows (1995) Introduction. In Featherstone and Burrows (eds) *op cit.*, pp. 1–20.

69. Dery, *op cit.*, p. 231.

70. Laurel (1993) *Computers as Theatre.*

71. Gibson (1984) *Neuromancer.*

72. Lupton, *op cit.*

73. Tomas (1989) The technophiliac body: on technicity in William Gibson's cyborg culture. *New Formations* 8: 113–129, 115.

74. Downey, Dumit and Williams (1995) Cyborg anthropology. *Cultural Anthropology* 10: 264–269; Holland (1995) Descartes goes to Hollywood: mind, body and gender in contemporary cyborg cinema. In Featherstone and Burrows (eds) *op cit.*, pp. 157–174.

75. Lupton, *op cit.*, p. 101.

76. Haraway (1985) A manifesto for cyborgs: science, technology, and social feminism in the 1980s. *Socialist Review* 80: 65–107; Haraway, *op cit.*

77. Haraway, (1991) *op cit.*, p. 150.

78. *Ibid.*, p. 180.

79. Dery, *op cit.*

80. *Ibid.*, p. 234.

81. Wolf (1991) *The Beauty Myth*; Ewen (1988) *All Consuming Images*.

82. Sobchack, *op cit.*

83. Jamison (1994) Contradictory spaces: pleasure and the seduction of the cyborg discourse. *The Arachnet Electronic Journal on Virtual Culture* 2(1).

84. Rheingold, *op cit.*; Featherstone and Burrows, *op cit.*

85. Poster (1995) Postmodern viralities, *op cit.*

86. Heim, *op cit.*; Jones (1995) Understanding community in an information age. In Jones (ed.) *op cit.*, pp. 10–35.

87. Jones, *op cit.*, Introduction.

88. Rheingold, *op cit.*

89. Robins, *op cit.*

90. Jones, *op cit.*, Introduction, p. 11.

91. Turkle, *op cit.*

92. Correll, *op cit.*

93. Luke (1993) Community and ecology. In Walker, S. (ed.) *Changing community*, pp. 207–221.

94. Habermas (1989) *The Structural Transformation of the Public Sphere*.

95. Sennett (1978) *The Fall of Public Man*.

96. Fernback and Thompson (1995) Virtual communities: abort, retry, failure?

97. McLaughlin, Osborne and Smith (1995) Standards of conduct on Usenet. In Jones (ed.) *op cit.*, pp. 90–111.

98. Rafaeli and Sudweeks (1996) Networked interactivity. *Journal of Computer-Mediated Communication* 2(4).

99. Baym, *op cit.*; Correll, *op cit.*; Reid, *op cit.*

100. Reid, *op cit.*, p. 183.

101. Argyle (1996) Life after death. In Shields (ed.) *op cit.*, pp. 133–142.

102. Weise (1996) A thousand aunts with modems. In Cherney and Weise (eds) *Wired Women: Gender and New Realities in Cyberspace*, pp. vii–xv.

103. Bromberg (1996) Are MUDs communities? In Shields (ed.) *op cit.*, pp. 143–152.

104. Fernback and Thompson, *op cit.*

105. Robins, *op cit.*

106. *Ibid.*

107. Jones, *op cit.*, Introduction.

108. Rheingold, *op cit.*

109. Sardar, *op cit.*, pp. 787–788.

110. Gray (1995) The sad side of cyberspace. *The Guardian* 10 April.

111. McLaughlin *et al.*, *op cit.*

112. Ogden (1994) Politics in a parallel universe: is there a future for cyberdemocracy? *Futures* 26: 713–729.

113. McLaughlin *et al.*, *op cit.*

114. Correll, *op cit.*

115. Robins, *op cit.*, p. 150.

116. Heim, *op cit.*
117. Hollifield and McCain (1995) A national network in the global village. *Social Science Computer Review* 13: 183–206.
118. Aycock (1993) Virtual play: Baudrillard online. *The Arachnet Electronic Journal on Virtual Culture* 1(7).
119. Signal-to-noise ratio is the number of worthwhile messages to the number of messages that contain material of little relevance.
120. Parks and Floyd (1996) Making friends in cyberspace. *Journal of Computer-Mediated Communication* 2(3).
121. Stallabrass (1995) Empowering technology: the exploration of cyberspace. *New Left Review* 78: 3–32
122. Brown (1994) The seven deadly sins of the information age. *Intermedia* 22(3).
123. McCellan (1994) Netsurfers. *The Observer* 13 February: 10. Cited in Fernback and Thompson, *op cit.*
124. Lajoie (1996) Psychoanalysis and cyberspace. In Shields (ed.) *op cit.*, pp. 153–169.
125. Davis (1993) Who killed LA? A political autopsy. *New Left Review* 199: 29–54.
126. Beamish (1995) Communities on-line: community-based computer networks.
127. Aoki, *op cit.*
128. Ross (1991) *Strange Weather: Culture, Science and Technology in the Age of Limits.*
129. Levy (1984) *Hackers: Heroes of the Computer Revolution.*
130. Ross, *op cit.*
131. Ross, *op cit.*
132. Gilboa (1996) Elites, lamers, Narcs and whores: exploring the computer underground. In Cherney and Reise (eds) *op cit.*, pp. 98–113.
133. Dery, *op cit.*; Schroeder, *op cit.*; Rushkoff (1994) *Cyberia: Life in the Trenches of Hyperspace.*
134. See Sterling (ed.) *Mirrorshades: The Cyberpunk Anthology.*
135. Edwards (1995) Cyberpunks in cyberspace: the politics of subjectivity in the computer age. In Star (ed.) *op cit.*, pp. 69–84.
136. Fitting (1991) The lessons of cyberpunk. In Penley, C and Ross, A. (eds) *Technoculture.*
137. Featherstone and Burrows, *op cit.*
138. Dery, *op cit.*
139. *Ibid.*, p. 51.
140. *Ibid.*, p. 52.
141. *Ibid.*, p. 329.
142. Rushkoff, *op cit.*, p. 17.
143. *Ibid.*, p. 260.
144. *Ibid.*, p. 34.
145. McKenna (1992) *Food of the Gods: The Search for the Original Tree of Knowledge.*
146. Dery, *op cit.*
147. Dery, *op cit.*
148. Sterling (1986) Preface. In Sterling (ed.) *op cit.*, p. xi.
149. Dery, *op cit.*
150. Featherstone and Burrows, *op cit.*
151. Jameson (1991) *Postmodernism, or, the Logic of Late Capitalism.*
152. Davis (1990) *City of Quartz*; Davis (1992) *Beyond Blade Runner.*
153. Gibson (1993) *Virtual Light.*
154. Tomas, *op cit.*; Stone, *op cit.*
155. Fitting, *op cit.*, p. 295.
156. Maffesoli (1989) The sociology of everyday life (epistemological elements). *Current Sociology* 37: 1–16.
157. *Ibid.*, p. 11.

158. Shields (1992) Spaces for the subject of consumption. In Shields, R. (ed.) *Lifestyle Shopping: The Subject of Consumption*, pp. 1–20.
159. Halfacree and Kitchin (1996) 'Madchester rave on': placing the fragments of popular music. *Area* 28: 47–55.
160. *Ibid.*
161. *Ibid.*
162. Maffesoli, *op cit.*
163. Correll, *op cit.*; Reid, *op cit.*; Bromberg, *op cit.*
164. Fitting, *op cit.*, p. 297.
165. McKenna, *op cit.*
166. Dery, *op cit.*, p. 39.
167. *Ibid.*, p. 70.
168. Dery, *op cit.*, pp. 41, 42.
169. Kirn (1993) Cyberjunk. *Mirabella* 24.
170. Gibson (1989) in McCellan, From here to reality. *The Face* 2(15): 70, cited by Hayward (1993) Situating cyberspace: the popularisation of virtual reality. In Hayward and Wollen (eds) *Future Visions: New Technologies of the Screen*, pp. 180–204, 185.

CHAPTER 5

1. Miller (1996) *Civilising Cyberspace*, p. vi.
2. Neustadt (1985) Electronic politics. In Forester, T. (ed.) *The Information Technology Revolution*.
3. Poster (1995) *The Second Media Age*, p. 27.
4. Thu Nguyen and Alexander (1996) The coming of cyberspacetime and the end of polity. In Shields (ed.) *Cultures of Internet: Virtual Spaces, Real Histories and Living Bodies*, pp. 99–124.
5. Poster, *op cit.*
6. Thu Nguyen and Alexander, *op cit.*, p. 118.
7. Lake (1994) Placing power/siting space: the politics of global and local in the New World Order. *Environment and Planning D: Society and Space* 12: 613–628.
8. *Ibid.*
9. Tolhurst *et al.* (1994) *Using the Internet.*
10. Thu Nguyen and Alexander, *op cit.*
11. *Ibid.*, pp. 109, 110.
12. *Ibid.*, p. 111.
13. Laudal (1995) One global community – many virtual worlds. *Electronic Journal on Virtual Culture* 3(3).
14. Interrogate the Internet (1996) Contradictions in cyberspace: collective response. In Shields (ed.) *op cit.*, pp. 125–132.
15. Schuler (1995) Public space in cyberspace. *Internet World* 6(12): 88–95.
16. Dutton (1996) Network rules of order: regulating speech in public electronic fora. *Media, Culture and Society* 18: 269–290.
17. *Ibid.*
18. Graham and Marvin (1996) *Telecommunications and the City.*
19. McChesney (1995) The Internet and US communication policy-making in historical and critical perspective. *Journal of Computer-Mediated Communication* 1(4).
20. Roszak (1994) *The Cult of Information*, quoting Marshall McLuhan, who, back in the 1960s, was championing the idea of a global, electronic village.
21. Brants, Huizenga and van Meerten (1996) The new canals of Amsterdam: an exercise in local democracy. *Media, Culture and Society* 18: 233–247.

22. *Ibid.*
23. *Ibid.*
24. Mitchell (1995) *City of Bits: Place, Space and the Infobahn.*
25. Lyon (1995) The roots of the information society idea. In In Heap, Thomas, Einon, Mason and MacKay (eds) *Information Technology and Society: A Reader.*
26. Mitchell, *op cit.*
27. Bilstad (1996) Obscenity and indecency on the Usenet: the legal and political future of alt.sex.stories. *Journal of Computer-Mediated Communication* 2(2).
28. A mail bomb consists of a massive file being posted to the offender's account which then overloads the mailer's ability to process it. Mass flaming consists of many messages being sent to an account so that it soon becomes full and inoperable. The most infamous case of mass flames concerns the law firm Canter and Siegel. They sent out an advertisement to a number of news list groups. In return they got over 30 000 messages, crashing their machine and leading to their removal by their Internet supplier.
29. Some individuals have taken it upon themselves to act as Net police. One famous example is Cancelmoose, who deletes unwanted spam from net lists. Cancelmoose always justifies his deletes and also provides information to sys-op's to reinstall the offending messages if they want. Cancelpoodle, however, has taken upon him/herself to delete all messages from the Church of Scientology (Maltz (1996) Customary law and power in Internet communities. *Journal of Computer-Mediated Communication* 2(1)).
30. Kollock and Smith (1994) Managing the virtual commons: cooperation and conflict in computer communities.
31. Cooke (1995) Are you decent? *Computer-Mediated Communications Magazine* 2(3).
32. Johnson (1996) Due process and cyberjurisdiction. *Journal of Computer-Mediated Communication* 2(1).
33. Kirsh, Phillips and McIntyre (1996) Recommendations for the evolution of cyberlaw. *Journal of Computer-Mediated Communication* 2(2).
34. Kirsh, *op cit.*
35. Shapiro (1995) Street corners in cyberspace: keeping on-line speech free. *Nation* 3 July: 10–14.
36. *Ibid.*, p. 10.
37. *Ibid.*
38. Beeson (1995) Next wave of censorship from the States? *Computer Mediated Communications Magazine* 1 August.
39. Schmeiser (1995) Can the US Congress define decency? *Computer Mediated Communications Magazine* 1 July.
40. Bilstad, *op cit.*
41. Lee (1996) Addressing anonymous messages in cyberspace. *Journal of Computer-Mediated Communication* 2(1).
42. Bilstad, *op cit.*
43. *Ibid.*
44. Elkin-Koren (1996) Public/private and copyright reform in cyberspace. *Journal of Computer-Mediated Communication* 2(2).
45. Samuelson (1996) Intellectual property rights and the global information economy. *Communications of the ACM* 39(1): 23–28.
46. *Ibid.*
47. Poster, *op cit., The Second Media Age*; Elkin-Koren, *op cit.*
48. Elkin-Koren, *op cit.*
49. Oberding and Norderhaug (1996) A separate jurisdiction for cyberspace? *Journal of Computer-Mediated Communication* 2(1).
50. *Ibid.*
51. Roszak, *op cit.*

52. Stallabrass (1995) Empowering technology: the exploration of cyberspace. *New Left Review* 78: 3–32.
53. Elkin-Koren, *op cit.*
54. Barratt (1996) *State of the Cybernation.*
55. See Dibbell (1994) A rape in cyberspace. *The Village Voice*, 26 December: 36–42.
56. Palme (1993) Legal and ethical aspects of computer-mediated communication. *The Arachnet Electronic Journal on Virtual Culture* 1(4).
57. Ogden (1993) Legal and ethical aspects of computer-mediated communication. *The Arachnet Electronic Journal on Virtual Culture* 1(4).
58. Roszak, *op cit.*
59. Miller *op cit.*
60. Oberding and Norderhaug *op cit.*
61. Jones (1995) Understanding community in an information age. In Jones, S.G. (ed.) *Cybersociety: Computer Mediated Communication and Community*, pp. 10–35, 23.
62. Thomas (1995) Access and inequality. In Heap *et al.* (eds) *op cit.*
63. Fernback and Thompson (1995) Virtual communities: abort, retry, failure?
64. Graham and Marvin, *op cit.*
65. *Ibid.*
66. Golding (1990) Political communication and citizenship: the media and democracy in an egalitarian social order. In Ferguson, (ed.) *Public Communication: The New Imperatives*, pp. 84–100, 90.
67. Miller, *op cit.*
68. Roszak, *op cit.*
69. Badgett and Sandler (1993) *Internet: From Mystery to Mastery.*
70. *Ibid.*
71. Mitchell, *op cit.*
72. Moss and Townsend (1996) Leaders and losers on the internet.
73. Hess (1995) *Science and Technology in a Multicultural World*, p. 16.
74. Lajoie (1996) Psychoanalysis and cyberspace. In Shields (ed.) *op cit.*, pp. 153–169.
75. Interrogate the Internet, *op cit.*
76. Dyrkton (1996) Cool runnings: the coming of cybereality in Jamaica. In Shields (ed.) *op cit.*, pp. 49–57.
77. *Ibid.*, p. 56.
78. Abiodun (1994) 21st century technologies: opportunities or threats for Africa? *Futures* 26: 944–963.
79. Penny (1994) Virtual reality as the completion of the Enlightenment project. In Bender and Druckery (eds) *Culture on the Brink*, pp. 231–248.
80. McLuhan (1964) *Understanding Media: The Extensions of Man*, pp. 358, 93
81. Waters (1995) *Globalisation.*
82. *Ibid.*
83. Sardar (1995) alt.civilisations.faq: cyberspace as the darker side of the West. *Futures* 27: 777–794, 779, 780, 781.
84. Peet (1986) The destruction of regional cultures. In Johnston and Taylor (eds) *A World in Crisis? Geographical Perspectives.*
85. Pryor and Scott (1993) Virtual reality: beyond Cartesian space. In Hayward and Wollen (eds) *Future Visions: New Technologies of the Screen*, p. 166–179.
86. Barlow (1991) Coming into the country. *Communications of the ACM* 343: 19–21.
87. Lyon (1994) *The Electronic Eye.*
88. Witmer (1996) Risky business: why people feel safe in sexually explicit on-line communication. *Journal of Computer-Mediated Communication* 2(4).
89. Krol (1992), cited in Witmer *op cit.*

90. Interrogate the Internet, *op cit.*, p. 129.
91. Druckery, *op cit.*, p. 9.
92. Mitterer and O'Neill (1992) The end of 'information': computers, democracy and the university. *Interchange* 23: 123–139; Poster, *op cit.*
93. Mitterer and O'Neill (*op cit.*) report that in 1990 the US government maintained 910 computer systems detailing records of citizens, 292 of which did not meet the Privacy Act Regulations; Roszak (*op cit.*) estimates that these systems hold between 2 and 4 billion overlapping files on individual citizens; by the end of 1996 the European Union's trans-European public administration network will be in place, allowing the transnational transfer of tax and customs information, statistics, social security data, etc.
94. Supermarkets are beginning to build consumer profiles, which are then used to target junk mail.
95. Kirsh *et al.*, *op cit.* report that marketing information has grown to be a $183 billion industry in the US alone.
96. Critical Art Ensemble (1995) Utopian promises – Net realities.
97. Graham and Marvin, *op cit.*
98. Chapman (1994) Making sense out of nonsense: rescuing reality from virtual reality. In Bender and Druckery (eds) *op cit.*, pp. 149-155.
99. The name of the store changes with whoever is telling the story.
100. Mitterer and O'Neill, *op cit.*
101. Poster, *op cit.*
102. Mitchell, *op cit.*
103. Poster, *op cit.*
104. Ross (1991) *Strange Weather: Culture, Science and Technology in the Age of Limits.*
105. Palfreman and Swade (1991) *The Dream Machine: Exploring the Computer Age.*
106. Lyon (1994) *op cit.*
107. Roszak, *op cit.*
108. Calcutt (1995) Computer porn panic: fear and control in cyberspace. *Futures* 27: 749–762.
109. *Ibid.*
110. Barlow (1994) Jackboots on the infobahn. *Wired* April: 40.
111. Robins and Hepworth (1988) Electronic spaces: new technologies and the future of cities. *Futures* 20: 155–176, 169.
112. Marx (1988) *Undercover: Police Surveillance in America.*
113. Graham and Marvin, *op cit.*
114. Shade (1996) Is there free speech on the Net? Censorship in the global information infrastructure. In Shields (ed) *op cit.*, pp. 11–32.
115. Squire (1996) Re-territorializing knowledge(s): electronic spaces and virtual geographies. *Area* 28: 101–103.
116. Shade, *op cit.*
117. Reid (1993) *Usenet Readership Summary Report.*
118. Furness (1993) Sex with a hard (disk) on: computer bulletin boards and pornography. *Wide Angle* 15(2): 19–37.
119. Dery, *op cit.*
120. Sardar, *op cit.*, p. 786.
121. Durkin and Bryant (1995) 'log on to sex': some notes on the carnal computer and erotic cyberspace as an emerging research frontier. *Deviant Behavior: An Interdisciplinary Journal* 16: 179–200, 180.
122. Kantrowitz *et al.* (1994), cited in Durkin and Bryant, *op cit.*, p. 189.
123. Calcutt, *op cit.*
124. Dery, *op cit.*, p. 207.
125. Parliamentary Select Committee for Home Affairs (1994) *Computer Pornography.*

126. Calcutt, *op cit.*

127. Dery, *op cit.*

128. DeLoach (1995) Why the 'big three' are lying low. *Computer-Mediated Communications Magazine* 1 August.

129. Rheingold (1991) *Virtual Reality.*

130. Dery, *op cit.*, p. 199.

131. Kane (1994) *Hitchhiker's Guide to the Electronic Highway.*

132. Gareth Branwyn, cited in Dery, *op cit.*, p. 199.

133. Argyle and Shields (1996) Is there a body in the net? In Shields (ed.) *op cit.*, pp. 58–69.

134. Tom Mandel discussing text sex on the WELLs discussion topic, 'Sex in virtual communities', cited by Dery, *op cit.*, p. 210.

135. Thu Nguyen and Alexander, *op cit.*

136. Witmer *op cit.*

137. Dery, *op cit.*

138. Correll, *op cit.*

139. Kramarae, *op cit.*

140. Dery, *op cit.*

141. Rheingold, *op cit.*

142. Dery, *op cit.*, p. 213.

143. Pryor and Scott, *op cit.*

144. Kramarae, *op cit.*

145. Ulrich (1992), cited in Kramarae, *op cit.*

146. Pryor and Scott, *op cit.*

147. Dery, *op cit.*, p. 195.

148. Rheingold, *op cit.*

149. Dery, *op cit.*

150. Janower, *op cit.*

151. Sardar, *op cit.*

152. Barratt, *op cit.*

153. Martin, *op cit.*

154. Thu Nguyen and Alexander, *op cit.*

155. Sardar, *op cit.*

156. Roszak, *op cit.*

Chapter 6

1. Druckery (1994) Introduction. In Bender and Druckery (eds) *Culture on the Brink*, pp. 1–12,10.

2. Peters (1990) Quoted in Thach and Woodman (1993) Organizational change and information technology: managing on the edge of cyberspace. *Organisational Dynamics* 23: 30–46.

3. Gibbs and Leach (1994) Telematics in local economic development. *Tijdschrift voor Econmische en Sociale Geografie* 85: 209–223.

4. Castells (1988) *The Informational City: Information Technology, Economic Restructuring and Urban–Regional Process*, p. 126.

5. Strangelove (1994) The internet as catalyst for a paradigm shift. *Computer Mediated Communications Magazine* 1(8).

6. Daniels (1995) Services in a shrinking world. *Geography* 80: 97–110; Martin (1995) *The Global Information Society*

7. Lyon (1995) The roots of the information society idea. In Heap, Thomas, Einon, Mason and MacKay (eds) *Information Technology and Society: A Reader.*

8. Hepworth (1990) Planning for the information city: the challenge and response. *Urban Studies* 27: 537–558, 538.

9. Goddard, Gillespie, Robinson and Thwaites (1985) The impact of new information technology on urban regional structure in Europe. In Thwaites and Oakley (eds) *The Regional Impact of Technological Change*, pp. 215–241; Ungerer (1990) *Telecommunications in Europe*.

10. Hall (1985) The geography of the fifth Kondratieff. In Hall and Markusen (eds) *Silicon Landscapes*.

11. Toffler (1980) *The Third Wave*.

12. Bell (1974) *The Coming Postindustrial Society*.

13. Lyon, *op cit*.

14. Bangemann Report (1994) *Europe and the Global Information Society: Recommendations to the European Council*.

15. Australian Computer Society (1994), cited in Martin *op cit*.

16. Makridakis (1995) The forthcoming information revolution: its impact on society and firms. *Futures* 27: 799–821.

17. Martin (1978) *The Wired Society*.

18. Stonier (1983) *The Wealth of Information*.

19. Robins and Webster (1989) *The Technical Fix*.

20. Stonier, *op cit.*, p. 214.

21. Robins and Webster, *op cit*.

22. Naisbett (1984) *Megatrends*. New York: Warner Books.

23. Kumar (1995) *From Postindustrial to Postmodern Society*.

24. Makridakis, *op cit*.

25. Warf (1989) Telecommunications and the globalisation of financial services. *Professional Geographer* 41: 257–271.

26. Langdale (1989) The geography of international business telecommunications: the role of leased networks. *Annals of the Association of American Geographers* 79: 501–522.

27. Robinson (1991) Globalization, telecommunications and trade. *Futures* 23: 801–814.

28. Castells (1996) *The Rise of the Network Society*.

29. Langdale, *op cit*.

30. Luke (1994) Placing power/siting space: the politics of global and local in the New World Order. *Environment and Planning D: Society and Space* 12: 613–628.

31. Harvey (1989) *The Condition of Postmodernity*.

32. Waters (1995) *Globalisation*.

33. Castells, *op cit.*, p. 348.

34. Langdale, *op cit*.

35. Glaser (1988) Telecommunications in banking. *IEEE International Conference on Communications 88*, pp. 1567–1571; Warf, *op cit*.

36. Warf (1995) Telecommunications and the changing geographies of knowledge transmission in the late 20th century. *Urban Studies* 32, 361–378.

37. Myers (1994) Gross reality of global statistics. *The Guardian* 2 May.

38. Castells (1996) *op cit*.

39. Graham and Marvin (1996) *Telecommunications and the City: Electronic Spaces, Urban Places*.

40. *Ibid*.

41. Daniels, *op cit*.

42. *Ibid*.

43. European Union (1996) *The Information Society*.

44. Roberts (1994) Fictitious capital, fictitious spaces: the geography of offshore financial flows. In Corbridge, Martin and Thrift (eds) *Money Power Space*.

45. Huws (1991) Telework: projections. *Futures* 23: 19–31.

46. Weijers, Meijer and Spoelman (1992) Telework remains 'made to measure': the large scale introduction of telework in the Netherlands. *Futures* 24: 1048–1055.

47. Huws, *op cit.*

48. Handy and Mokhtarian (1996) The future of telecommuting. *Futures* 28: 227–240.

49. US Department of Transportation (1993) *Transportation Implications of Telecommuting.*

50. Martin (1995) *op cit.*

51. Weijers *et al.*, *op cit.*

52. Martin (1995) *op cit.*

53. Weijers *et al.*, *op cit.*

54. European Union, *op cit.*

55. Handy and Mokhtarian, *op cit.*

56. Selby (1995) Telecottages in their context: the Welsh experience.

57. Ducatel and Halfpenny (1993) Telematics for the community? An electronic village hall for East Manchester. *Environment and Planning C: Government and Policy* 11: 367–379.

58. Warf (1995) *op cit.*.

59. *Ibid.*

60. Cronin, *op cit.*

61. Dabinett and Graham (1994) Telematics and industrial change in Sheffield, UK. *Regional Studies* 28: 605–617.

62. Rayport and Sviokla (1995) Exploiting the virtual value chain. *Harvard Business Review*, November/December: 75–85.

63. Cronin, Overfelt, Fouchereaux, Manzvanzvike, Cha and Sona (1994)) The internet and competitive intelligence: a survey of current practice. *International Journal of Information Management* 14: 204–222.

64. Cronin, *op cit.*

65. *Ibid.*

66. Dabinett and Graham, *op cit.*

67. Cronin, *op cit.*

68. Johnston (1993) Teleworking as an enabler factor for economic growth and job creation in Europe, cited by Graham and Marvin, *op cit.*

69. Castells (1996) *op cit.*

70. *Ibid.*, pp. 238–239.

71. Davis (1993) Cyberspace and social struggle. *Computer Underground Digest* 28, cited in Graham and Marvin, *op cit.*

72. Castells, *op cit.*

73. Kumar, *op cit.*

74. Castells (1996) *op cit.*.

75. Robins and Webster, *op cit.*

76. Kumar, *op cit.*

77. Cronin (1994) *Doing Business on the Internet.*

78. Malone and Rockhart (1991) Computers, networks and the corporation. *Scientific American* 267: 92–99.

79. Naisbett, *op cit.*, p. 282.

80. Castells, *op cit.*

81. Graham and Marvin, *op cit.*

82. Ter Hart and Piersma (1990) Direct representation in international financial markets. *Tijdschrift voor Econmische en Sociale Geografie* 81: 82–92.

83. Castells, *op cit.*

84. Graham (1993) Changing communications landscapes. *Cities* 10: 158–166.

85. Graham and Marvin *op cit.*

86. *Ibid.*

87. Boghani, Kimble and Spencer (1991) *Can Telecommunications Help Solve America's Transportational Problems?*, cited in Graham and Marvin, *op cit.*

88. Mokhtarian (1988) An empirical evaluation of the travel impacts of teleconferencing. *Transportation Research A* 22: 283–289.

89. Graham and Marvin, *op cit.*

90. *Ibid.*

91. Castells, *op cit.*

92. Daniels, *op cit.*

93. Alles, Esparza and Lucas (1994) Telecommunications and the large city–small city divide: evidence from Indiana cities. *Professional Geographer* 46: 307–316.

94. Daniels, *op cit.*

95. Graham and Marvin, *op cit.*, p. 139.

96. Morgan (1992) Digital highways: the telecommunications era. *Geoforum* 23: 317–332.

97. Warf, *op cit.*

98. Hepworth, *op cit.*

99. Alles *et al.*, *op cit.*

100. Hepworth, *op cit.*

101. Graham, *op cit.*

102. Warf, *op cit.*

103. Gibbs and Leach *op cit.*

104. Daniels, *op cit.*

105. Castells, *op cit.*

106. Richardson (1994) Telebased customer services. *Communicore*, newsletter of Newcastle PICT Centre No. 2, cited in Graham and Marvin, *op cit.*

107. Castells, *op cit.*

108. Moss (1987) Telecommunications and the future of cities. *Urban Studies* 24: 33–44.

109. Mitchell, *op cit.*, pp. 107, 163.

110. Choo (1995) National computer policy management in Singapore: planning an intelligent Island. *Proceedings of the 58th Annual Meeting of the American Society for Information Science*, pp. 152–156.

111. Choo, *op cit.*

112. Batty (1991) Urban information networks: the evolution and planning of computer-communications infrastructure. In Brotchie, Batty, Hall and Newton (eds) *Cities of the 21st Century*, pp. 139–158.

113. Zukin (1992) *Landscapes of Power.*

114. Poster (ed.) (1988) *Jean Baudrilard: Selected Writings.*

115. Sorkin (ed.) (1992) *Variations on a Theme Park.*

116. Castells and Hall (1995) *Technopoles: Mines and Foundries of the Information Economy.*

117. Jameson (1991) *Postmodernism, or, the Logic of Late Capitalism.*

118. Jacobs (1996) *Edge of Empire: Postcolonialism and the City.*

119. Goodwin (1993) The city as a commodity: the contested spaces of urban development. In Kearns and Philo (eds) *Selling Places: The City as Cultural Capital, Past and Present.*

120. Lash and Urry (1994) *Economies of the Sign and Spaces.*

121. Kearns and Philo (1993) Culture, history, capital: a critical introduction to the selling of places. In Kearns and Philo (eds) *op cit.*

122. Roszak, *op cit.*, p. 29.

123. *Ibid.*, pp. 21-23.

124. Makridakis, *op cit.*

125. *Ibid.*

Chapter 7

1. Castells is probably the only analyst to date to make a concerted effort to develop and explore the entwining of the cultural, social, political and economic implications of cyberspatial technologies. In his book, *The Rise of the Network Society*, he develops a grand narrative centred on a notion of an emerging 'space of flows' as the spatial and temporal bases of society are transformed.
2. Critical Art Ensemble (1995) Utopian promises – Net realities.
3. *Ibid.*
4. Sawheeny (1996) Information superhighway: metaphors as midwives. *Media, Culture and Society* 18: 291–314.
5. Mitchell (1995) *City of Bits: Space, Place and the Infobahn.*
6. Barratt (1996) *State of the Cybernation.*

LIST OF PLATES

LIST OF FIGURES

LIST OF TABLES

ACKNOWLEDGEMENTS

I would like to thank Gill Alexander of the School of Geosciences, Queens University of Belfast for redrawing and adapting most of the figures. Of the other figures and plates, Figures 2.6 and 2.7 have been reproduced from Batty, M. and Barr, R. (1994) The electronic frontier: Exploring and mapping cyberspace, *Futures* 26: 699–712, with the kind permission of Butterworth Heinemann; Figures 6.3 and 6.4 have been reproduced from Graham, S. and Marvin, S. (1996) Telecommunications and the City, with the kind permission of Routledge; Plate, Chapter 1, Virtual skyscrapers has been reproduced from Lamm, S., Reed, D. and Scullin, W.H. (1996) Realtime geographic visualisation of WWW traffic, *Computer Networks and ISDN Systems* 28(7–11): 1457–1468 with the kind permission of Elsevier Science – NL, Sara Burgerhartstraat 25, 1055 KV Amsterdam, The Netherlands; Plate 1.3 has been reproduced with the kind permission of the Centre for Advanced Spatial Analysis, University College London; Plate, Chapter 3, Virtual architecture has been reproduced from Bray, T. (1996) Measuring the Web, *Computer Networks and ISDN Systems* 28(7–11): 993–1005 with the kind permission of Elsevier Science; Plate, Chapter 4, Virtual Bologna has been reproduced with the kind permission of Leda Guidi, Project Manager, Bologna Civic Network; and Plate, Chapter 5, http://www.election.co.uk/, was reproduced with the kind permission of The Internet Factory Ltd.

References

Abiodun, A.A. (1994) 21st century technologies: opportunities or threats for Africa? *Futures* 26: 944–963.

Alles, P., Esparza, A. and Lucas, S. (1994) Telecommunications and the large city–small city divide: evidence from Indiana cities. *Professional Geographer* 46: 307–316.

Alter, J. (1995) The couch potato vote. *Newsweek*, 27 Feb: 30.

Aoki, K. (1994) Virtual communities in Japan. Paper presented at the Pacific Telecommunications Council Conference.

Argyle, K. (1996) Life after death. In Shields, R. (ed.) *Cultures of Internet: Virtual Spaces, Real Histories and Living Bodies*. London: Sage, pp. 133–142.

Argyle, K. and Shields, R. (1996) Is there a body in the net? In Shields, R. (ed.) *Cultures of Internet: Virtual Spaces, Real Histories and Living Bodies*. London: Sage, pp. 58–69.

Aronowitz, S. (1994) Technology and the future of work. In G. Bender and T. Druckery (eds) *Culture on the Brink: Ideologies of Technology*. Seattle, WA: Bay Press, pp. 15–29.

Aycock, A. (1993) Virtual play: Baudrillard online. *The Arachnet Electronic Journal on Virtual Culture* 1(7).
http://www.monash.edu.au/journals/ejvc/ejvcv1n7.html

Aycock, A. (1995) 'Technologies of the Self': Foucault and internet discourse. *Journal of Computer-Mediated Communication* 1(2).
http://207.201.161.120/jcmc/vol1/issue2/aycock.html

Aycock, A. and Buchignani, N. (1995) The e-mail murders: reflections on 'dead' letters. In Jones, S.G. (ed.) *Cybersociety: Computer Mediated Communication and Community*. London: Sage, pp. 184–227.

Badgett, T. and Sandler, C. (1993) *Internet: From Mystery to Mastery*. New York: MIS Press.

Balsamo, A. (1995) Forms of technological embodiment: reading the body in contemporary culture. In Featherstone, M. and Burrows, R. (eds) *Cyberspace, Cyberbodies and Cyberpunk: Cultures of Technological Embodiment*. London: Sage, pp. 215–238.

Bangemann Report (1994) *Europe and the Global Information Society: Recommendations to the European Council*. Brussels: European Union.

Barlow, P.W. (1991) Coming into the country. *Communications of the ACM* 343: 19–21.

Barlow, P. (1994) Jackboots on the infobahn. *Wired* April: 40.

Barratt, N. (1996) *State of the Cybernation*. Kogan Paul, London.

Batty, M. (1991) Urban information networks: the evolution and planning of computer-communications infrastructure. In Brotchie, J., Batty, M., Hall, P. and Newton, P. (eds) *Cities of the 21st Century*. London: Longman, pp. 139–158.

Batty, M. (1996) Virtual geography, unpublished manuscript. University College London.

Batty, M. and Barr, R. (1994) The electronic frontier: exploring and mapping cyberspace. *Futures* 26: 699–712.

Baym, N.K. (1995) From practice to culture on Usenet. In Star, S.L. (ed.). *The Cultures of Computing*. Oxford: Blackwell, pp. 29–52.

Beamish, A. (1995) Communities on-line: community-based computer networks, MA thesis, MIT.
http://alberti.mit.edu/arch/4.207/anneb/thesis/toc.html

Bechar-Israeli, H. (1995) From <Bonehead> to <cLoNeHEAd>: nicknames, play, and identity on Internet Relay Chat. *Journal of Computer-Mediated Communications* 1(2).
http://207.201.161.120/jcmc/vol1/issue2/bechar.html

Beeson, A. (1995) Next wave of censorship from the States? *Computer-Mediated Communication Magazine* 2(8).
http://www.december.com/cmc/mag/1995/aug/last.html

Bell, D. (1974) *The Coming Postindustrial Society: A Venture in Social Forecasting*. Harmondsworth: Penguin.

Bellman, B., Tindimubona, A. and Arias, A. Jr (1993) Technology transfer in global networking: capacity building in Africa and Latin America. In Harasim, L. (ed.) *Global Networks: Computers and International Communication*. Cambridge, MA: MIT Press, pp. 237–254.

Benedikt (1991) Introduction. In Benedikt, M. (ed.) *Cyberspace: First Steps*. Cambridge, MA: MIT Press.

Berman, M. (1992) Why modernism still matters. In Lash, S. and Friedman,J. (eds) *Modernity and Identity*. Oxford: Blackwell.

Bijker, W. and Law, J. (1992) *Shaping Technology, Building Society: Studies in Sociotechnical Change*. London: MIT Press.

Bilstad, B.T. (1996) Obscenity and indecency on the Usenet: the legal and political future of alt.sex.stories. *Journal of Computer-Mediated Communication* 2(2). http://207.201.161.120/jcmc/vol2/issue2/bilstad.html

Boghani, A., Kimble, E. and Spencer, E. (1991) *Can Telecommunications Help Solve America's Transportational Problems?* Cambridge, MA: Arthur D. Little Inc.

Boman, D.K. (1995) International survey: virtual environment research. *Computer* June: 57–65.

Borsook, P. (1996) The memoirs of a token: An aging Berkeley feminist examines Wired. In Cherney, L. and Reise, E.R. (eds) *Wired Women: Gender and New Realities in Cyberspace*. Seattle, WA: Seal Press.

Bowonder, Miyake and Linstone (1994) The Japanese institutional mechanisms for industrial growth: a systems perspective – part 1. *Technological Forecasting and Social Change* 47: 229–254.

Brail, S. (1996) The price of admission: harrassment and free speech in the wild, wild west. In Cherney, L. and Reise, E.R. (eds) *Wired Women: Gender and New Realities in Cyberspace*. Seattle, WA: Seal Press, pp. 141–157.

Brants, K., Huizenga, M. and van Meerten, R. (1996) The new canals of Amsterdam: an exercise in local democracy. *Media, Culture and Society* 18: 233–247.

Bromberg, H. (1996) Are MUDs communities? Identity, belonging and consciousness in virtual worlds. In Shields, R. (ed.) *Cultures of Internet: Virtual Spaces, Real Histories and Living Bodies*. London: Sage, pp. 143–152.

Brown, L. (1994) The seven deadly sins of the information age. *Intermedia* 22(3).

Brown, S. (1995) Postmodernism, the wheel of retailing and the will to power. *International Review of Retail, Distribution and Consumer Research* 5, 387–414.

Bruckman, A.S. (1993) Gender swapping on the Internet, paper presented at the Internet Society, San Fransisco, August. ftp://ftp.media.mit.edu/pub/asb/papers/gender-swapping.txt

Bruckman, A. and Resnick, M. (1995) The MediaMOO project: constructionism and professional community. *Convergence* 1(1). ftp://ftp.media.mit.edu/pub/asb/papers/convergence.txt

Calcutt, A. (1995) Computer porn panic: fear and control in cyberspace. *Futures* 27, 749–762.

Castells, M. (1988) *The Informational City: Information Technology, Economic Restructuring and the Urban–Regional Process*. Oxford: Blackwell.

Castells, M. (1996) *The Rise of the Network Society*. Oxford: Blackwell.

Castells, M. and Hall, P. (1995) *Technopoles: Mines and Foundries of the Information Economy*. London: Routledge.

Cerf, V. (1995) Foreword. In Salus, P. *Casting the Net: From ARPANET to INTERNET and Beyond. . ..* Reading, MA: Addison-Wesley.

Chapman, G. (1994) Making sense out of nonsense: rescuing reality from virtual reality. In Bender, G. and Druckery, T. (eds) *Culture on the Brink: Ideologies of Technology*. Seattle, WA: Bay Press, pp. 149–155.

Choo, C.W. (1995) National computer policy management in Singapore: planning an intelligent island. In *Proceedings of the 58th Annual Meeting of the American Society for Information Science*, 9–12 October, Chicago. Volume 32: 152-156

Clerc, S. (1996) Estrogen brigades and 'big tits' threads: media fandom online and off. In Cherney, L. and Reise, E.R. (eds) *Wired Women: Gender and new realities in cyberspace*. Seattle, WA: Seal Press. pp. 73-97.

Cloke, P., Philo, C. and Sadler, D. (1991) *Approaching Human Geography: An Introduction to Contemporary Theoretical Debates*. Paul Chapman Publ. London

Cooke, K. (1995) Are you decent? *Computer-Mediated Communication* 2(3).
http://sunsite.unc.edu/cmc/mag/1995/mar/decency.html

Correll, S. (1995) The ethnography of an electronic bar: The lesbian cafe. *Journal of Contemporary Ethnography* 24: 270-298.

Coyle, K. (1996) How hard can it be? In Cherney, L. and Reise, E.R. (eds) *Wired Women: Gender and New Realities in Cyberspace*. Seattle, WA: Seal Press, pp. 42–55.

Coyle, R. (1993) The genesis of virtual reality. In Hayward, P. and Wollen, T. (eds) *Future Visions: New Technologies of the Screen*. London: British Film Institute, pp. 148–165.

Critical Art Ensemble (1995) Utopian promises – Net realities.
http://www.well.com/user/hlr/texts/utopiancrit.html

Cronin, B., Overfelt, K., Fouchereaux, K., Manzvanzvike, T., Cha, M. and Sona, E. (1994) The internet and competitive intelligence: a survey of current practice. *International Journal of Information Management* 14: 204–222.

Cronin, M.J. (1994) *Doing Business on the Internet*. New York: Von Nostrand Reinhold.

Crook, S., Pakulski, J. and Waters, M. (1992) *Postmodernization: Change in Advanced Society*. London: Sage.

Dabinett, G. and Graham, S. (1994) Telematics and industrial change in Sheffield, UK. *Regional Studies* 28: 605–617.

Danet, B., Ruedenberg-Wright, L. and Rosenbaum-Tamari, Y. (1996) 'Hmmm . . . Where's that smoke coming from?' Writing, play and performance on Internet Relay Chat. *Journal of Computer-Mediated Communication* 2(4).
http://207.201.161.120/jcmc/vol2/issue4/danet.html

Daniels, P. (1995) Services in a shrinking world. *Geography* 80: 97–110.

Davis, J. (1993) Cyberspace and social struggle. *Computer Underground Digest* 5 November: 28.

Davis, M. (1990) *City of Quartz*. London: Verso.

Davis, M. (1992) *Beyond* Blade Runner: *Urban Control, the Ecology of Fear*. Westfield, NJ: Open Magazines Pamphlets.

Davis, M. (1993) Who killed LA? A political autopsy. *New Left Review* 199: 29–54.

Dear, M. (1988) The postmodern challenge: reconstructing human geography. *Transactions of the Institute of British Geographers* 13: 262–274.

DeLoach, A. (1995) Why the 'big three' are lying low. *Computer-Mediated Communication*, 1 August.
http://sunsite.unc.edu/cmc/mag/1995/aug/deloach.html

Dery, M. (1996) *Escape Velocity: Cyberculture at the End of the Century*. London: Hodder & Stoughton.

Dibbell (1994) A rape in cyberspace. *The Village Voice* 21 December: 36–42.

Downey, G.L., Dumit, J. and Williams, S. (1995) Cyborg anthropology. *Cultural Anthropology* 10: 264–269.

Druckery, T. (1994) Introduction. In Bender, G. and Druckery, T. *Culture on the Brink: Ideologies of Technology*. Seattle, WA: Bay Press, pp. 1–12.

Ducatel, K. and Halfpenny, P. (1993) Telematics for the community? An electronic village hall for East Manchester. *Environment and Planning C: Government and Policy* 11: 367–379.

Durkin, K.F. and Bryant, C.D. (1995) 'log on to sex': some notes on the carnal computer and erotic cyberspace as an emerging research frontier. *Deviant Behavior: An Interdisciplinary Journal* 16, 179–200.

Dutton, W.H. (1996) Network rules of order: regulating speech in public electronic fora. *Media, Culture and Society* 18: 269–290.

Dyrkton, J. (1996) Cool runnings: the coming of cybereality in Jamaica. In Shields, R. (ed.) *Cultures of Internet: Virtual Spaces Real Histories and Living Bodies*. London: Sage.

Edge, D. (1995) The social shaping of technology. In Heap, N., Thomas, R., Einon, G., Mason, R. and MacKay, H. (eds) *Information Technology and Society: A Reader*. Milton Keynes: Open University Press.

Edwards, P.N. (1995) Cyberpunks in cyberspace: the politics of subjectivity in the computer age. In Star, S.L. (ed.) *The Cultures of Computing*, Oxford: Blackwell, pp. 69–84.

Elkin-Koren, N. (1996) Public/private and copyright reform in cyberspace. *Journal of Computer-Mediated Communication* 2(2).
http:// 207.201.161.120/jcmc/vol2/issue2/elkin.html

Ellis, S.R. (1991) Nature and origins of virtual environments: a bibliographic essay. *Computing Systems in Engineering* 2(4): 321–347.

Ellis, S. (1994) What are virtual environments? *IEEE Computer Graphics and Applications* January: 17–22.

Emberley, P. (1988) Technology, values and nihilism. *Science, Technology and Politics* 3: 41–58.

Encardacao, J., Gobel, M. and Rosenblum, L. (1994) European activities in virtual reality. *IEEE Computer Graphics and Applications* January: 66–74.

Escobar, A. (1994) Welcome to Cyberia: notes on the anthropology of cyberculture. *Current Anthropology* 35: 211–231.

European Union (1996) *The Information Society*. Luxembourg: Office for Official Publications of the European Communities.

Ewen, S. (1988) *All Consuming Images: The Politics of Style in Contemporary Culture*. New York: Basic Books.

Featherstone, M. and Burrows, R. (1995) Cultures of technological embodiment: an introduction. In Featherstone, M. and Burrows, R. (eds) *Cyberspace, Cyberbodies and Cyberpunk: Cultures of Technological Embodiment*. London: Sage, pp. 1–20.

Fernback, J. and Thompson, B. (1995) Virtual communities: abort, retry, failure? Paper presented at the annual convention of the International Communication Association, Albuquerque, New Mexico.
http://www.well.com/user/hlr/texts/VCcivil.html

Fitting, P. (1991) The lessons of cyberpunk. In Penley, C and Ross, A. (eds) *Technoculture*. Minneapolis, MN: University of Minnesota Press.

Foucault, M. (1978) *The History of Sexuality*, Vol. 1. New York: Pantheon.

Foucault, M. (1979) *Discipline and Punish, the Birth of a Prison*. New York: Vintage.

Furness, M. (1993) Sex with a hard (disk) on: computer bulletin boards and pornography. *Wide Angle* 15(2), 19–37.

Gibbs, D. and Leach, B. (1994) Telematics in local economic development. *Tijdschrift voor Econmische en Sociale Geografie* 85: 209–223.

Gibson, W. (1984) *Neuromancer*. London: Gollancz.

Gibson, W. (1993) *Virtual Light*. New York: Bantam Spectra.

Gilboa, N. (1996) Elites, lamers, Narcs and whores: exploring the computer underground. In Cherney, L. and Reise, E.R. (eds) *Wired Women: Gender and New Realities in Cyberspace*. Seattle, WA: Seal Press, pp. 98–113.

Gillespie, A. and Williams, H. (1988) Telecommunications and the reconstruction of regional comparative advantage. *Environment and Planning A* 20: 1311–1321.

Glaser, P. (1988) Telecommunications in banking. In *IEEE International Conference on Communications 88, Conference Record*. Philadelphia, PA: IEEE, pp. 1567–1571.

Goddard, J.B., Gillespie, A.E., Robinson, J.F. and Thwaites, A.T. (1985) The impact of new information technology on urban regional structure in Europe. In Thwaites, A.T. and Oakley, R.P. (eds) *The Regional Impact of Technological Change*. London: Frances Pinter, pp. 215–241.

Golding, P. (1990) Political communication and citizenship: the media and democracy in an egalitarian social order. In Ferguson, M. (ed.) *Public Communication: The New Imperatives*. London: Sage.

Golledge, Loomis, Klatzky, Flury and Yang (1991) Designing a personal guidance system to aid navigation without sight; progress on the GIS component. *International Journal of Geographical Information Systems* 5: 373–395.

Goodwin, M. (1993) The city as a commodity: the contested spaces of urban development. In Kearns, R. and Philo, C. (eds) *Selling Places: The City as Cultural Capital, Past and Present*. Oxford: Pergamon Press.

Graham, S. (1993) Changing communications landscapes: threats and opportunities for UK cities. *Cities* 10: 158–166.

Graham, S. and Marvin, S. (1996) *Telecommunications and the City: Electronic Spaces, Urban Places*. London: Routledge.

Gray, C.H. and Driscoll, M. (1992) What's real about virtual reality? Anthropology of, and in, cyberspace. *Visual Anthropology Review* 8: 39–49.

Gray, J. (1995) The sad side of cyberspace. *The Guardian*. 10 April.

Gregory, D. (1994) *Geographical Imaginations*. Oxford: Blackwell.

Griswold, W. (1994) *Cultures and Societies in a Changing World*. Thousand Oaks, CA: Pine Forge Press.

Guattari, F. (1992) Regimes, pathways, subjects (translated by Massumi, B.). In Crary, J. and Kwinter, S. (eds.) *Zone 6: Incorporations*. Cambridge, MA: MIT Press, p. 18.

Habermas, J. (1989). *The Structural Transformation of the Public Sphere: An Inquiry into Bourgeois Society* (translated by T. Burger and F. Lawrence). Cambridge, MA: MIT Press (first published in 1962).

Halfacree, K. and Kitchin, R.M. (1996) 'Madchester rave on': placing the fragments of popular music. *Area* 28: 47–55.

Hall, K. (1996) Cyberfeminism. In Herring, S. (ed.) *Computer Mediated Communication*. Amsterdam: John Benjamins.

Hall, P. (1985) The geography of the fifth Kondratieff. In Hall, P. and Markusen, A. (eds) *Silicon Landscapes*. London: Allen & Unwin.

Handy, S.L. and Mokhtarian, P.L. (1996) The future of telecommuting. *Futures* 28: 227–240.

Haraway, D. (1985) A manifesto for cyborgs: science, technology, and social feminism in the 1980s. *Socialist Review*, 80: 65–107.

Haraway, D. (1991) A cyborg manifesto: science, technology, and socialist-feminism in the late twentieth century. In *Simians, Cyborgs and Women*. London: Free Association Press.

Hardy, H.E. (1993) The history of the Net, master's thesis. Grand Valley State University. http://www.ocean.ic.net/ftp/doc/nethist.html

Hart, J.A., Reed, R.R. and Bar, F. (1992) The building of the internet: implications for the future of broadband networks. *Telecommunications Policy* 16: 666–689.

Harvey, D. (1989) *The Condition of Postmodernity: An Enquiry into the Origins of Cultural Change*. Oxford: Blackwell.

Hauben, M, (1995) The Net and Netizens: The impact the Net has on People's lives. Preface. http://www.cs.columbia.edu/hauben/CS/netizen.txt

Hayles, K. (1993) Virtual bodies and flickering signifiers. *October* 66: 69–91.

Hayward, P. (1993) Situating cyberspace: the popularisation of virtual reality. In Hayward, P. and Wollen, T. *Future Visions: New Technologies of the Screen*. London: British Film Institute, pp. 180–204.

Heim, M. (1991) The erotic ontology of cyberspace. In Benedikt, M. (ed.) *Cyberspace: First Steps*. Cambridge, MA: MIT Press, pp. 59–80.

Heim, M. (1995) The design of virtual reality. In Featherstone, M. and Burrows, R. (eds) *Cyberspace, Cyberbodies and Cyberpunk: Cultures of Technological Embodiment*. London: Sage, pp. 65–78.

Hepworth, M. (1990) Planning for the information city: the challenge and response. *Urban Studies* 27: 537–558.

Herring, S.C. (1993) Gender and democracy in computer-mediated communication. *Electronic Journal of Communication* 3(2): 1–17.

Hess, D.J. (1995) *Science and Technology in a Multicultural World: The Cultural Politics of Facts and Artifacts*. New York: Columbia University Press.

Hillier, B. and Hanson, J. (1984) *The Social Logic of Space*. Cambride: Cambridge University Press.

Hillman, J. (1991) *Revolution or Evolution? The Impact of Information and Communication Technology on Buildings and Places*. London: Royal Institution of Chartered Surveyors.

Holland, S. (1995) Descartes goes to Hollywood: mind, body and gender in contemporary cyborg cinema. In Featherstone, M. and Burrows, R. (eds) *Cyberspace, Cyberbodies and Cyberpunk: Cultures of Technological Embodiment*. London: Sage, pp. 157–174.

Hollifield, A. and McCain, T.A. (1995) A national network in the global village: US policy goals for an international network. *Social Science Computer Review* 13: 183–206.

Huws, , U. (1991) Telework: projections. *Futures* 23; 19–31.

Interrogate the Internet (1996) Contradictions in cyberspace: collective response. In Shields, R. (ed.) *Cultures of Internet: Virtual Spaces, Real Histories and Living Bodies*. London: Sage, pp. 125–132.

Jacobs, J. (1996) *Edge of Empire: Postcolonialism and the City*. London: Routledge.

Jameson, F. (1991) *Postmodernism, or, the Logic of Late Capitalism*. Durham, NC: Duke University Press.

Jamison, P.K. (1994) Contradictory spaces: pleasure and the seduction of the cyborg discourse. *The Arachnet Electronic Journal on Virtual Culture* 2(1).
http://www.monash.edu.au/journals/ejvc/jamison.html

Jencks, C. (1989) *What Is Post-Modernism?*, 3rd edn. London: Academy Editions.

Johnson, D.R. (1996) Due process and cyberjurisdiction. *Journal of Computer-Mediated Communication* 2(1).
http://207.201.161.120/jcmc/vol2/issue1/due.html

Jones, S.G. (1995) Introduction: from where to who knows. In Jones, S.G. (ed.) *Cybersociety: Computer Mediated Communication and Community*. London: Sage, pp. 1–9.

Jones, S.G. (1995) Understanding community in an information age. In Jones, S.G. (ed.) *Cybersociety: Computer Mediated Communication and Community*. London: Sage, pp. 10–35.

Kahaner (1994) Japanese activities in virtual reality. IEEE *Computer Graphics and Applications* January: 75–78.

Kane, P. (1994) *Hitchhiker's Guide to the Electronic Highway*. New York: MIS Press.

Kapor, M. (1993) Where is the digital highway really heading? The case for Jefferson information policy. *Wired* 1(3): 53–59.

Kearns, R. and Philo, C. (1993) Culture, history, capital: a critical introduction to the selling of places. In Kearns, R. and Philo, C. (eds) *Selling Places: The City as Cultural Capital, Past and Present*. Oxford: Pergamon Press.

Kirn, W. (1993) Cyberjunk. *Mirabella* 24.

Kirsh, E.M., Phillips, D.W. and McIntyre, D.E. (1996) Recommendations for the evolution of cyberlaw. *Journal of Computer-Mediated Communication* 2(2).
http://207.201.161.120/jcmc/vol2/issue2/kirsh.html

Kollock, P. And Smith, M. (1994) Managing the virtual commons: cooperation and conflict in computer communities.
http://www.sscnet.ucla.edu/soc/csoc/vcommons.htm

Kramarae, C. (1995) A backstage critique of virtual reality. In Jones, S.G. (ed.) *Cybersociety: Computer Mediated Communication and Community*. London: Sage, pp. 36–56.

Kroker, A. and Weinstein, M. (1994) *Data Trash: The Theory of the Virtual Class*. Montreal: New World Perspectives.

Kumar, K. (1995) *From Postindustrial to Postmodern Society: New Theories of the Contemporary World*. Oxford: Blackwell.

Lajoie, M. (1996) Psychoanalysis and cyberspace. In Shields, R. (ed.) *Cultures of Internet: Virtual Spaces, Real Histories and Living Bodies*. London: Sage, pp. 153–169.

Lake, T.W. (1994) Placing power/siting space: the politics of global and local in the New World Order. *Environment and Planning D: Society and Space* 12: 613–628.

Lakoff, R. (1975) *Language and Women's Place*. New York: Harper Colophon Books.

Langdale, J.V. (1989) The geography of international business telecommunications: the role of leased networks. *Annals of the Association of American Geographers* 79: 501–522.

Lanier, J. (1989) Virtual environments and interactivity: windows to the future (panel session). *Computer Graphics* 23(5): 8.

Lanier, J. and Biocca, F. (1992) An insider's view of the future of virtual reality. *Journal of Communication* 42.

Lash, S. and Urry, J. (1994) *Economies of the Sign and Spaces*. London: Sage.

Laudal, T. (1995) One global community – many virtual worlds. *Electronic Journal on Virtual Culture* 3(3).

http://www.monash.edu.au/journals/ejvc/laudal.html

Laurel, B. (1991) *Computers as Theatre*. Reading, MA: Addison-Wesley.

Leary, T. (1994) How I became an amphibian. In *Chaos and Cyberculture*. Berkeley, CA: Ronin.

Lee, G.B. (1996) Addressing anonymous messages in cyberspace. *Journal of Computer-Mediated Communication* 2(1).

http:// 207.201.161.120/jcmc/vol2/issue1/anon.html

Lemke, J. (1994) Cultural dynamics and virtual culture. *The Arachnet Electronic Journal on Virtual Culture* 2(1).

http://www.monash.edu.au/journals/ejvc/lemke.html

Lemos, A. (1996) The labyrinth of Minitel. In Shields, R. (ed.) *Cultures of Internet: Virtual Spaces, Real Histories and Living Bodies*. London: Sage, pp. 33–48.

Levy, S. (1984) *Hackers: Heroes of the Computer Revolution*. New York: Anchor Books.

Light, J.S. (1995) The digital landscape: a new space for women? *Gender, Place and Culture* 2(2): 133–146.

Luke, T. (1993) Community and ecology. In Walker, S. (ed.) *Changing Community: The Graywolf Annual Ten*. St Paul, MN: Graywolf Press, pp. 207–221.

Lupton, D. (1995) The embodied computer/user. In Featherstone, M. and Burrows, R. (eds) *Cyberspace, Cyberbodies and Cyberpunk: Cultures of Technological Embodiment*. London: Sage, pp. 97–112.

Lyon, D. (1988) *The Information Society: Issues and Illusions*. Oxford: Polity Press.

Lyon, D. (1994) *Postmodernity*. Milton Keynes: Open University Press.

Lyon, D. (1994) *The Electronic Eye: The Rise of the Surveillance Society*. Oxford: Polity Press.

Lyon, D. (1995) The roots of the information society idea. In Heap, N., Thomas, R., Einon, G., Mason, R. and MacKay, H. (eds) *Information Technology and Society: A Reader*. Milton Keynes: Open University Press.

Machover, C. and Tice, S.E. (1994) Virtual reality. *IEEE Computer Graphics and Applications* January: 15–16.

Mackenzie, D. and Wajcman, J. (1985) *The Social Shaping of Technology*. Milton Keynes: Open University Press.

Maffesoli, M. (1989) The sociology of everyday life (epistemological elements). *Current Sociology* 37, 1–16.

Makridakis, S. (1995) The forthcoming information revolution: its impact on society and firms. *Futures* 27: 799–821.

Malone, T.W. and Rockhart, J.F. (1991) Computers, networks and the corporation. *Scientific American* 267: 92–99.

Maltz, T. (1996) Customary law and power in Internet communities. *Journal of Computer-Mediated Communication* 2(1).

http://207.201.161.120/jcmc/vol2/issue2/custom.html

Martin, L.H., Gutman, H. and Hutton, P.H. (eds) (1988) *Technologies of the Self: A Seminar with Michel Foucault*. Amherst, MA: University of Massachusetts Press.

Martin, J. (1978) *The Wired Society*. Englewood Cliffs, NJ: Prentice Hall.

Martin, W.J. (1995) *The Global Information Society*. London: Aslib Gower.

Marvin, L-E. (1994) Spoof, spam, lurk and lag: the aesthetics of text-based virtual realities. *Journal of Computer-Mediated Communication* 1(2).

http:// 207.201.161.120/jcmc/vol1/issue2/marvin.html

Marx, G.T. (1988) *Undercover: Police Surveillance in America*. Berkeley, CA: University of California Press.

McCaffery, L. (1991) Introduction: in the desert of the real. In McCaffery, L. (ed.) *Storming the Reality Studio: A Casebook of Cyberpunk and Postmodern Fiction*. London: Duke University Press, pp. 1–16.

McCaffery, L. (1991) An interview with William Gibson. In McCaffery, L. (ed.) *Storming the Reality Studio: A Casebook of Cyberpunk and Postmodern Fiction*. London: Duke University Press, pp. 263–285.

McCellan, J. (1994) Netsurfers. *The Observer*, 13 February.

McChesney, R.W. (1995) The internet and US communication policy-making in historical and critical perspective. *Journal of Computer-Mediated Communication* 1(4).

http://207.201.161.120/jcmc/vol1/issue4/vol1no4.html

McKenna, T. (1992) *Food of the Gods: The Search for the Original Tree of Knowledge: A Radical History of Plants, Drugs and Evolution*. New York: Bantam.

McLaughlin, M.L., Osborne, K.K. and Smith, C.B. (1995) Standards of conduct on Usenet. In Jones, S.G. (ed.) *Cybersociety: Computer Mediated Communication and Community*. London: Sage, pp. 90–111.

McLuhan, M. (1964) *Understanding Media: The Extensions of Man*. New York: Macmillan.

Miller, S. (1996) *Civilising Cyberspace: Power, Policy and the Information Superhighway*. New York: ACM Press.

Mitchell, W.J. (1995) *City of Bits: Space, Place and the Infobahn*. Cambridge, MA: MIT Press.

Mitterer, J. and O'Neill, K. (1992) The end of 'information': computers democracy and the university. *Interchange* 23: 123–139.

Mnookin, J.L. (1996) Virtual(ly) law: the emergence of law in LambdaMOO. *Journal of Computer-Mediated Communication* 2(1).

http://207.201.161.120/jcmc/vol2/issue1/

Mokhtarian, P.L. (1988) An empirical evaluation of the travel impacts of teleconferencing. *Transportation Research A* 22: 283–289.

Morgan, K. (1992) Digital highways: the telecommunications era. *Geoforum* 23: 317–332.

Morley, D. and Robins, K. (1995) *Spaces of Identity: Global Media, Electronic Landscapes and Cultural Boundaries*. London: Routledge.

Morris, M. and Ogan, C. (1994) The internet as mass medium. *Journal of Computer-Mediated Communication* 1(4).

http://207.201.161.120/jcmc/vol1/issue4/

Morse, M. (1994) What do cyborgs eat? Oral logic in an information society. In Bender, G. and Druckery, T. (eds) *Culture on the Brink: Ideologies of Technology*. Seattle, WA: Bay Press, pp. 157–189.

Moss, M.L. (1987) Telecommunications and the future of cities. *Urban Studies* 24: 33–44.

Moss, M.L. and Townsend, A. (1996) Leaders and losers on the internet.
http://www.nyu.edu/urban/research/internet/internet.html

Myers, N. (1994) Gross reality of global statistics. *The Guardian*, 2 May.

Naisbett (1984) *Megatrends*. New York: Warner Books.

Neustadt, R.M. (1985) Electronic politics. In Forester, T. (ed.) *The Information Technology Revolution*. Oxford: Blackwell.

Oberding, J.M. and Norderhaug, T. (1996) A separate jurisdiction for cyberspace? *Journal of Computer-Mediated Communication* 2(1).
http://207.201.161.120/jcmc/vol2/issue2/juris.html

Ogden, J. (1993) Legal and ethical aspects of computer-mediated communication. *The Arachnet Electronic Journal on Virtual Culture* 1(4).
http://www.monash.edu.au/journals/ejvc/ejvcv1n4.html

Ogden, J. (1994) Politics in a parallel universe: is there a future for cyberdemocracy? *Futures* 26: 713–729

O'Neill, J.E. (1995) The role of ARPA in the development of the ARPANET, 1961–1972. *IEEE Annals of the History of Computing* 17(4): 76–81.

Palfreman, J. and Swade, D. (1991) *The Dream Machine: Exploring the Computer Age*. London: BBC Books.

Palme, J. (1993) Legal and ethical aspects of computer-mediated communication. *The Arachnet Electronic Journal on Virtual Culture* 1(4).
http://www.monash.edu.au/journals/ejvc/palme.v1n4.

Parks, M.R. and Floyd, K. (1996) Making friends in cyberspace. *Journal of Computer-Mediated Communication* 1(4).
http://207.201.161.120/jcmc/vol1/issue4/vol1no4.html

Parliamentary Select Committee for Home Affairs (1994) *Computer Pornography*. London: HMSO.

Peet, R. (1986) The destruction of regional cultures. In R.J. Johnston and P.J. Taylor (eds) *A World in Crisis? Geographical Perspectives*. Oxford: Blackwell.

Peet, R. and Thrift, N. (1989) Political economy and human geography. In Peet, R. and Thrift, N. (eds) *New Models in Geography: The Political-Economy Perspective*, vol. 1. London: Unwin-Hyman, pp. 1-27

Penley, C. and Ross, A. (1991) *Technoculture*. Minneapolis, MN: University of Minnesota Press.

Penny, S. (1994) Virtual reality as the completion of the Enlightenment project. In Bender, G. and Druckery, T. (eds) *Culture on the Brink: Ideologies of Technology*. Seattle, WA: Bay Press, pp. 231–248.

Peters (1990) Quoted in Thach and Woodman (1993) Organizational change and information technology: managing on the edge of cyberspace. *Organisational Dynamics* 23: 30–46.

Pile, S. and Thrift, N. (1995) *Mapping the Subject: Geographies of Cultural Transformation*. London: Routledge.

Plant, S. (1993) Beyond the screens: film, cyberpunk, and cyberfeminism. *Variant* 14: 12–17.

Plant, S. (1996) On the matrix: cyberfeminist simulations. In Shields, R. (ed.) *Cultures of Internet: Virtual Spaces, Real Histories and Living Bodies*. London: Sage, pp. 170–184.

Polis, M.F., Gifford, S.J. and McKeown Jr, D.M. (1995) Automating the construction of large scale virtual worlds. *Computer* July: 57–65.

Poster, M. (ed.) (1988) *Jean Baudrilard: Selected Writings*. Cambridge: Polity Press.

Poster, M. (1995a) *The Second Media Age*. Oxford: Polity Press.

Poster, M. (1995b) Postmodern virtualities. In Featherstone, M. and Burrows, R. (eds.) *Cyberspace, Cyberbodies and Cyberpunk: Cultures of Technological Embodiment*. London: Sage, pp. 79–96.

Postman, N. (1992) *Technopoly: The Surrender of Culture to Technology*. New York: Vintage Books.

Pratt, D., Zyda, M. and Kelleher, K. (1995) Virtual reality: in the mind of the beholder. *Computer* 17–19.

Pryor, S. and Scott, J. (1993) Virtual reality: beyond Cartesian space. In Hayward, P. and Wollen, T. (eds.) *Future Visions: New Technologies of the Screen*. London: British Film Institute, pp. 166–179.

Rafaeli, S. and Sudweeks, F. (1996) Networked interactivity. *Journal of Computer-Mediated Communication* 2(4).
http://207.201.161.120/jcmc/vol2/issue4/rafaeli.sudweeks.html

Rayport, J.F. and Sviokla, J.J. (1995) Exploiting the virtual value chain. *Harvard Business Review* November/December: 75–85.

Reid, B. (1993) *Usenet Readership Summary Report*. Palo Alto, CA.

Reid, E. (1995) Virtual worlds: culture and imagination. In Jones, S.G. (ed.) *Cybersociety: Computer Mediated Communication and Community*. London: Sage, pp. 164–183.

Rheingold, H. (1991) *Virtual Reality*. New York: Touchstone.

Rheingold, H. (1994) *The Virtual Community: Surfing the Internet*. London: Minerva.

Ribarsky, W., Bolter, J., Op den Bosch, A. and van Teylingen, R. (1994) Visualization and analysis using virtual reality. *IEEE Computer Graphic and Applications*, January: 10–12.

Roberts, S. (1994) Fictitious capital, fictitious spaces: the geography of offshore financial flows. In Corbridge, S., Martin, R. and Thrift, N. (eds) *Money Power Space*. Oxford: Blackwell.

Robins, K. (1995) Cyberspace and the world we live in. In Featherstone, M. and Burrows, R. (ed.) *Cyberspace, Cyberbodies and Cyberpunk: Cultures of Technological Embodiment*. London: Sage, pp. 135–156.

Robins, K. and Hepworth, M. (1988) Electronic spaces: new technologies and the future of cities. *Futures* 20: 155–176.

Robins, K. and Webster, F. (1989) *The Technical Fix*. London: Macmillan.

Robinson, P. (1991) Globalization, telecommunications and trade. *Futures* 23: 801–814.

Rosenau, P.M. (1992) *Postmodernism and the Social Sciences: Insights, Inroads and Intrusions*. Princeton, NJ: Princeton University Press.

Ross, A. (1991) *Strange Weather: Culture, Science and Technology in the Age of Limits*. London: Verso.

Roszak, T. (1994) *The Cult of Information*. Berkeley, CA: University of California Press.

Rushkoff, D. (1994) *Cyberia: Life in the Trenches of Hyperspace*. London: Flamingo.

Salus, P. (1995) *Casting the Net: From ARPANET to Internet and beyond. . ..* Reading, MA: Addison-Wesley.

Samuelson, P. (1996) Intellectual property rights and the global information economy. *Communications of the ACM* 39(1): 23–28.

Sardar, Z. (1995) alt.civilisations.faq: cyberspace as the darker side of the West. *Futures* 27: 777–794.

Sawheeny, H. (1996) Information superhighway: metaphors as midwives. *Media, Culture and Society* 18: 291–314.

Schmeiser, L. (1995) Can the US Congress define decency? *Computer-Mediated Communication Magazine* 1 July.
http:// http://sunsite.unc.edu/cmc/mag/1995/jul/lisa.html

Schroeder, R. (1994) Cyberculture, cyborg post-modernism and the sociology of virtual reality technologies: surfing the soul of the information age. *Futures* 26: 519–528.

Schuler, D. (1995) Public space in cyberspace. *Internet World* December: 89–95.

Selby, J. (1995) Telecottages in their context: the Welsh experience, unpublished undergraduate dissertation, University of Wales, Swansea.

Sennett, R. (1978) *The Fall of Public Man*. New York: Alfred A. Knopf.

Shade, L. R. (1994) Gender issues in computer networking. *Electronic Journal on Virtual Culture* 2(3).
http://www.monash.edu.au/journals/ejvc/shade.v2n3

Shade, L.R. (1996) Is there free speech on the Net? Censorship in the global information infrastructure. In Shields, R. (ed) *Cultures of Internet: Virtual Spaces, Real Histories and Living Bodies*. London: Sage.

Shapiro, A.L. (1995) Street corners in cyberspace: keeping on-line speech free. *Nation* 3 July: 10–14.

208

Sherman, B. and Judkins, B. (1992) *Glimpses of Heaven, Visions of Hell*. London: Hodder & Stoughton.

Shields, R. (1992) Spaces for the subject of consumption. In Shields, R. (ed.) *Lifestyle Shopping: The Subject of Consumption*. London: Routledge, pp. 1–20.

Shields, R. (1996) Introduction: virtual spaces, real histories and living bodies. In Shields, R. (ed.) *Cultures of Internet: Virtual Spaces, Real Histories and Living Bodies*. London: Sage, pp. 1–10.

Slouka, M. (1996) *War of the Worlds: The Assault on Reality*. London: Abacus.

Sobchack, V. (1995) Beating the meat/surviving the text, or how to get out of this century alive. In Featherstone, M. and Burrows, R. (eds) *Cyberspace, Cyberbodies and Cyberpunk: Cultures of Technological Embodiment*. London: Sage, pp. 205–214.

Soja, E. (1989) *Postmodern Geographies: The Reassertion of Space in Critical Social Theory*. London: Verso.

Sorkin, M. (ed.) (1992) *Variations on a Theme Park: The New American City and the End of Public Space*. New York: Hill & Wang.

Squire, S.J. (1996) Re-territorializing knowledge(s): electronic spaces and virtual geographies. *Area* 28: 101–103.

Stallabrass, J. (1995) Empowering technology: the exploration of cyberspace. *New Left Review* 78: 3–32.

Sterling, B. (ed.) *Mirrorshades: The Cyberpunk Anthology*. London: HarperCollins.

Stix, G. (1993) Domesticating cyberspace. *Scientific American* 269(2): 85–92.

Stone, A.R. (1991) Will the real body please stand up? Boundary stories about virtual cultures. In Benedikt, M. (ed.) *Cyberspace: First Steps*. Cambridge, MA: MIT Press, pp. 81–118.

Stone, A.R. (1995) Sex and death among the disembodied: VR, cyberspace, and the nature of academic discourse. In Star, S.L. (ed.) *The Cultures of Computing*. Blackwell: Oxford, pp. 243–274.

Stonier, T. (1983) *The Wealth of Information: A Profile of the Postindustrial Economy* London: Methuen.

Strangelove, M. (1994) The internet as catalyst for a paradigm shift. *Computer-Mediated Communication Magazine* 1(8).
http://sunsite.unc.edu/cmc/mag/1994/dec/shift.html

Sutton, L.A. (1996) Cocktails and thumbtacks in the Old West: what would Emily Post say? In Cherney, L. and Reise, E.R. (eds) *Wired Women: Gender and New Realities in Cyberspace*. Seattle, WA: Seal Press, pp. 169–187.

Ter Hart, H.W. and Piersma, J. (1990) Direct representation in international financial markets: the case of foreign banks in Amsterdam. *Tijdschrift voor Econmische en Sociale Geografie* 81: 82–92.

Thach, L. and Woodman, R.W. (1993) Organizational change and information technology: managing on the edge of cyberspace. *Organisational Dynamics* 23: 30–46.

Thomas, R. (1995) Access and inequality. In Heap, N., Thomas, R., Einon, G., Mason, R. and MacKay, H. (eds) *Information Technology and Society: A Reader*. Milton Keynes: Open University Press.

Thu Nguyen, D. and Alexander, J. (1996) The coming of cyberspacetime and the end of polity. In Shields, R. (ed.) *Cultures of Internet: Virtual Spaces Real Histories and Living Bodies*. London: Sage, pp. 99–124.

Toffler, A. (1980) *The Third Wave*. London: Pan.

Tolhurst W.A. *et al.* (1994) *Using the Internet*, special publication. Indianapolis, IN: Que Corporation.

Tomas, D. (1989) The technophiliac body: on technicity in William Gibson's cyborg culture. *New Formations* 8: 113–129.

Tomas, D. (1991) Old rituals for new space: rites de passage and William Gibson's cultural model of cyberspace. In Benedikt, M. (ed.) *Cyberspace: First Steps*. Cambridge, MA: MIT Press, pp. 31–48.

Ungerer, H. (1990) *Telecommunications in Europe*. Commission of the European Communities.

US Department of Transportation (1993) *Transportation Implications of Telecommuting*. Washington DC, April.

Walker (1985) Is there a service economy? *Science and Society* 49: 42–83.

Warf, B. (1989) Telecommunications and the globalisation of financial services. *Professional Geographer* 41: 257–271.

Warf, B. (1995) Telecommunications and the changing geographies of knowledge transmission in the late 20th century. *Urban Studies* 32, 361–378.

Waters, M. (1995) *Globalisation*. London: Routledge.

We, G. (1994) Cross-gender communication in cyberspace. *The Arachnet Electronic Journal on Virtual Culture* 2(3).
http://www.monash.edu.au/journals/ejvc/we.v2n3

Weijers, T., Meijer, R. and Spoelman, E. (1992) Telework remains 'made to measure': the large scale introduction of telework in the Netherlands. *Futures* 24: 1048–1055.

Weise, E.R. (1996) A thousand aunts with modems. In Cherney, L. and Weise, E.R. (eds) *Wired Women: Gender and New Realities in Cyberspace*. Seattle, WA: Seal Press, pp. vii–xv.

White, L. (1978) *Medieval Technology and Social Change*. Oxford: Oxford University Press.

Wilson, L. (1994) Cyberwar, God and television: interview with Paul Virilio. CTHEORY.
http://english-www.hss.cmu.edu/ctheory/a-cyberwar—god.html

Winner, L. (1986) *The Whale and the Reactor: A Search for the Limits in an Age of High Technology*. Chicago, IL: University of Chicago Press.

Winner, L. (1993) Upon opening the black box and finding it empty: social constructivism and the philosophy of technology. *Science, Technology, and Human Values* 18: 362–378.

Winner, L. (1994) Three paradoxes of the information age. In Bender, G. and Druckery, T. (eds) *Culture on the Brink: Ideologies of Technology*. Seattle, WA: Bay Press, pp. 191–197.

Witmer, D.F. (1996) Risky business: why people feel safe in sexually explicit on-line communication. *Journal of Computer-Mediated Communication* 2(4).
http://207.201.161.120/jcmc/vol2/issue4/witmer.html

Witmer, D.F. and Katzman, S.L. (1996) On-line smiles: does gender make a difference in the use of graphical accents? *Journal of Computer Mediated Comunications* 2(4).
http://207.201.161.120/jcmc/vol1/issue4/witmer1old.html

Wolf, N. (1991) *The Beauty Myth: How Images of Beauty are Used Against Women*. New York: William Morrow.

Woods, L. (1995) A question of space. In Aronowitz, S. and Menser, A. (eds) *Technoculture*. New York: Routledge.

Woodward, K. (1994) From virtual cyborgs to biological time bombs: technocriticism and the material body. In Bender, G. and Druckery, T. (eds) *Culture on the Brink: Ideologies of Technology*. Seattle, WA: Bay Press.

Woolley, B. (1992) *Virtual Worlds: A Journey in Hype and Hyperreality*. Harmondsworth: Penguin.

Zakon, R.H. (1996) Hobbes' internet timeline.
http://info.isoc.org/guest/zakon/internet/History/HIT.html

Zukin, S. (1992) *Landscapes of Power*. Berkeley, CA: University of California Press.

INDEX

Page numbers in *italics* refer to Figures and Plates; those in **bold** refer to Tables

Index compiled by Annette Musker